PRAISE FOR *LIQUID HANDCUFFS*

"In *Liquid Handcuffs*, Helen Redmond fearlessly takes on the militarization of methadone clinics. Her searing analysis, which ends with a call to dramatically retool drug policy and uplift peer-led activist organizations, is crucial reading for those of us who work and live in health and social service systems."

—HELENA HANSEN, MD, PhD, professor at UCLA's David Geffen School of Medicine and coauthor of *Whiteout*

"This is not just a book—it's a reckoning, exposing how too many methadone clinics have failed their patients in the service of the imperatives of market medicine, racial capitalism, and the carceral state. Helen Redmond harnesses decades of lived experience, frontline practice, and the perspectives of patients themselves to rip the curtain back on one of the most dehumanizing medical regimes in the United States. In some of the most compelling abolitionist writing in medicine to appear in some time, she leaves us with one conclusion: Methadone clinics are not broken systems in need of reform; they are punishment by design. *Liquid Handcuffs* is not just for health care practitioners, policymakers, or substance use patients, but for anyone who has ever thought critically or had questions about American medicine itself."

—SAMUEL KELTON ROBERTS, Jr., PhD, associate professor of history and sociomedical sciences at Columbia University and author of *Infectious Fear*

"Methadone is an inherently political issue, and this brilliant book takes apart its dark history and offers what should be an encouraging future."

—JOHANN HARI, *New York Times* best-selling author of *Chasing the Scream*

"We have needed a book that critiques the methadone clinic system and Helen Redmond delivers with this page-turner. Painstakingly researched, it is filled with powerful stories of methadone patients that will make readers furious. The book lays out the contradictory history of methadone. It is a lifesaving medicine, but for fifty years it has been locked inside punitive clinics that imprison people instead of freeing them."

—PATT DENNING, PhD, coauthor of *Over the Influence*

"Reading *Liquid Handcuffs* was personal. As a mother of a daughter who takes methadone, I have lived the realities Helen Redmond so boldly exposes. Methadone saved my daughter's life—but only because I had the means, the voice, and the relentless will to get her to a clinic an hour away every single day, and to advocate fiercely against a system designed to punish rather than support. This book confirms what I witnessed firsthand: methadone clinics operate less like health care facilities and more like parole offices. . . . With sharp analysis and profound compassion, Redmond documents how opioid treatment programs in the United States operate under a carceral model born out of the War on Drugs, not evidence-based medicine. Through patient stories, historical context, and frontline advocacy, she lays bare a system built on surveillance, shame, and control. This is not just a critique of policy—it's a cry for justice. . . . If you care about public health, human rights, or ending the overdose crisis, read this book. And if you've ever loved someone who needed methadone, you'll see them on every page."

—KATHLEEN COCHRAN, founder of Moms for All Paths to Recovery

"This compelling book will save countless lives if read by people who struggle with opioid addiction, or who live with them, or who really want to help them, or who have power over them. Helen Redmond brings the voices of methadone patients out of the closet in making a persuasive case for desegregating the role of methadone in the medical system."

—ETHAN A. NADELMANN, JD, founder of the Drug Policy Alliance

"Any overseas visitor who has been shocked by the sight of long lines of distressed people queueing in US cities will appreciate this eye-opening and well-researched book. It exposes the historical class- and race-based fear and distrust underpinning this distinctively American way of distributing an essential medicine. Helen Redmond argues vehemently against this system, versions of which have been adopted by other countries, in favor of some form of physician and pharmacy-based provision. Taking into account the dangers of lax prescribing, international readers will be provoked to consider: What would more humane and effective regulation look like in their own country?"

—SUSANNE MACGREGOR, honorary professor at the London School of Hygiene and Tropical Medicine

"*Liquid Handcuffs* does a masterful job of telling the story of methadone. . . . Having worked in the front lines of addiction medicine for over thirty years, I have seen first-hand the transformative impact of methadone. However, this is often undermined by punitive and cruel systems of dispensing. *Liquid Handcuffs* is an important read for anyone involved with addiction and makes an impassioned case for policymakers to abolish the methadone clinic system."

—MARK TYNDALL, MD, professor of medicine at the School of Population and Public Health, University of British Columbia

"A visionary insight into the problems of our current methadone clinic system. . . . Redmond masterfully takes the reader on a journey to better understand this vital topic and gives us a sobering reality of what needs to be done to truly take the shackles off methadone." ·

—WILLIAM AMARQUAYE, PharmD, clinical pharmacist at Tampa General Hospital

"As an advocate for pregnant women, including those who used drugs, I came to learn about the life-saving benefits of methadone treatment. Sadly, that knowledge was quickly followed by lessons in the dehumanizing way in which this vital treatment is regulated in the United States, and the particular barriers to such treatment for pregnant women. It was with extreme relief and gratitude that I read Helen Redmond's much-needed exposé of the methadone treatment system and its baked-in culture of cruelty. Redmond offers a vision of the kind of affordable, respectful, and compassionate health care that we all deserve."

—LYNN M. PALTROW, JD, founder of Pregnancy Justice (formerly National Advocates for Pregnant Women)

"*Liquid Handcuffs* lifts the lid on the stigma and discrimination that people who take methadone experience across the globe. Helen Redmond sheds a much-needed spotlight on the problems people have accessing this life-saving medication, and the book will no doubt be a catalyst for change."

—FIONA PATTEN, former Australian politician, harm reduction activist, and author of *Sex, Drugs and the Electoral Roll*

"*Liquid Handcuffs* unabashedly confronts the racist and classist system that allows for the dehumanization of methadone clients. Abolition of the current clinic system is the only way to liberate this lifesaving medication."

— JESS TILLEY, director of the New England Drug Users Union

LIQUID HANDCUFFS

Policing and Punishment in
Methadone Clinics and the Future
of Opioid Addiction Treatment

HELEN REDMOND, LCSW

North Atlantic Books
Huichin, unceded Ohlone land
Berkeley, California

North Atlantic Books
Huichin, unceded Ohlone land
2526 Martin Luther King Jr Way
Berkeley, CA 94704 USA
www.northatlanticbooks.com

Cover photo © Andrea Colarieti via Getty Images
Cover design by Jasmine Hromjak
Book design by Happenstance Type-O-Rama

Printed in the United States of America

Liquid Handcuffs: Policing and Punishment in Methadone Clinics and the Future of Opioid Addiction Treatment is sponsored and published by North Atlantic Books, an educational nonprofit that collaborates with partners to develop cross-cultural perspectives; nurture holistic views of art, science, the humanities, and healing; and seed personal and global transformation by publishing work on the relationship of body, spirit, and nature.

North Atlantic Books's publications are distributed to the US trade and internationally by Penguin Random House Publisher Services. For further information, visit our website at www.northatlanticbooks.com.

The authorized representative in the EU for product safety and compliance is Eucomply OÜ, Pärnu mnt 139b-14, 11317 Tallinn, Estonia, hello@eucompliancepartner.com, +33757690241.

DISCLAIMER: The following information is intended for general information purposes only. The publisher does not advocate illegal activities but does believe in the right of individuals to have free access to information and ideas. Any application of the material set forth in the following pages is at the reader's discretion and is their sole responsibility.

Library of Congress Cataloging-in-Publication data is available from the publisher upon request.
ISBN: 979-8-88984-239-2 (paperback)
ISBN: 979-8-88984-240-8 (ebook)

1 2 3 4 5 6 7 8 9 KPC 31 30 29 28 27 26

To all the people who take methadone,
we see you, we hear you.
Y a Eduardo, fuiste amado.

CONTENTS

INTRODUCTION

Anyone who knows me knows that I am not a morning person. I love to sleep in. I might read a book, listen to music, scroll through Instagram on my phone, think about the day ahead, or just look at the sky and daydream. I never have to think about getting to a place every morning to take a medication and that if I was late, and the door was locked, I wouldn't get it. A three-month supply of Enbrel is delivered to my door by UPS. I track the package online and know when it will arrive. There is always a stock of it in my refrigerator. I cannot function without it. My friend Melissa is not so lucky. She takes methadone. Melissa texted me and said she overslept and missed the Saturday dose. The clinic is closed on Sundays. That meant she would miss two doses and experience withdrawal symptoms. Her weekend was ruined, and she would stay in bed to ride it out, not to daydream. The only thing on Melissa's mind would be getting to the clinic early Monday morning to get dosed. She is not free.

That's why I wrote this book. People who take methadone are not free. The carceral clinic system that controls access to this lifesaving medication has total control over patients' lives. The truth is, patients are prisoners in this system. It is enraging.

The audacious goal of *Liquid Handcuffs: Policing and Punishment in Methadone Clinics and the Future of Opioid Addiction Treatment* is to catalyze a movement to abolish methadone clinics. To free the people trapped inside.

The other reason for this book is that I couldn't find any that radically critiqued the clinic system and called for abolition. There is a huge void that needs to be filled. Many more books need to be published that expose the inhumanity of methadone clinics, which are also called opioid treatment programs (OTPs). People who take methadone need to write accounts. Staff who work in clinics—nurses, counselors, doctors, directors—need to tell their stories. This book should not be the only critique of OTPs.

A canon of books is needed to explain how a system that so ruthlessly oppresses people who just want to take methadone and get on with their lives has been allowed to stand without any significant reform for *fifty years*! Iterations of the US system exist across the world and accounts need to be written by people in those countries who are also not free. The methadone clinic system needs to be documented in other ways too: podcasts, documentaries, social media, explainer videos, oral histories, photographs.

What influenced and informed this book project? I'm a medical social worker who has worked with people who use drugs for decades, and my practice is grounded in antiracism and the philosophy of harm reduction. I'm a documentary filmmaker and I've made two documentaries about methadone. As a journalist, I write about aspects of the War on Drugs with a focus on the politics of methadone for the *Filter* website.

I first encountered methadone when I worked in a hospital and outpatient care center in Chicago. It was part of my job to help patients enroll in OTPs. It was the 1990s, before lab-manufactured, super deadly fentanyl displaced humble plant-based heroin. Right away something seemed off. I could rarely talk to anyone at the clinic. Staff didn't return calls, and when they did, they often spoke negatively about my patients. But the stories I heard about what happened inside clinics changed me. My hope is that by reading this book, it will change you too. I found out about the ways patients are controlled, from daily dosing to observed urines. The list of clinic-generated harms is endless, and it was punish, punish, punish, then punish some more. My patients' hatred of the clinic and staff was justified.

I had the sinking realization that these opioid treatment *prisons* that thousands of vulnerable patients/hostages endure on a daily basis were a well-kept secret. Back then, no one was paying attention to or even cared about what occurred inside these programs. They weren't on the radar of policymakers, the public, or the corporate media. And so the suffering went on, unseen. The methadone clinic system is purposely invisible. It isn't intended to be seen because if we see it, we'll start to get angry. I had to figure out a way to make the invisible visible.

In 2012 I moved to New York City, the home of the founders of methadone, doctors Vincent Dole, Marie Nyswander, and Mary Jeanne Kreek. Working on the Lower East Side, I helped clients in a supportive housing program get into methadone treatment. I'll never forget a meeting I attended at a clinic to advocate for my client. Javier wanted to go to a conference in upstate New York and needed take-home bottles. The staff refused because he had missed several doses and counseling appointments within the last month. I was shocked at the level of contempt they had for Javier during the meeting and the refusal to recognize that his desire to participate in a conference was a positive thing and should be supported. To staff, he was just a junkie fuckup who didn't follow the rules. Javier had told me many times that he despised going to the clinic and how he felt abused by the staff. He would wake up early and arrive at the clinic in Midtown Manhattan in the dark. As the sun came up, hundreds of people on their way to work rushed past the long line he stood in. Javier said it was humiliating. It made him feel like he could never get out of the clinic's "liquid handcuffs" and become one of the workers streaming by on their way to a job and a different life. He dropped out of treatment and later died of a fentanyl-related overdose. The methadone clinic system killed Javier. I was enraged.

My co-filmmaker Marilena Marchetti and I finished our feature-length documentary, *Liquid Handcuffs: A Documentary to Free Methadone*, in 2019. It was filmed in six countries. I interviewed lots of patients and staff for the documentary and discovered even more things that I didn't like about OTPs. We held several screenings of the film in New York City. Afterward, there were panel discussions featuring people who took methadone. It was a start.

Then I found an article by Peter Vanderkloot that rocked my world. His ground-breaking piece, published in 2001, "Methadone: Medicine,

Harm Reduction or Social Control," linked the way the medication is dispensed to drug prohibition. The methadone clinic system is a creation of the War on Drugs, the Drug Enforcement Administration (DEA) designed it, and at the same time the clinic system is a refuge from the war on drugs. People who take methadone swap the dangers of illicit drug use—arrest, incarceration, violence, overdose, and death—for a safe supply of the medication in a setting that punishes, monitors, and controls them. OTPs are a battleground, another front in the drug war. Vanderkloot concludes the article by calling for abolishing the clinic system and for prescription parity. It made complete sense. It's a root cause solution. I became a clinic abolitionist.

Over time, I also became an OTP rageaholic. I found a fellow rageaholic in Dr. Ruth Potee. I watched a video of her on YouTube speaking at a conference in 2022.[1] The title of her presentation was "WTF Methadone—What Is the Future?" It blew me away. Potee's critique of the DEA was badass, and she dropped this bomb: "First of all, if this room was filled with DEA agents, I would still say the exact same thing I'm about to say. . . . Public enemy number one to treatment is the DEA." WTF methadone for real! I'd never heard a doctor so boldly call out the drug warriors. During her talk, Potee used the words *criminal, carceral*, and *parole* to describe OTPs and introduced the idea of a "methadone industrial complex" that makes enormous profits. Her brilliant presentation both explained and excoriated the American methadone clinic system. She confessed that she is rageful every single day. But here's the thing: Dr. Potee is the medical director of four methadone clinics in Massachusetts. Why does Potee work in the opioid treatment prisons that she so convincingly condemns? This was one of the first of many contradictions in the weird world of methadone that you'll learn about in *Liquid Handcuffs*.

Then COVID-19 hit like a category 5 hurricane and didn't let up for two years. The brutal realities of long-term systemic inequality in the United States were exposed. A bright beam of light was trained on strict OTP regulations in a way like never before. Suddenly the invisible became visible. Federal and state agencies that regulate clinics were forced to allow more take-home medication so patients and staff wouldn't die. It was as if Moses had parted a sea of liquid methadone and patients were finally able to escape. Louise Vincent, the executive director of the National Survivors Union said, "It took a pandemic to get more take-homes." She was right.

It was critical to document the historic changes that were taking place in OTPs. Marilena and I filmed interviews with patients and staff inside and outside clinics in five states in the second year of the pandemic. The result was our short film, *Swallow THIS: A Documentary About Methadone and COVID-19*. Then we launched a cross-country tour using it to make the case for clinic abolition. It was the experience of a lifetime to meet and be in conversation with so many folks who take methadone and with clinic staff. But this Rip Van Winkle methadone moment of waking up wouldn't last.

As a result of my documentaries and articles about methadone, I've become a small magnet for patients around the United States who are frustrated, want real change, and are keen to share their experiences in methadone clinics. I've invited some of them to write for *Filter* so readers can hear directly from people with lived experience.

Janet Urdahl, a former executive director of an OTP, contacted me asking for help to reform her clinic. I told her I could not. But I made a short video of Urdahl for *Filter* and she blows the whistle on the culture of cruelty in for-profit clinics. Staff in some OTPs are fed up. I read this on an email list: "I am transitioning out of working at this clinic due to an atmosphere of hostility, a culture of wanting to 'punish' clients, and unethical, immoral practices as I've seen with the methadone clinic system in general."

People also started to hate on me for criticizing the clinic system, for my abolitionist stance, and for opposing methadone reform legislation. In various forums, participants attacked me and said shut up, that I couldn't have an opinion because I didn't take methadone or work in an OTP. I was called an "unhinged troublemaker" and warned that I don't speak on behalf of methadone patients. I don't. I speak for myself. And I won't shut up. Because of my position that clinics are oppressive and must be shut down, several people declined to be interviewed for this book.

It has been a long and winding road to write *Liquid Handcuffs*. On the way, I've learned about methadone from an empathic, generous, knowledgeable, funny, and ever-growing cast of characters from Kabul to Knoxville, Lisbon to Los Angeles, New Delhi to New York City.

I am convinced that the only way to free people who take methadone is to abolish the clinic system. If this book convinces you, then it has done its job.

Some book housekeeping notes:

I wasn't able to include the voices of the dozens of people I interviewed for the book, but please know you have influenced how I think about methadone.

I use person-centered language to describe people who take methadone and use drugs throughout the book, except when doing so becomes intolerably repetitive. Always, I strive to be respectful.

When I quote people who take methadone, I use both full names, one name, or a pseudonym for privacy purposes.

Errors or omissions are mine.

Finally, lovely readers, I leave you with a comment Melissa posted on social media:

I got to get myself all winterized to commute to the methadone clinic to receive 1 dose of my medication by a nurse through a hole in the glass. Today there were 2 folks in wheelchairs, 4 with walkers, 2 on oxygen, more canes than I could count. This isn't sustainable. #freemethadone

1

THE AMERICAN METHADONE CLINIC SYSTEM: "Who Do I Have to Blow?"

A methadone patient is monitored more closely than a paroled murderer.

—EDWIN SALSITZ, MD

Indulge me. Imagine you take a medication that is vital to your health: as vital as oxygen or water. You can't go a single day without it because you are completely dependent on it to think, to work, to take care of your family, to just be *you*. And if you miss a dose? A withdrawal hellscape awaits: extreme muscle and bone pain, intense cravings, vomiting, insomnia, severe anxiety, cramps, cold sweats, fever, and bouts of diarrhea. Death might actually be preferable. What kinds of indignities would you endure to avoid that experience? How far would you go to get the drug that literally saves your life every day?

Be honest: You would do whatever it takes to get it—and it, in this case, is methadone. And the only way to legally obtain this medication that mercifully binds to mu-opioid receptors and blocks the brain from telling the body to revolt is to attend a special clinic six or seven days a week and be observed by a nurse swallowing the medication. These methadone clinics, also known as opioid treatment programs (OTPs), are licensed and regulated through a partnership between the Drug Enforcement Administration (DEA) and the Substance Abuse and Mental Health Services Administration (SAMHSA). That the DEA, a police organization that is waging the War on Drugs, is involved in the dispensing of methadone is outrageous. They are ignorant about the nature of addiction and believe that methadone is a dangerous drug and that adults who take it cannot be trusted. That SAMHSA, an agency composed of medical doctors, addiction experts, and researchers who do understand the importance of methadone to treat addiction, collaborates with DEA drug warriors is also outrageous. Their decades-long partnership has denied people who need methadone their freedom.

Methadone is a full agonist, synthetic opioid used to treat addiction to heroin, fentanyl, and prescription opioids like OxyContin. It eliminates intense cravings and withdrawal. The medication is the gold standard of treatment. It was discovered by doctors Vincent Dole, Marie Nyswander, and Mary Jeanne Kreek at Rockefeller University in the 1960s. A report by the National Academy of Sciences Institute of Medicine (IoM) concluded, "Methadone maintenance has been the most rigorously studied drug treatment modality and has yielded the most incontrovertibly positive results. . . . Consumption of all illicit drugs, especially heroin, declines. Crime is reduced, fewer individuals become HIV positive, and individual functioning is improved."[1]

The IoM also noted that methadone can be taken as a maintenance medication with few negative side effects. In reviewing clinic regulations, though, the researchers also concluded, "Current policy puts too much emphasis on protecting society from methadone, and not enough on protecting society from the epidemics of addiction, violence, and infectious diseases that methadone can help reduce."[2] The report was published in 1995.

Tragically, society is still being protected *from* methadone. That's because the drug has been locked inside a singularly oppressive penal institution that is anchored in a culture of cruelty and surveillance. The DEA, SAMHSA, and OTPs have created dense layers of nonsensical arbitrary rules and regulations that make entering and staying in a program a frustrating and humiliating daily ordeal. In the midst of an ongoing overdose crisis, just one in five adults received medication to treat opioid addiction, with women and African Americans substantially less likely to have access.[3] Longer retention in methadone treatment is associated with better patient outcomes, and research indicates the first twelve months are critical to patient success. Studies over decades show that the majority of patients drop out during the first year of methadone treatment,[4] with one study showing that 64 percent of patients discontinue use of medication prior to six months.[5]

Yet drug warriors and callous bureaucrats in these federal agencies, along with clinic staff, shift the blame to patients. They don't "follow the rules," they don't "take recovery seriously," or—the biggest lie of all—patients are "not ready for treatment." Patients don't fail methadone treatment; the treatment fails them. Methadone itself is a tool of harm reduction. But the clinics that control methadone are a system of harm *production* that drives people out of treatment and back to a toxic supply of street drugs. Over one million Americans have died from opioid-related overdoses. Methadone has been proven to cut the overdose death rate by 59 percent.[6] It is criminal that OTPs take a medication with such demonstrated, lifesaving benefits and make it difficult to access.

Carceral Clinics

Imagine you've just stepped off a crowded bus after a second subway transfer, or you've just driven a white knuckled harrowing hour during a snowstorm, and you pull up to an unmarked concrete building with frosted windows that is surrounded by a tall black steel fence in the "seedy part of town." It's 5 a.m. There is a line of people snaking around the block. You join it. This is where you come to swallow one dose of liquid methadone six or seven days a week.

Every interaction between patients and staff in the methadone clinic system is marked by a lack of trust, surveillance, coercion, and punishment. Patients are not allowed to possess their own medication. Instead, a constantly changing cast of counselors, security guards, physicians, and nurses control access, robbing patients of autonomy while exerting control over their lives well beyond the walls of the OTP.

This massive power imbalance, which is rarely acknowledged, creates an environment that keeps patients passive, afraid, anxious, and obedient. In no other health care setting are patients with chronic medical conditions at the complete mercy of staff and constantly threatened with being cut off their medication and forced into withdrawal. This practice is a human rights violation and contravenes the Hippocratic Oath and the Nursing Code of Ethics, which declare "do no harm" and promote "autonomy in decision-making and justice."

Commuting to a clinic is a lifelong proposition. A counselor said to Louis Jones, a former methadone patient in New York City, "Till death do we part." Patients routinely talk about OTPs using carceral language. They are on chemical parole or a chemical tether, restrained by liquid hand-cuffs; attending the clinics constitutes a life sentence; the clinic is a ball and chain; patients are lifers. Indeed, the relationship between staff and patients models a prisoner-guard relationship. The clinic assigns everyone an ID number, and some nurses use that instead of the name of a person to confirm their identity and dose.

> I had no idea what I was getting into. In the beginning, it didn't bother me having to go to the clinic six days a week because it gave me a reason to wake up every morning. But after a year passed, I realized it was a prison because I couldn't go anywhere without having this drug with me, and I couldn't get take-home bottles. I don't care if I was going to the clinic once a month or once a week, it was still a prison.
>
> —FRANCINE, New York

The resemblance to prisons is a feature, not a bug, of the clinic system. Methadone clinics were designed to segregate, control, and monitor patients, much like penal institutions. When a person enters a clinic, they lose their freedom and basic human rights. Uniformed security guards are the first personnel patients encounter. Some clinics hire off-duty cops. The job description for a security officer at Montefiore OTPs in the Bronx includes managing the waiting area and directing patients to medicating windows; exercising constant vigilance of patients, staff, and visitors; and performing perimeter patrols, including loitering patrols. The job qualification section states "military experience preferred."[7]

Loitering or "hanging around" the vicinity of clinics is taken very seriously. This is because the neighborhoods OTPs are located in have opposed their opening and are looking for reasons to shut them down.[8] When the Greater Harlem Coalition complained about loitering at a Mount Sinai OTP in Harlem, the management agreed to "contract a new, more reputable security firm and staff their new building with retired New York Police Department (NYPD) sergeants and install additional security measures inside the buildings, such as metal detectors and security cameras."[9]

A sign posted on the door and in windows of the Family Guidance Center in Chicago threatened: "If you are seen loitering or lingering around the building or the surrounding area, you will immediately be placed on involuntary withdrawal." The sign speaks volumes about the oppression of people who take methadone. That a health care facility would force a patient into withdrawal for simply lingering in the vicinity of the clinic is barbaric.

Policing patients is a core function of clinic security guards, and police officers in the community have harassed and arrested patients on their way to the program and while waiting in line outside. The Beyond Methadone study in New York City found that nearly four in ten patients surveyed reported being stopped and frisked by police outside their clinic, and seven in ten respondents witnessed someone else being frisked or harassed by police while entering or leaving the clinic.[10] A methadone patient explained, "The police arrested a few of the people on the program. . . . If they need a spot to meet their quotas, they just come to the methadone programs and mess with people, search them for no reason. . . . I have missed a dose because of the police."[11]

At a New York City clinic I filmed in for my first documentary, a guard sat in a raised booth in front of the entrance to the medicating area. As patients arrived, he ordered them to throw take-out coffees, plastic water bottles, and cans of soda into a large trash bin. This was a security measure to prevent diversion of methadone. Inside the booth, a bank of monitors displayed camera feeds from all areas of the clinic and tracked the movement of people inside and outside the building. This is how patients are caught loitering or breaking other clinic rules. Doug was in line waiting for the clinic to open and got into a brief pushing match with another patient who cut the line. No one was hurt, but later staff confronted him with the footage of the altercation and kicked him out of the clinic permanently for fighting.

Security officers are stationed in OTPs for another critical reason. At the American Association for the Treatment of Opioid Dependence (AATOD) conference I attended in 2022, Dr. Kenneth B. Stoller, the director of Johns Hopkins Broadway Center for Addiction in Baltimore, stated, "Security is there to make staff feel safe." But safe from whom? The pervasive presence of uniformed security personnel and hyper-surveillance in clinics creates an atmosphere of criminality and hostility while reinforcing the power imbalance.

Many clinics operate in old run-down buildings with unmarked facades surrounded by razor wire–topped fences in abandoned, deindustrialized zones full of detritus to deter NIMBY protests. A clinic in East Harlem has separate entrances for patients and staff.[12] Iron bars on windows and roll-down metal security gates are common. Clinic interiors are austere and cold, with artificial lighting, drab colors, and ceiling mounted cameras. Methadone clinics have long embodied hostile architecture before it became a thing on Instagram. There is no art, beauty, or comfort in clinics because of their prison-like environment.

In dense urban areas like New York City, OTPs hide in plain sight with no signage and tinted windows. An unmarked storefront clinic on the Lower East Side has graffiti sprayed across it and the glass is blacked out. In 1971 a methadone program that was closed by the DEA transferred all their patients to the *Gold Star Mother*, a decommissioned Staten Island ferryboat that was docked at Battery Park on the Hudson River. "Every weekday, 450 former heroin addicts climb a gangway to the *Gold Star Mother*. . . . After showing their credentials and submitting to tests, they climb to the upper deck. At what used to be the refreshment stand (the soft drink machines have not yet been removed) they receive one-day dosages of methadone."[13] Two OTPs in Boston located on "Methadone Mile" are around the corner from the Suffolk County House of Corrections.[14] A coincidence? In rural Pennsylvania, an OTP is housed in a cross between a shipping container and a trailer. A concrete building with no windows in Baltimore accommodated a storefront church, the New Life Evangelical Baptist Church, and a methadone clinic.[15]

OTPs are purposely invisible. They're not businesses the public is supposed to see or be able to identify. The only thing that gives them away is the people standing in long lines outside the building. Imagine having to spend any amount of time inside or even outside such a dismal and depressing place for years on end.

The Culture of Cruelty

In 2021 the National Survivors Union, a grassroots coalition of drug users, both former and active, published "The Methadone Manifesto."[16] It was the first systematic critique of the clinic system by people who take methadone. The group identified a deep-rooted "culture of cruelty" in methadone clinics. It consists of strict attendance requirements, supervised dosing, urinalysis, mandated counseling, "earning" take-home doses, bottle recalls, limited dosing hours, and much more. The cruelty that patients endure daily is covered up by a culture of concealment. The public, politicians, health care providers, and the media don't know what happens in methadone clinics.

The culture of cruelty begins with an attendance requirement that can only be understood via the clinic imperative to surveil and control patients. From the start, clinic staff don't trust patients to take methadone as prescribed, often citing the potential for overdose or diversion, which is selling it on the street. So, for the first three months, everyone is mandated to come to the program six days a week, and in some states, seven. It is a commitment that extracts an enormous amount of time, money, and energy from patients. Patients commute daily to swallow a single dose of methadone under the watchful eye of a nurse. It forces people to prioritize traveling to a clinic instead of other things like work, family, education, or relaxation. Generally, people try to get medicated at a clinic that is close to where they live, but that isn't always possible because 80 percent of US counties don't have a single OTP.[17]

In large cities like Boston, Chicago, New York City, and San Francisco, there is mass transit, but it is often unreliable. In 2023 it was announced that the MTA in New York City was facing "the greatest crisis in its long history."[18] Train delays are an everyday occurrence. Funding for public transportation has declined and has led to the elimination of bus routes, fewer trains, and longer wait times.

Being dependent on the operation of both buses and trains is precarious, but that is exactly the situation Laura, who lives on Staten Island, finds herself in. She takes a bus to the ferry, then gets on an uptown train. Depending on the day, time, and the state of transit delays, it can take up to two hours one-way to reach her clinic. For those with mobility issues, the commute is even more difficult when there are no elevators or escalators or they are closed for repair. There are zero OTPs in Wyoming, so people have to cross state lines to get methadone.[19] In rural areas, clinics are often hundreds of miles away, which makes a car a necessity. What could go wrong? Flat tires, engine trouble, road closures, construction, accidents, and traffic.

Round-trip travel six or seven days a week isn't cheap, and costs rise most years. In New York City a one-way subway fare is $2.90 as of 2025. Jenna, who is unemployed, stands at the entrance in a Brooklyn station and asks passengers for a "swipe" of their MetroCard. When desperate, she has jumped the turnstile and risked arrest for fare evasion. A one-way fare to ride the Bay Area Rapid Transit system in Northern California could cost over $7. For those who drive, the average cost of a gallon of regular gas in Nevada is $4. Exacerbating this transportation nightmare is that people who take methadone are disproportionately low-income, so the expense of getting to an OTP takes a big bite out of an already tight budget. The attendance requirement combined with an expensive and long commute for many causes patients to miss doses and to drop out of treatment.

> *I honestly wish they would just understand I have a house and job I am trying very hard to maintain, and going two hours out of my way before work is really just hard sometimes. People might call me lazy, but if I am really tired, I just don't go. I won't risk getting in trouble at my job. A counselor said I didn't want recovery enough because if I did, I would get up early and get to the clinic with more than enough time to travel back home to be at my place of employment.*
> —LIZ, Illinois

Extreme weather events have become more common in the United States because of climate change: heat waves, floods, wildfires, and hurricanes. As a result of weather emergencies, mass transportation and highways are closed and authorities advise staying home. That is not an option for people on methadone. In 2012, when Hurricane Sandy slammed into New York City, patients still had to go to the clinic. They trudged through dangerous streets with downed power lines because the entire subway system was shut down. In 2013, Elizabeth Brico was five months pregnant and living in Boulder, Colorado, when a flood inundated the city and her methadone clinic closed. She was told to go to a clinic in Denver, but no public buses were running. Brico's counselor then arranged for a FEMA helicopter to fly her there, but fortunately she got dosed at a hospital in Boulder.[20] In 2024, an extreme cold event flooded and shut down an OTP in Seattle. Over one thousand patients were transferred to other clinics that were much farther away. There was an increase in missed doses and patients dropping out of treatment.[21] It makes no sense to travel to an OTP during extreme weather because it puts the lives of patients, as well as clinic staff, in grave danger.

Narrow Windows

Compounding the stress of killer commutes is the narrow window of time that OTPs are open. Dosing hours can differ widely from one clinic to another and can change with no notice and for no apparent reason. In general, clinics are not open for eight consecutive hours during the day, nor are there late evening hours. One exception is a clinic in Phoenix that is open twenty-four hours, seven days a week.[22] A typical weekday schedule is 6:30 a.m. to 2:30 p.m. Some clinics reserve the first hour for patients with verified employment. Saturdays are the most restrictive, with dosing hours typically from 8 a.m. to 10:45 a.m. Getting medicated on Saturday is vital because patients get a take-home bottle for Sunday when the clinic is closed. Patients who drive report that they regularly exceed speed limits to get to the clinic on time. It's called the "Indy 500."

When the clinic door closes, patients are effectively locked out. Dozens of patients have told me that if they were late, even by *one minute*, staff wouldn't open the door. The reason doesn't matter. If you miss the dosing window, fuck you, no methadone.

I got to the clinic at 10:04. The door was locked. I was confused because I thought the clinic was open until noon on Saturdays. I knocked and eventually someone came out and I was like, 'Look, I'm so sorry. I had an issue with the kids.' And they're like, 'Sorry, it's past 10 o'clock.' Staff said this would be a lesson to me that I need to be on time. They're closed on Sundays. Now I was going to miss two doses. Staff told me that I better show up on time on Monday, and if I didn't, they would drop my dose down to 40 mg. The anxiety was so severe I almost burst into tears. I went to the street and got enough fentanyl for two days, just to keep the withdrawal at bay.

—BILL, Pennsylvania

I was about five minutes late. Security wouldn't let me in. My reaction was, I went out and got a couple bags of dope and then I went back and knocked on the door again. Security came to the small window in the door and I held up

16

the bags of dope so he could see them. I had an attitude. If you don't give me access to something I need, I'll go serve myself.

—HECTOR, New York

Even if a patient is late because of a mass shooting, no methadone.

You'll probably appreciate the most American thing I've ever experienced at the methadone clinic. This week we had a mass shooting a block away from the main street splitting downtown. I take the bus and bring my bike. I was only a few blocks away when it happened. We were stopped for around thirty minutes. I thought about getting off and making a mad dash on my bike but without info on if the shooter was at large, I decided that'd probably be a bad idea. It looked like I'd get to the clinic with fifteen minutes to spare but traffic was so crazy I arrived five minutes late. No exceptions for late arrivals even when you're late due to a mass shooting. I wanted to laugh and cry at the same time.

—MELISSA, Virginia

Having medication withheld for tardiness is a major point of conflict in clinics and can lead to patients becoming verbally abusive to staff. Clinics can punish these responses by putting a patient on a "contract," transferring them to another clinic, or expulsion. Denying patients their medication is a mortal threat, and some patients will understandably react in an angry way. Missing a dose can set up patients to buy illicit opioids, like Bill and Hector, from street dealers who are always open and offer to deliver. Still others are so angry and humiliated at being locked out that they leave treatment. Clinic-generated relapses are extremely dangerous in the era of fentanyl.

Supervised Humiliation

The medicating area is where patients feel their criminalized status and lack of freedom most viscerally. Signs admonishing them are everywhere:

Attention. Stop. Please wait until you are called.

Reminder when at the medicating window, No: eating, drinking, reading, cell phones.

Remove: dark glasses, headphones, items from the medication counter.

You must speak to the nurse after medication.

Please, no distractions or interruptions while nurse is medicating.

Quiet, please, medication being dispensed.

Help prevent medication errors: no talking.

Answer your name promptly or you will be medicated last.

No profanity in the clinic please.

The posters full of commands make it clear: If you want methadone, keep your mouth shut and stand in line quietly until it's your turn. Nurses are stationed behind a wall of thick plexiglass, which symbolizes that patients are feared and not trusted. For some international contrast, in Portugal, methadone vans are deployed in the community. I rode along with staff in Porto. At each location the van door opened and patients approached a nurse who dispensed liquid methadone into a cup from a plastic bottle perched on the seat next to her. There was no security guard.

The medication window is where arguments with nurses often occur. Patients report waiting in long lines only to be told they won't be medicated until they meet with their counselor or provide a urine specimen, or that their take-home bottles have been rescinded.

> *I get that clients can be emotionally charged, but maybe if the staff didn't spring life-altering changes on you at the dosing window or have the power to make such a life-altering impact with impunity, they wouldn't have to fear their clients.*
>
> —KEISHA, Texas

Supervised dosing is why OTPs exist. An expensive, computerized dispensing system calculates the exact dose of methadone, and a bright-colored liquid drips into a plastic cup and is passed through the opening of the plexiglass window (in carceral language, a chuckhole). The nurse watches the patient as they drink the liquid and then asks them to lift up their tongue for inspection or to speak. This is to ensure that the medication has been swallowed so it can't be diverted and sold as "spit-back." This is when a patient holds the liquid in their mouth and, once outside, spits it into a container.

Methadone clinics are founded on the idea that the medication they dispense is a privilege, not a right. There is no other area of health care where patients have to demonstrate on a daily basis that they deserve their medicine and are watched while they ingest it. Can you imagine daily supervised use of Viagra, birth control pills, Lipitor, or insulin?

Pissed Off

When a patient walks into a methadone program, their body no longer belongs to them, and constant urine testing is a potent reminder. Screening urine for substances is an invasive form of surveillance, and it has become completely normalized. The results, positive or negative, "clean" or "dirty," inform all treatment decisions. Urine is screened for alcohol, benzodiazepines, cannabis, cocaine, and opioids.

Federal rules require eight random drug tests per year, but twenty-six states, including California, Texas, and Maine, require more drug screenings than federally mandated.[23] Some clients are tested weekly, and there is a "random drop": The patient is not informed in advance. Refusal is considered a positive.

But how to get all that urine? In ten states, staff "directly observe the collection of urine," meaning they watch the genitals of clients while they pee.[24] For survivors of sexual trauma, it can be retraumatizing. Patients who can't produce a urine specimen on demand are in trouble. The SOAR clinic handbook explains: "If a patient has an inability to provide a sample when requested, they are instructed to sit in the lobby and drink water until a sample is provided. If a patient fails to provide a sample by the close of business or leaves the lobby, the scheduled dose of methadone is forfeited for the day."[25] Staff give instructions in how to urinate correctly.

A patient who attends a SOAR clinic in Pennsylvania sent me a photo of a poster in the bathroom: "For our male clients: Please make sure you are standing directly in front of the toilet when asked to give a urine sample. For our female clients: Please make sure you are sitting straight on the toilet when asked to give a urine sample. If you don't, your sample will not be accepted and you will forfeit your dose for the day."

Some clinics use cameras to observe urination. It's called a "monitored drop." This method raises issues around privacy. Methadone programs might claim urination is just observed and not recorded, but patients are concerned that staff might film the live video on their cell phone and use it for nefarious purposes, like posting it on social media.

Patients rightly fear urine testing because the results can lead to punishment. To avoid that, some sneak in "clean" urine or add chemicals to the sample. There are thousands of sites on the internet that offer products and advice on how to beat a drug test. The availability of these tools has triggered yet more suspicion and surveillance of patients. Some clinics now take two samples using different methods.

My clinic does direct observation for every patient, every single time. They have nurses dedicated to only drug testing and they stand in the bathroom with you for your random UA every month. They're at least mindful about standing near the door as far away from you as possible and aren't staring right at you the whole time, but it still sucks. I'm extremely pee shy and even after like eight and a half years of doing an observed UA every month, I was still having so much trouble peeing with them being in the bathroom with me. I finally got switched to mouth swabs because I had other urinary issues and it was honestly the single most positive change for me at the clinic in my almost 10 years there.

—BUNNYGIRL93XO, Methadone Harm
Reduction Forum, Reddit

I literally switched clinics because I couldn't stand the observed UAs. My old clinic wanted me to learn to self-catheterize myself to deal with them. It caused me a lot of health issues and anxiety. I could never go back to observed UAs.

It's a shame. I would've had more rights on federal or state probation then I do voluntarily seeking treatment.

—JERSEY_GIRL666, Methadone Harm
Reduction Forum, Reddit

MedMark makes it clear on their website that peeing in a cup is mandatory: "When you walk in for your assessment, you'll have to be prepared to provide a urine specimen for a drug screen. In fact, the heroin treatment center can ask you to retest just about any time, any day. You probably aren't going to like that, but those are the rules. If you choose not to participate or if you don't pass your drug test, you may not be able to receive your methadone or Suboxone."[26] This isn't an empty threat. OTPs regularly withhold medication for noncompliance, or remove the "privilege" of take-home doses. A clinic counselor reported to a colleague that he told a patient her urine was positive, and she would lose all her take-home bottles. The woman asked, "Who do I have to blow to keep them?"

New technologies that are marketed as nonintrusive (though they still are) have transformed the practice of urine testing. Saliva can be collected via swabbing the mouth, and strands of hair and fingernail clippings can be analyzed for drugs. The United States Drug Testing Laboratory uses fingernails and can test for seventeen substances. A company brochure explains, "A wealth of new data brings fingernail testing to the forefront of toxicology. . . . As the nail grows in thickness, it creates layers of drug history." Not enough fingernails? They suggest collecting toenails instead.[27]

The for-profit drug-testing industry is a cornerstone of the methadone-industrial complex. Screening urine for banned substances is lucrative and business is booming. OTPs, drug courts, and drug rehabilitation programs are three of the most reliable customers because of the high frequency of testing. Methadone patients are customers for life, and testing can be pricey. With or without insurance, the cost can run over four thousand dollars.[28] If a drug test is positive and a patient wants a confirmation, they must pay out of pocket. The charges associated with drug screening are high, and if eliminated, it would reduce the expense of taking methadone. But for lab owners, urine testing is "liquid gold," so it continues.

The Take-Away Bottle Game

Getting take-home bottles of methadone is the number-one goal of every patient for a simple reason: it reduces the time spent traveling to the clinic and being subjected to the alienating culture of cruelty. It also provides a modicum of freedom. But it's a zero-sum game with an ever-changing series of obstacles that stacks the deck against the majority of patients. I call it the "take-away bottle game." Are you ready to play? Patients can get bottles to take home only after complying with a sequenced set of requirements that can change at any moment. More on these below. It's almost impossible not to lose some or all the bottles for a raft of petty reasons and to maintain clinic profit margins. Clinics bill insurance every time a nurse supervises a dose and loses money when it's unsupervised, so there is a powerful financial incentive to enforce daily attendance. That's the game, and it's full of gotcha moments that force patients to start all over again.

> *You have to earn take-home bottles. It's a privilege, and it takes time to earn them.*
> —CATHERINE, New York

The federal guidelines lay out the time frame required for earning "take-home privileges." SAMHSA's treatment standards, codified in the 2015 *Federal Guidelines for Opioid Treatment Programs*, reinforce the carceral nature of OTPs. Their main concern in allowing unsupervised dosing is "to limit the potential for diversion of opioid agonist treatment medications to the illicit market."[29]

During the first ninety days of treatment, patients are limited to one take-home bottle, usually on Sunday and on holidays. All other doses must be supervised, which means daily attendance. In the second ninety days of treatment, two take-home bottles are allowed. In the remaining months of the first year, a patient may be given a maximum six-day supply of take-home medication. After one year of continuous treatment, they can receive a maximum two-week supply, and after two years, they can receive a maximum one-month supply. Days, months, years: A key determinant of getting take-home doses is "time in treatment," another carceral concept that is similar to "time served."

Because these numbers are guidelines and are not enforceable by SAMHSA, states can do whatever they want. State opioid treatment authorities (SOTA) are a leading player in the take-away bottle game, often imposing even stricter regulations. Ten states go beyond federal rules by prohibiting take-home doses in the first thirty days of treatment, and seven prohibit this practice during the first ninety days.[30] Some states cap the number of take-homes and give no explanation why. For years Indiana allowed up to twenty-eight take-home bottles, then dropped it down to a stingy six, then bumped it back up to the current fourteen. Prior to the pandemic, West Virginia, one of the epicenters of the opioid overdose crisis, only allowed up to six take-home doses of methadone after the first year and up to fourteen after two years, based on compliance with counseling and drug screenings.[31]

Along with rigid time frames within which a person earns take-home doses, there is a list of criteria that determines whether a patient is responsible enough to handle methadone for unsupervised use. Patients are evaluated as "stable" or "less stable" using eight benchmarks:

1. Absence of recent abuse of drugs (opioid or nonnarcotic) and alcohol.

2. Regularity of clinic attendance.

3. Absence of serious behavioral problems at the clinic.

4. Absence of known recent criminal activity, e.g. drug dealing.

5. Stability of the patient's home environment and social relationships.

6. Length of time in comprehensive maintenance treatment.

7. Assurance that take-home medication can be safely stored within the patient's home.

8. Whether the rehabilitative benefit the patient may derive from decreasing the frequency of clinic attendance outweighs the potential risks of diversion.[32]

With no other medication is a person's ability to take it assessed by a wildly subjective criteria of "stable" or "less stable." Why would SAMHSA create such unattainable barriers to patients getting take-home medication? Why focus on alleged criminal behavior, drug dealing, or diversion at all?

The eight criteria set the bar so high that many patients will never get more than a few bottles per week and almost never the liberatory fourteen or twenty-eight. They focus on an individual's ability to comply with unmeasurable and arbitrary rules instead of considering whether taking methadone at home would improve a patient's life, keep them in treatment, and, during an opioid overdose crisis, keep them alive.

The first benchmark, "absence of recent abuse of drugs," fails to recognize that not all drug use is abuse. If a person is addicted to opioids, it doesn't automatically mean their use of other substances is problematic. Moreover, alcohol is legal, and 74 percent of Americans live in a state where marijuana is legal for either recreational or medical use.[33] But the use of either drug can result in zero take-home bottles. This means that patients are forbidden to do what millions of other Americans do every single day: enjoy a glass of wine or a bottle of beer, smoke a pre-rolled joint, or eat a cannabis-infused edible. OTPs have the power to enforce total abstinence of all substances, legal or illegal.

Rebecca Smith, a sixty-five-year-old woman in Detroit, lost thirteen take-home bottles of methadone after testing positive for alcohol. She drank wine during a toast at her grandson's high-school graduation party.[34] The clinic accused her of having a drinking problem. The consequences were devastating. Smith was forced to choose her medication over her job, and within a few weeks she was late on rent.[35]

According to SAMHSA guidelines, "The results of toxicological tests are an essential component in making decisions regarding take-home medication privileges; however, treatment decisions should not be based solely on toxicology screening results."[36] But they are, in every OTP. It's often the sole reason for loss of take-home bottles.

What constitutes "regular" clinic attendance is open to interpretation. In the real world, it will be "irregular" at times. Patients miss doses or counseling appointments due to illness, transportation delays, no child care, and inflexible work hours. But in the monochrome world of methadone, none of that matters.

The stipulation that patients have a stable home environment and social relationships is discriminatory. How does having "stable relationships," whatever that means and however it is determined, impact a person's ability to swallow their medication outside an OTP? It's reasonable to assume that a good percentage of patients already do that with other prescribed medications.

The demand that a person has stable housing discriminates against those who are street homeless, live in shelters, or move frequently. Patients on methadone are motivated to take the medication daily because it has such positive effects on mental and physical health, maintaining employment, or completing educational coursework. SAMHSA's eight criteria ignore the underlying drivers of inequality, racism, and poverty that disproportionately deny people of color, who are also more likely to be homeless and poor, take-home doses. It's hard to believe that the eight criteria weren't deliberately designed to make it impossible for patients to win the take-away bottle game.

OTPs are the most important and powerful player in this game. They are free to ignore the guidelines crafted by SAMHSA, but in the case of state regulations, clinics usually follow them. Additional stricter and vague regulations are often added by OTPs. A social worker told me that to get more take-homes, patients in her program had to prove that they were doing "something positive during the day."

Bring Bottles Back

Did you think the take-away bottle game was over? It is not. The bottles themselves play a key role in the game via bottle recall, yet another way OTPs surveil and control patients. Without warning, an OTP will contact a patient to inform them they have a short window of time, usually twenty-four hours, to bring all bottles back for inspection. Medication must be carried in an approved lockbox. No other medications, not even other opioids, are required to be transported in a secure container to a clinic. These black lockboxes are stigmatizing and denote that something inside is either dangerous or valuable, which can put a patient at risk for theft or assault. The nurse counts every bottle to confirm the correct number. Each one is obsessively examined to see if the medication has been taken as prescribed and for bottle tampering or diversion.

> *I came right away. Like, I was there within the hour. The first thing was, they made me give urine, and I remember it was a twelve-panel instant test. The nurse came into the room and asked me to unlock my medicine box. She opened the empty bottles and looked inside. She lined up all the unopened bottles on the table and got down at eye level to inspect them to see if they were all the same. And she really checked them. She would kind of tap or flick at the edges to see if they came up easily and then held the bottles up like two feet over the table by the edges of the seals to see if they fell. I felt so intimidated by her. Then she found a bottle with no label. As a result, I lost all my take-homes. It didn't matter that the nurse, a different one who gave me the bottles two weeks before, forgot to attach a label. The bottle recall was when my anxiety and anger really started; before that I felt like the poster child for the methadone clinic.*
> —JORDAN, Michigan

The practice of recalling bottles further restricts patient mobility. How could someone possibly travel out of state or out of the country if at any moment the clinic might demand a bottle recall? This perverse policy forces people to make an OTP the center of their world. A patient from Connecticut told me that when she and her partner, who was also on methadone, bought a house, a major consideration was how close it was to the clinic. Not how close it was to beaches, stores, schools, parks, work, family, or friends; *the clinic.*

In 2002 the National Alliance for Methadone Advocates (NAMA) published a policy statement to address this problem:

> NAMA knows of numerous instances where bottle recall becomes a means to control patients. Patients who travel for business and are called must return to the clinic within a specified time no matter the expense. This can mean a costly airline ticket or even loss of their job. NAMA knows of instances where patients were not able to return because they were out of town. Upon their return and finding out about the recall, they contacted their clinic to find that all their take-home privileges had been revoked for lengthy periods of time. In fact, some patients were told that they must start all over to get the privileges they once had.[37]

Some OTPs don't do bottle recalls, but this doesn't mean the containers aren't regularly checked by nurses. At scheduled intervals, patients return empty bottles that are checked before new ones are dispensed, and during this inspection the possibility always looms that they'll be taken away.[38] NAMA's "Guidelines for Bottle Recall" don't propose ending the practice but state that it should only be used in "special circumstances," while noting additional problems: "Bottle recall can quickly become an abusive policy and should never be used for an entire clinic; these policies create a clinic atmosphere that is anti-therapeutic and anti-methadone and hinders the free movement of patients who are American citizens protected by the Constitution."[39]

Think of a medication you currently take or have taken in the past. Could you comply with all eight criteria, produce zero positive urine screenings, win the take-away bottle game, and earn the privilege of swallowing your medication in the convenience and privacy of your home?

Treatment Trauma

Why would any client talk honestly about their problems with a counselor who has the power to destroy their lives? And yet, in OTPs, it's a thing. Methadone patients are forced to accept counseling in an adversarial environment where they are not trusted and where they are continually monitored and penalized for a host of rule infractions. Mandated counseling violates the most basic ethics of therapy. For example, if a person reveals they're using drugs, their counselor has the authority to revoke take-home bottles, increase or decrease their dose, or to "administratively discharge" them from treatment. Moreover, they can report them to child welfare agencies, parole officers, and drug court judges. No true therapeutic alliance can be built in these circumstances. It's simply not safe to tell the truth. I asked people about counseling services. What I heard over and over was, "We tell them what they want to hear" and "I can't be honest." One person shared that therapy sessions consisted mostly of talking about their dogs.

Edith Springer, a trailblazer in the US harm reduction movement, started taking methadone in the 1970s. In an interview she told me: "I wanted to get off heroin, and I tried to by myself many times and failed. And I heard about methadone from my doctor. The counselors were social workers and it was run by psychiatrists. And they treated me like a criminal. They didn't believe anything I said. I hated the program."[40]

A common complaint was the revolving door of counseling staff: "a new graduate every other month." This constant turnover creates a challenging situation for patients who are expected to talk about traumatic life events again and again. Patients also shared with me that there were counselors who sincerely care about their health and well-being and even bent or broke the rules to protect them, but that doesn't change the fact that they wield enormous power and control over them.

> *There is someone they refer to as my counselor, but the name has changed so frequently I am not even certain I have ever met with them. This is a situation I am quite happy with, as the counseling is a waste of my time, unwanted, and unneeded.*
>
> —DANIELLE, Arizona

Most counselors have a bachelor's degree or a certification as a Credentialed Alcoholism and Substance Abuse Counselor (CASAC). To become a CASAC, only a high school diploma or GED is needed. In addition, employment in a clinic usually requires a minimum of one year of work experience in addiction counseling. Requiring only a basic level of education and minimal experience is problematic. The majority of people with a chronic and persistent opioid addiction have a mental health diagnosis: post–traumatic stress disorder (PTSD), bipolar, major depression, or anxiety. Many are survivors of domestic violence, rape, or physical and sexual abuse. Well-paid, experienced, licensed clinicians with advanced degrees are needed to work with patients who have such complex and intersecting social and mental health needs. This mismatch between inexperienced counselors and high-need patients results in ineffective, unethical counseling and leads to staff desensitization, burnout, and high rates of turnover.

> *The staff here are a bunch of rude, ghetto trash bags. People come here to get help and just get treated like animals by these so-called "counselors." Attitudes are unbelievable. I've never seen anything like it. They seemed bothered that they even have to do their jobs.*
> —GOOGLE REVIEW OF A METHADONE
> CLINIC IN NEW YORK CITY

The counselors in methadone clinics are unlike those in other settings because they are centrally involved in policing and punishing patients. At Montefiore methadone clinics, the job description explicitly states that counselors "directly supervise the collection of toxicology samples for all patients when required" and "monitor patient response to methadone medication treatment through individual counseling and toxicology review."[41] How, after your counselor stares at your genitals during urination, do you go back to their office for a mandated counseling session and feel safe to talk about anything?

OTPs claim that counseling is essential for patient recovery, but studies show that there isn't any significant increase in positive outcomes or program retention related to counseling.[42] It's not that therapy isn't important;

the problem is coerced counseling with a person who has inadequate education and experience *and* the authority to punish. Patients who want therapy should be referred to outside agencies. But then clinics would lose money—every counseling session is billable. What passes for therapy is actually treatment trauma.

> *Slow and inept, this clinic treats patients like human garbage who don't deserve any respect. The most rude and lazy clinicians I have ever encountered. The counselors dismiss needs. They can call you for billing issues but won't call if you need late clinic or guest dosing. I am an advocate for overdose prevention and medication-assisted treatment, but this clinic keeps you in a state of anxiety and relapse circles.*
>
> —GOOGLE REVIEW OF A METHADONE
> CLINIC IN NEW YORK CITY

As one counselor explained, "It is sad, but the only control we have over them is through their medication, so if they start messing up, the only way we can control them is if we detox them. But it's never more than five milligrams or so, but the minute they know you are detoxing them, they straighten out."[43] There is no other group of patients who are systematically terrorized with being denied their medication. In any other field of medicine, deliberately denying someone their life-saving medication as a punishment would be grounds for a lawsuit, disciplinary action, or license suspension.

Peter Vanderkloot, in his seminal article "Methadone: Medicine, Harm Reduction or Social Control," explains, "Counselors with life experience are almost exclusively anti-methadone graduates of therapeutic communities whose personal difficulties with abstinence frequently add resentment and envy to their preexisting hostility to methadone."[44] Employing counselors with a therapeutic communities (TCs) background can harm patients. They are pressured to accept low doses of methadone and urged to taper off quickly, which are setups for relapse. The controversial documentary *Methadonia* follows a group of people who take methadone in New York City. It contains several scenes where a counselor uses TC tactics to bully, confront, and shame participants. At one point she tells them to shut up![45]

Why are staff so willing, and often seem to enjoy, punishing patients struggling with an addiction? The answer is the degrading, zero-tolerance, carceral clinic environment that desensitizes them to the suffering they cause. It leads to a profound loss of empathy for patients. Inflicting the culture of cruelty becomes normalized and needs no justification or acknowledgment. Punishment is reframed as "care," and a culture of concealment allows staff to avoid accountability or consequences for the mistreatment of patients.

2

SUBSTITUTING ONE DRUG FOR ANOTHER: Discovering Methadone to Treat Opioid Addiction

I have no vested interest in their being off drugs. I like them whether they're off or on.

—MARIE NYSWANDER, MD

D
r. Vincent Dole has often been credited as the one who discovered methadone, but without the work of doctors Marie Nyswander and Mary Jeanne Kreek, this synthetic opioid wouldn't have become the gold standard of treatment for addiction or landed on the World Health Organization's list of essential medicines.[1] The trio's work revolutionized the field of addiction and also polarized it. The sites for methadone research took place at two radically different institutions, one rural, one urban: The US Public Health Service Hospital, commonly referred to as the Narcotic Farm, or "Narco," in bucolic Lexington, Kentucky, and Rockefeller University on the wealthy Upper East Side of Manhattan. Dr. Nyswander worked at both.

Back to the Future: "Narco" and the War on Drugs

In 1914, the Harrison Narcotic Act was passed. It required narcotics manufacturers, sellers, and distributors to register with the Bureau of Internal Revenue under the US Treasury Department. There was an ambiguous phrase in the act that said a physician could prescribe narcotics in good faith and "in the course of his professional practice only," which implied, without specifying, a constraint on the authority of the medical profession to dispense narcotics. In 1919 the Supreme Court ruled against narcotic maintenance.[2]

This resulted in patients being forced to buy opioids from the illicit market with predictable, negative consequences. By the 1920s, about half of all prisoners were jailed on drug-related offenses. The Boggs Act of 1951 and The Narcotic Control Act of 1956 set mandatory sentences of two to ten years for narcotics convictions.[3] As a result of the increasing criminalization of narcotics, the prison population exploded. To decrease the numbers and to find a cure for addiction, federal officials built Narco to treat drug users and to conduct research. It was an era long before Institutional Review Boards, ethical considerations, or informed consent. Patients at Narco were a mixed-gender multiracial group of people who were convicted of drug offenses or who "volunteered" for the experiments and at any time could withdraw. But incarcerated people can never give true consent, and people with a drug dependence are especially vulnerable.

The Narcotic Farm became a world-renowned center for drug treatment and research, employing thousands of nurses, doctors, and researchers over the forty years of its existence. Narco was built on fertile farmland and funded by the New Deal–era Works Project Administration. Opening in 1935, the sprawling complex of foreboding art deco concrete buildings had massive steel doors at the entrance and barred windows.[4] It was a peculiar and unique fusion of a federal prison, an inpatient hospital drug rehabilitation program, and the Addiction Research Center (ARC).[5] For even more cognitive dissonance, it was run jointly by the Bureau of Prisons *and* the Public Health Service.

No one contributed to putting more people behind bars than Harry J. Anslinger, the first commissioner of the Federal Bureau of Narcotics (FBN), the forerunner of the DEA. For thirty-two long years he waged a violent, relentless war on Black people who used narcotics and cannabis.[6] He had a particular hatred for Black jazz musicians and singers, believing the clubs they played in encouraged drug use and "race mixing."[7] Anslinger hounded the great jazz vocalist Billie Holiday, who had a lifelong heroin addiction, until she died. She was warned by the FBN never to sing the anti-lynching song "Strange Fruit" in public. But she did. At one point in the singer's career, she was sentenced on drug charges to a year in Federal Prison Camp, Alderson, in West Virginia.[8] She wanted treatment for her addiction but was denied. In June 1959 Holiday was arrested in a New York City hospital room while suffering from withdrawal symptoms. She was finally given methadone to ease her suffering. But after ten days the medication was discontinued, and she went back into withdrawal.[9] Holiday died the following month at age forty-four from heart failure and liver disease. The way that Billie Holiday was tortured by both police and hospital staff reveals the deep-seated roots of racism and hatred of drug users that existed then and now in law enforcement and in the US health care system.

Methadone was a focus of research at the ARC. In one experiment, morphine was administered to 115 men who had a history of a narcotic addiction. Test subjects were detoxed, readdicted to the drug, then abruptly put into withdrawal. Then they received a shot of methadone, which was found to quickly relieve withdrawal symptoms.[10] Researchers pioneered the use of methadone in detoxing patients and establishing safe therapeutic dosage levels. But they didn't discover methadone's potential as a maintenance medication; that was left to doctors Dole, Nyswander, and Kreek.

Treatment for addiction consisted of individual and group therapy as well as recreational and vocational therapy. Sports, art, and music classes were offered. Narco became a temporary resting place for some of the most famous jazz musicians addicted to drugs and a refuge from Anslinger's racist war on their music. At the prison, interracial bands were formed, and concerts featuring jazz giants Sonny Rollins, Red Rodney, Chet Baker, and Bennie Green were held in the 1,300-seat auditorium.[11]

"Work therapy" was central to the mission of Narco, and the prison depended on free labor to clothe and feed prisoners. Planting and harvesting crops as well as caring for and slaughtering animals were all in a day's work down on the farm. For city slickers like Stanley Novick, a Brooklynite steeped in the ways of modern life, the hard physical labor was a nightmare: "I got a job in the dairy milking cows. Here I am a teenager from New York City milking cows at four o'clock in the morning. Cows have a nasty habit of pooping all over the place. . . . I said I've got to get out of here."[12] And he did. Novick would later become the first president of NAMA. All the fresh air, healthy food, exercise, therapy, table tennis, and picking kale were no match for the power of opioids. When patients left Narco, the rate of relapse was over 90 percent.[13]

In the early 1970s, Narco opened the Matrix program. It was a shift away from the Freudian-based psychiatry that Dr. Nyswander was trained in toward TCs. The foundation of TC drug rehabilitation is "The Game." It's a type of group counseling, also called "attack therapy," where people are confronted, bullied, and shamed. Charles Dederich, who founded the original TC, Synanon, invented The Game. In 1958, he opened a storefront drug treatment program in Santa Monica, California.[14] Dederich had a drinking problem and had attended Alcoholics Anonymous (AA) meetings. At Synanon, like AA, he insisted on complete abstinence from all substances. Dederick never understood the nature of drug addiction and said, "The use of narcotics is stupid. What Synanon is dealing with is addiction to stupidity."[15] Synanon devolved into a cult that gradually became more violent under Dederich's authoritarian and perverse leadership. Heads were shaved, men were forced to get vasectomies, and women to abort pregnancies.[16] This brutal approach to treating heroin addiction failed, but the influence and tactics of the model can still be found in most drug treatment settings today, including methadone clinics.

In 1975, a scandal over the ethics of drug research resulted in Narco closing. A congressional hearing revealed that researchers had recruited patients as test subjects for Central Intelligence Agency–funded LSD experiments from 1953 to 1962. The program was called MKUltra.[17]

Over four decades of operation, the Narcotic Farm created a set of contradictory theories about addiction and treatment. Researchers believed addiction was a brain disease, *and* it was a character defect that needed to be aggressively confronted. Today the National Institute on Drug Abuse (NIDA) defines addiction as a chronic, relapsing brain disorder characterized by compulsive drug-seeking and use despite adverse consequences. The definition from the American Society of Addiction Medicine (ASAM) states, "Addiction is a treatable, chronic medical disease involving complex interactions among brain circuits, genetics, the environment, and an individual's life experiences."[18] Both organizations support the use of medication to treat opioid use disorder.

What was learned and piloted at Narco laid the foundation for the next wave of medications to treat for opioid addiction, both methadone and, later, buprenorphine. The shuttering of the ARC created a diaspora of staff and patients who fanned out across the country. From California to New York, they created community-based drug treatment programs. Former patients became counselors practicing attack therapy in TCs and eventually in many methadone programs.[19]

Nyswander on the Farm and in Harlem

In 1945, Dr. Marie Nyswander took a job at The Narcotic Farm. She was twenty-six. In an extensive interview with *Village Voice* journalist Nat Hentoff, she explains, "The year I spent at Lexington was the most miserable I'd ever know. Because of the way I'd been raised, I was totally unequipped to cope with the attitudes which prevail in a prison, and that essentially is what

Lexington is. I'd never had anything to do with addicts before, and when I left, I never wanted to see another one as long as I lived."[20] Nyswander would eat her words about never working with addicts again. She came from a politically liberal family in the North and was exposed to Marxist ideas and to non-Western cultures. Nyswander was miserable at Narco because of the appalling racism of the Jim Crow South. She was called a "nigger-lover" and an "addict-lover" by staff. But Nyswander's antiracism allowed her to develop relationships with Black prisoners that were built on trust and respect and that continued throughout her career. "Most of the negro patients were particularly kind to me," she told Hentoff. "They'd play jazz for me, something they usually did only for themselves. At night they'd often sneak milk shakes into my room. They kept me going, asking nothing of me."[21]

During the year Nyswander spent at Narco, she learned to detox patients from opioids with methadone. She would use this knowledge in the future in community and medical settings and would go on to become an internationally recognized leader for her work in addiction at Bellevue Hospital and Rockefeller University in New York City.[22]

Nyswander's first foray into community-based treatment was in partnership with the East Harlem Protestant Parish Narcotics Office in the 1960s. Trained in psychoanalysis, she offered "storefront psychiatry" to people who lived in the neighborhood. The individual therapy she provided didn't cure addiction, but working in the community profoundly changed her ideas about drug users. "I was seeing 'addicts' outside of prison. . . . I realized that the stereotypes of the 'dangerous drug fiend' were wrong."[23] Nyswander understood addiction on a personal level too. She admitted how difficult it was to quit smoking cigarettes because of the intense cravings for nicotine and noted the similarities to quitting heroin. Nyswander started smoking at the age of fourteen and was never able to stop. She died from cancer in 1986.[24]

Vincent Dole was changed by what he saw in Harlem too. He lived in Rye, New York, a wealthy coastal suburb in Westchester County. Five days a week he took the Metro-North train to New York City and got off at the 125th street stop in Harlem. Dole would walk to the elevated Third

Avenue subway station to catch a train to the campus of Rockefeller University on the Upper East Side. Walking down the street he saw crowds of people using drugs, nodding out on sidewalks, or sleeping in doorways.[25] Dole said, "I had the sense of moving between two highly privileged oases through a truly epidemic sea of misery. I began to realize that nobody in my community of scientists or people in Rye had any concept of that world. We were essentially living in the midst of an epidemic and ignoring it."[26] Dole decided he wouldn't ignore the misery, and it triggered a scientific quest to understand the nature of narcotic addiction and to research methadone as a treatment. He discovered Nyswander's work with drug users in Harlem and asked her to join him at Rockefeller.

Doling Out Methadone

In 1964 they began clinical trials of methadone hydrochloride. The impetus for the research was New York City jails that were filled with thousands of people dependent on heroin. To participate, a person needed to have at least a four-year history of injecting heroin and repeated relapses. During the first phase, patients were hospitalized for a month and gradually brought up to a blockading dose of methadone, then in the second phase, discharged to an outpatient clinic. Patients attended the clinic five days a week for witnessed dosing, got take-homes for the weekend, and had their urine tested. Dole and Nyswander created a methadone dispensing system based on surveillance and a lack of trust in patients. The final phase 3 was reached "when the subject has become a stable and socially productive member of the community, and can be treated as an ordinary medical patient. . . . He must be acceptably employed (either in a job or at school, or if a woman, as a homemaker), and have no further problems with drugs or alcohol."[27] This is the origin of ranking and sorting patients into stable and unstable categories with the end goal of creating the "model methadone patient."

The findings of the four-year study were groundbreaking and demonstrated that a daily dose of the long-acting synthetic opioid eliminated cravings for heroin with few side effects. Doctors Dole, Nyswander, and Kreek believed that their research proved that opioid addiction caused a permanent metabolic change in the brain that required the long-term use of methadone. The medication wasn't to be used to medically withdraw patients from opioids; maintenance was the standard of care. Their position that addiction was a chronic, relapsing brain disease was as debated in the 1960s as it is today. Nevertheless, their discovery was a pivotal moment in the development of medication that would treat addiction, free people from chasing illegal opioids, and allow them to avoid incarceration and overdose death. But in significant ways the research conclusions created a monster because it connected crime to addiction, and patients were designated "criminal-addicts." Their study linked taking methadone with lowering crime rates, something no other medication has ever been tasked with doing.

Dole and Nyswander said of the study results, "Drug-related crime has been sharply reduced by the blockade of narcotic drug hunger. Prior to treatment 91 percent of the patients had been in jail, and all of them had been more or less continuously involved in criminal activities."[28] It's important to recognize that these patients would not have committed offenses and been jailed if they had been maintained on a legal supply of opioids. Harry Anslinger's war on drugs made it illegal for doctors to do this as they had done in the past. Drug prohibition is the real crime. Consistently connecting methadone to crime reduction led to viewing people who take methadone not as human beings struggling with the social determinants of addiction—poverty, racism, trauma, discrimination—but as violent lawbreakers whose addiction drove crime rates. The consequences of this connection created the stigmatizing carceral clinic system where patients are treated like criminals.

Harassment and Surveillance

For much of their professional careers, Nyswander and Dole were harassed by Anslinger's agents. Year after year they endured personal and professional attacks on their research. Nyswander said she didn't possess a narcotics license for years to avoid the scrutiny of the bureau and entrapment. She wasn't "prepared emotionally or financially for court battles."[29] Nonetheless, FBN informers were sent to her office in East Harlem to find out if she referred patients to doctors who did prescribe narcotics. Agents surveilled her self-financed Narcotic Addiction Research Project, which offered therapy to drug users. "A representative of the bureau was at every one of our staff meetings," she told Hentoff. "What concerned him was if the therapists were asking the right questions to make absolutely sure whether their patients were still on drugs. It was impossible to communicate to him that we didn't care."[30] The bullies at the bureau interfered with research Nyswander and Dole conducted at Rockefeller University. They objected to their clinical trials because they were designed to maintain patients on methadone, which they vehemently opposed. Agents showed up in person to threaten Nyswander and Dole and to tell them they were breaking the law. The agents advised them to stop, or they would be "put out of business" or go to jail. According to Dole, agents infiltrated clinics and stole records, spread false rumors that they fabricated data to discredit their research, and called them liars.[31]

The through line in treating addiction in the United States is the powerful policing role of the DEA via their generously funded drug war. The criminalization of drug users made it impossible to create a humane, patient-centered methadone clinic system despite the efforts of Dole, Nyswander, and many others. The specter of Harry Anslinger stalks doctors to this day. His modern-day agents, equipped with state-of-the-art digital surveillance technology, continue to monitor physicians who prescribe opioids via their DEA number as well as the pharmacists who dispense them.[32] To the detriment of patients, the intrusive role of the DEA has been accepted and normalized. DEA personnel are welcomed to speak at the conferences of ASAM and AATOD.[33] The enforcers of prohibition shouldn't be allowed at these meetings, and they shouldn't be involved in addiction treatment. They are police, not doctors. It's past time to get them out of medicine.[34]

Office-Based Opioid Treatment

Dole and Nyswander wanted methadone to be prescribed by doctors outside of OTPs. Nyswander knew her counterparts in Britain could prescribe diamorphine (heroin) and patients collected it at a pharmacy. Published in 1956, her book *The Drug Addict as a Patient* includes an appendix titled "The British Approach."[35] To that end, in 1983 they created an office-based methadone maintenance pilot program at Rockefeller University. To qualify, patients had to be employed and have no illicit drug use or positive urine screenings for several years. It was only for those deemed stable. The medication was prescribed by a physician and a month's supply was picked up at an on-site pharmacy. In 1985, the program moved to Beth Israel. The idea was to transfer patients into the practices of physicians who had never worked in a methadone clinic to determine if they could treat addiction within their practices.[36] Office-based opioid treatment (OBOT), as it came to be called, was a resounding success and liberatory for patients.[37] Unfortunately, this effective prescribing model, which normalized the lives of a small group of methadone patients, was never duplicated on a large scale. A network of seven methadone medical maintenance programs was opened in New York, but most have closed. One program that continues to operate is housed in the Vincent P. Dole Treatment and Research Institute for Opiate Dependence at New York–Presbyterian.[38]

Nyswander and Dole watched as the methadone clinic system, controlled by the DEA, SAMHSA, and state opioid treatment authorities, became overly regulated and excessively punitive. A zero-tolerance mentality took hold, and kicking patients out of treatment for any rule violation became routine. In a prescient article, they wrote:

> Without mutual respect, an adversarial relationship develops between patients and staff, reinforced by arbitrary rules and the indifference of persons in authority. Patients held in contempt by the staff continue to act like addicts and the overcrowded facility becomes a public nuisance. Understandably, methadone maintenance programs today have little appeal to the communities or to the majority of heroin addicts on the street.[39]

The contradictory reality is that the pioneers of methadone founded a clinic system that monitored, controlled, and distrusted patients and later created OBOT, which allowed a few hundred model methadone patients to be treated with dignity and respect outside the carceral clinic system.

Dole and Nyswander were a product of their time and ahead of their time. Nyswander was a harm reductionist before that was a thing. She accepted patients into her practice in Harlem who were active drug users because she didn't believe that total abstinence was necessary to start treatment. In her research on methadone, she recognized the importance of hiring people with lived experience to be involved in the work.[40] Nyswander wanted to supply patients with legal opioids to prevent death. "I hope that you're not seeing another life lost in the cause of the Federal Bureau of Narcotics," she cynically told Hentoff after hearing about a patient who had overdosed and was in a coma. "I lose five to twenty addicts a year from overdose. . . . How can people accept these needless deaths?"[41] Tragically, we are still asking that question. Nyswander believed addiction was a medical problem, not a criminal one. At the time that was viewed as heretical, but it was a vital contribution to the nascent field of addiction medicine. Nyswander's bold commitment to work with people dependent on narcotics in an era when the medical profession had largely abandoned them was the driving force behind the revolutionary research that discovered methadone.

Dole, who died in 2006 at the age of ninety-three, lived to see the siloed clinic system devolve even further into a complex bureaucracy that was so dysfunctional it was easier to buy heroin on the street than to get methadone in a clinic. He witnessed how the early promise of methadone liberating patients collided with the creation of a carceral clinic system that exercised massive control over them and embedded societal stigma. During the AIDS epidemic, when sharing needles was one of the leading causes of virus transmission, strict methadone regulations weren't changed to save lives. In 1996 Dole attended a methadone conference in France. He reported that access to the medication had increased in European countries. He lamented, "The stagnation of our treatment situation in the United States is really looking very foolish compared to the application of methadone treatment in Europe. But they don't have the same bureaucracy that tends to hinder us here."[42]

Every year AATOD gives out the Nyswander-Dole "Marie" Award: "Award recipients have devoted themselves to improving the lives of patients in our treatment system." In 2015, Jason Kletter, the president of the for-profit, private equity–backed BayMark Health Services, a methadone clinic chain, and Yngvild K. Olsen, the director for the Center for Substance Abuse Treatment at SAMHSA and a former clinic medical director, received the Marie Award.[43] Kletter and Olsen haven't improved the lives of patients; they've kept them chained to a crusty old clinic system where they have to prove seven days a week that they deserve to swallow a single dose of methadone. On their watch, the rate of overdose deaths— needless deaths, as Nyswander believed—has skyrocketed year after year while the lifesaving medication that cuts overdose deaths by over half has remained in prison.[44] Nyswander and Dole wouldn't applaud these recipients of the Marie Award. They would be turning over in their graves.

The year that Dole died, Beth Israel Medical Center named a methadone clinic after him, the Vincent P. Dole Clinic. I visited on a hot sunny day in July. The G Train dropped me of in the Gowanus neighborhood of Brooklyn. It's a long trek from the subway station that can only remind patients of how little their lives and time are valued. The OTP can be found in a gentrified industrial zone that still smells of its polluted past. Despite the odor of sewage from the Gowanus Canal, it's being promoted as a new center of Brooklyn's art scene. In 2010 the canal was put on the Environmental Protection Agency's Superfund list. Along the scenic route to the clinic, I passed the Pottery Studio, a gleaming Tesla showroom, and a lumber liquidator. There are beautiful murals painted on the walls of the low-slung building that houses the Salvation Army Donation Center. When I turned onto 12th Street, I was greeted by a fleet of parked sanitation trucks that reeked of garbage. Each one had a sign: "Don't Do NYC

Dirty." The Dole program is on the second floor of a decrepit, four-story, yellow brick building at the end of the road. It is sandwiched between a sprawling Lowe's Home Improvement and the loading dock for BIG Reuse, a thrift store and donation drop-off hub. The entranceway was dirty, and the scuffed doors were held open by an orange traffic cone. I walked up a gray ramp and found the elevator. Next to it was a wall covered by a huge poster advertising Retro Fitness, a gym on the third floor. It showed a toned woman exercising exuberantly and exclaimed: "It Becomes Something You Constantly Crave." Unfortunately I wasn't able to visit Dole's namesake clinic because I arrived after 10:45 a.m. and it was closed.

True to the template that methadone clinics must hide in plain sight, there were no signs directing patients to the program on the second floor. Not one, inside or out. The only hint that an OTP might be on the premises was a label stuck to a metal mailbox on the first floor. It read "Beth Israel Medical Center." But the exercise junkies know who is one floor below. Reviews of Retro Fitness on the Yelp website reveal some of them don't like the Dole Clinic:

> I just canceled my membership as I really hate the fact that it is in the same building as a methadone clinic. . . . There will be shady characters in the stairwell, elevator, and hanging out outside. There's a security guard but who knows what could happen.

> They definitely don't let you know when signing up there is a methadone program in the building. Upon entering the facility you are riding the elevator or taking the stairs with drug addicts.

> On the second floor in the same building is a really gross methadone clinic. Don't even walk out into that floor; avoid it.[45]

Google reviews reveal that some patients don't like the Dole Clinic either, but for different reasons:

> The whole vibe is filled with anger and contempt. I would not recommend setting foot in this place unless it's a matter of life and death. I refuse to believe this is how New Yorkers would treat patients seeking help for a drug addiction . . . basically treated like an eight-year-old in jail.

It's too isolated to reach if you don't drive. Three long blocks to walk in winter with diabetic leg problems. If you don't drive stay away from Dole.

Slow, there are constantly lines, and the staff is not at all friendly. The nurses act like they're doing you favors, and just a general air of rudeness surrounds the place.

If you are looking for compassion and understanding, this clinic is not the place for you. They treat their patients like lowlife scum.

This place sucks.[46]

That a clinic named after Dr. Dole would be found near a canal that is a toxic sewage dump, and that patients would despise the staff, would have disappointed him, but not come as a surprise.

3

RICHARD NIXON, THE WAR ON DRUGS, AND METHADONE

The struggles and victories of the Black power and civil rights movements against white supremacy in the 1960s changed the consciousness of millions of Americans. As a result, it was no longer acceptable to be publicly, openly racist. That was a problem for President Richard Nixon. "Tricky Dick" had to find a way to reinforce racial capitalism, and using coded language and hidden agendas became his go-to. Nixon combined his hatred of Black people with his hatred of drugs and launched the War on Drugs. At an infamous press conference in June 1971, Nixon forcefully declared, "America's public enemy number one is drug abuse. In order to fight and defeat this enemy, it's necessary to wage a new, all-out offensive."[1]

His remarks were a master class in deception and scapegoating. The words used to describe a serious health problem, addiction, were steeped in the language of war and violence. There were foes to be defeated. Nixon promoted a "law and order" agenda, and enforcement disproportionately targeted communities of color. The focus on dismantling structural inequalities ended, and a backlash against interventions to end poverty and inequality began.[2] Public enemy number one was not unemployment, racial injustice, police brutality, or lack of access to health care and affordable housing; it was drugs and crime.

John Ehrlichman, a Watergate coconspirator, made a startling confession in 1994 that revealed the president's true motivations:

> The Nixon campaign in 1968, and the Nixon White House after that, had two enemies: the antiwar left and black people. . . . We knew we couldn't make it illegal to be either against the war or black, but by getting the public to associate the hippies with marijuana and blacks with heroin, and then criminalizing both heavily, we could disrupt those communities. We could arrest their leaders, raid their homes, break up their meetings, and vilify them night after night on the evening news. Did we know we were lying about the drugs? Of course we did.[3]

Ehrlichman's confession is crucial in understanding how the development of the methadone clinic system became racialized, connected to criminality, and highly stigmatized.

Nixon's drug war budget included something surprising after his "get tough" talk: millions of dollars for the creation of a federally coordinated, national drug treatment system that promoted methadone maintenance treatment. The funding for treatment programs increased from $33.5 million in 1970 to a whopping $350.3 million in 1973, while the funding for law enforcement increased from $8.5 million to $45.7 million. By 1973, these programs were treating over 70,000 people.[4]

Drugs, Crime, Racism

The Nixon administration sought to link drug addiction to crime.[5] To that end, the former president created the drug-crime train (D-C train), and he demanded everyone get onboard. It wasn't hard to find fellow passengers because of the hatred of drug users and the fear of crime, real or imagined. It is a gift that keeps on giving—politicians are guaranteed to get elected and reelected while funneling billions to police agencies to wage the drug war. Every president since Nixon has been on the D-C train and used it to pass harsh drug laws that disproportionately impact communities of color and fuel mass incarceration. It set up a "tough on crime" dynamic that made it hard to oppose legislation that imprisoned more people and to support funding for drug treatment for fear of being labeled the opposite, "soft on crime."

There was another hidden motivation in Nixon's promotion of the drug-crime connection: the Southern strategy, which appealed to racist white voters in the south who opposed civil rights and desegregation. H. R. Haldeman, a Nixon adviser, recalled that he deliberately pursued a Southern racial strategy: President Nixon "emphasized that you have to face the fact that the whole problem is really the blacks. The key is to devise a system that recognizes this while not appearing to."[6] Methadone clinics became part of that system and a form of both controlling Black people and treating their addiction.

Nixon hired two white psychiatrists, Dr. Jerome Jaffe and Dr. Robert DuPont, to build a system to dispense methadone. In DuPont they found a researcher who was already on the drug-crime train. Harvard-educated, DuPont was patrician in demeanor and had drop-dead confidence. His early research centered on linking crime to heroin addiction and ignoring the social determinants of both.

Nixon's advisers paid close attention to DuPont's research, and they liked what they saw, in particular, his study of heroin use among the incarcerated in a Washington, DC, jail. From an estimated 1,000 inmates, who were mostly Black, DuPont and his colleagues interviewed 225 prisoners and collected 129 urine samples. The researchers found that 45 percent either reported their addiction to heroin or had positive urine screenings, and that nearly one of every two inmates was addicted to heroin. The study also estimated that maintaining a heroin habit cost about $44 a day. In a widely circulated journal article, they concluded, "The addict's constant need for funds to support his heroin habit apparently leads him to commit street robberies as frequently as does the nonaddict. Thus, the addict poses a very real threat to property as well as to persons in the community."[7]

These statements are pure fearmongering. Crime fell as methadone became more widely used, and DuPont asserted that it was attributed directly to the medication. Reduction in rates of crime are never the result of one policy, but DuPont's research reinforced the notion that addiction and crime were intrinsically linked. Never mind that testing positive for opioids doesn't automatically mean a person has an addiction, and even though some people who use drugs commit crimes, not all do.

DuPont went on to establish the Narcotics Treatment Administration (NTA), and it became the model for treating heroin addiction. Methadone clinics expanded to greater DC, and thousands of residents received the medication, 95 percent of whom were Black. DuPont testified at the Congressional Select Committee on Crime that there were lower arrest rates among program participants and they had the highest treatment retention rates.[8]

From the outset, methadone programs relied heavily on urine surveillance to evaluate outcomes and success. Patients were never trusted to honestly report drug use.[9] The NTA utilized computerized systems in the early 1970s, and data on urine testing were analyzed and reported via the NTA's new Bureau of Computer Systems. Patients had to give urine samples twice a week. Weekly data reported the percentage of "dirty" urine tests. This stigmatizing terminology became widely adopted by staff and patients, who referred to their own urine tests as "clean" or "dirty." Program success was defined by "clean" urine, as if the complexity of a person's life could be understood solely by a bodily fluid in a plastic cup.

As heroin and crime became conflated and racialized, methadone maintenance treatment was aimed at urban Black communities, first and foremost as a crime reduction intervention. DuPont, obsessed with drug-crime metrics, said, "The relationship between an effective treatment program for addict-clients and an effective program of crime prevention for the larger community is readily apparent."[10] He was always a supporter of punishment and control of patients: "Over the years I have been less attracted to permissive methadone treatment and more attracted to a stricter standard for program participation, including tests to detect use of other drugs and sanctions for failure to meet program goals, including cessation of nonmedical drug use and criminal behavior and promotion of gainful employment."[11]

Methadone's Golden Boy

In 1971 Dr. Jerome Jaffe stood behind Nixon at the infamous press conference announcing that drug abuse was public enemy number one. Despite the slight smile on his face, Jaffe seemed nervous. Perhaps it was because Tricky Dick said with presidential authority twice that Jaffe would "report directly to me."[12] The doctor only discovered at a meeting prior to the press conference that he was appointed to head the newly created Special Action Office for Drug Abuse Prevention (SAODAP). The purpose of the office was to marshal the resources of the federal government to develop a comprehensive, nationwide drug treatment system. It played an integral role in establishing methadone treatment programs across the country and defining methadone regulations.

Jaffe was an alumnus of Narco in Lexington, where he spent two years counseling prisoners and learned how methadone was used to medically withdraw patients from opioids.[13] He was politically progressive, relished a challenge, and was a workaholic and a calculated risk-taker. Jaffe's life's mission was to help people struggling with drug dependence, whether it was heroin or nicotine.

Two incidents of Jaffe going rogue stand out: one in New York and one in Illinois. While working at the Albert Einstein College of Medicine in the Bronx, he did something unheard of: He prescribed injectable oxymorphone to patients. The FBN found out and sent an agent to his office to threaten him, but somehow Jaffe managed to convince the agent that it was just a few patients and therefore no big deal. The FBN left him alone.[14] He also wrote prescriptions for methadone that patients picked up at a pharmacy. In Chicago, Jaffe worked at Billings Hospital on the South Side, and he was the head of the newly created Illinois Drug Abuse Program. During the process of opening a methadone clinic, a jazz clarinetist who had Hodgkin lymphoma told Jaffe he was refused treatment at Billings when staff discovered he was a heroin user. Infuriated, he wrote a prescription for methadone on the spot, despite warnings from colleagues that he was jeopardizing the program. Ethically he believed it was the right thing to do, and for good measure, he prescribed methadone for a dozen more patients.[15] A month later the clinic officially opened.

Jaffe's approach to addiction was full of contradictions. While he genuinely cared for his patients and would break rules for them on occasion, he embraced many punitive and humiliating aspects of drug treatment—constant urine testing, observed dosing, and the vicious attack therapy that is the hallmark of TCs. Jaffe got on the D-C train too and said his goal was to make services "available that no addict could say he committed a crime because he couldn't get treatment."[16] Jaffe instituted a program called Treatment Alternatives to Street Crime and believed that if law enforcement cracked down on the supply of drugs, more people would enter treatment. This is a profound misunderstanding of what motivates people to seek help. Moreover, his eponymous Jaffe Report stated that a major justification for federal funding of methadone programs was that it would lead to a decline in arrest and imprisonment rates, while also noting the need for a comprehensive range of services including counseling and employment assistance.[17] While decreasing arrests and incarceration is important, the Jaffe Report links methadone to crime. Later, Jaffe became a big supporter of drug treatment courts, which is ironic because they have a long history of not allowing participants to take or to stay on methadone.

GI Junkies and Golden Flow

A president with many secrets, Nixon needed Jaffe's help. GIs in Vietnam were using heroin. Studies found that 34 percent of soldiers had used heroin and 20 percent displayed symptoms of dependence.[18] Vietnam bordered the

Golden Triangle of Myanmar, Thailand, and Laos. These countries supplied cheap heroin to soldiers both bored and traumatized by a bloody war for nothing that they were losing. The president and the Pentagon were concerned that combat-trained GIs returning to the United States with a heroin habit would wreak havoc on society. Jaffe was drafted to solve the "GI junkie" crisis.

During a clandestine meeting in Washington with Pentagon generals, Jaffe laid out a program of universal drug testing of soldiers in Vietnam. To Jaffe's credit, he insisted the men not be court-martialed for testing positive, which required changing the Uniform Code of Military Justice.[19] Nicknamed Operation Golden Flow by the military, it was up and running within two and a half weeks, and Jaffe secretly flew to Vietnam to see the operation in action.[20] In order to go back to the United States, which soldiers were desperate to do, they had to test negative for opiates. Jaffe said, "The new development of urine testing made it feasible to test the roughly 1,000 people who were leaving Vietnam every day. Testing had an immediate effect. . . . The word got out very quickly that there is no way to leave this place if you're using heroin."[21] The results of thousands of urine tests revealed that a small percentage of soldiers, less than 5 percent, were using heroin, a rate well below what had been initially estimated.

The success of Operation Golden Flow made Dr. Jaffe the golden boy of the Nixon administration. Now he could turn his full attention to the SAODAP. The office controlled federal funding of treatment programs, and Jaffe opened methadone clinics and residential abstinence-based programs across the country. The office financed over four hundred addiction treatment programs in over three hundred cities between 1971 and 1973, a nationalized system that provided free or low-cost access to methadone, outpatient drug treatment, and medically supervised withdrawal. By 1973 these programs were treating over 70,000 people. SAODAP created more treatment capacity in two years than in the previous fifty years combined.[22] It was a huge accomplishment in a short span of time and is a testament to what a "big government" program can achieve when it wants to and has sufficient funding.

Despite the uneven rollout of methadone, long waiting lists in some cities, and criticism from abstinence zealots, people could finally get treatment that eliminated their cravings for heroin. Word spread around the country that methadone worked. One patient explained: "I live a normal life. I don't have to scheme to get drugs. . . . Taking it once a day is an enormous advantage. My life has stabilized one hundred percent. If you weigh assets and liabilities, methadone has been a good thing for me. Not only a good thing, the only thing."[23] It was a golden moment, but it wouldn't last. Jaffe had a hunch that the Nixon administration would at some point defund drug treatment: "I had the feeling from the very first day that the willingness to look at the demand side rather than the law enforcement approach might be a transient phenomenon, that it might pass, and we would go back to our old ways of more and more law enforcement, and I was right."[24]

The president was laser-focused on funding treatment because of the fear of heroin-addicted soldiers returning from Vietnam and the need to at least appear to reduce crime to get reelected. When both were favorably resolved, he escalated the drug war and got rid of Jaffe. The doctor's days were always numbered because the legislation creating SAODAP contained a sunset provision terminating the office in 1975. Nixon never intended to keep expanding and allocating millions for a national drug treatment system.

Then the "lock 'em up and throw away the key" era was launched by New York Governor Nelson Rockefeller. He proposed draconian legislation mandating sentences up to life in prison with no possibility of parole for selling any amount of drugs. Nixon countered with a mandatory sentence of five years. Jaffe wrote a memo criticizing Nixon's shift away from treatment, and it was leaked to the press, which infuriated the White House.[25] Jaffe had been played, and he resigned in 1973.

Locking Methadone Up

In the mid-1960s, until 1972, the administering of methadone varied widely from city to city and state to state. The medication was parked in a legal gray zone, and federal and state regulations, if they even existed, were in flux and unevenly enforced. Physicians could write a prescription for methadone to be picked up at a pharmacy.[26] There were few restrictions on take-home medication, and doctors made the decision of how many to allow, if any.

New, strict regulations were enacted by the FDA and the FBN in 1972. The regulations were designed to increase control over patients and take control away from doctors to use their clinical judgment. Every aspect of dispensing and ingesting methadone, down to the initial starting dose of thirty milligrams, was dictated by federal regulation. Doses above one hundred milligrams required justification and prior approval by the FDA and the state authority. Dosages for pregnant patients were to be kept "as low as possible" if continued treatment was deemed necessary. Clinics had to offer counseling, rehabilitation, and vocational services. All patients had to attend six days a week for supervised dosing, and the most take-home medication that was allowed was two days.[27] These rigid rules harmed patients because withdrawal symptoms cannot be adequately managed at low induction doses and may harm the fetus. Daily dosing leads to treatment dropout. To compound these problems, clinics hired counselors from TCs who were hostile to methadone and believed it was "substituting one addiction for another." They pressured patients to taper off quickly, setting them up for relapse, overdose, and death. It would be difficult to design a more traumatizing, degrading, and massively inconvenient clinic system for patients to obtain a lifesaving medication if one tried.

The Controlled Substances Act (CSA) played a key role in the establishment of the methadone clinic system. The DEA enforces the nation's drug laws, and its authority is derived from the CSA, which divides drugs into five schedules.[28] The drugs listed in Schedule I are those considered to have a high potential for misuse and no current accepted medical use; these include heroin and cannabis. Wrong. These substances have numerous medicinal uses. Cannabis, or medical marijuana, is prescribed to treat nausea, seizures, and a host of other maladies, while heroin-assisted treatment for opioid use disorder is available in Canada and Europe.[29] This is evidence that the DEA is incapable of accurately assessing the state of medical and scientific knowledge about drugs.[30] At any time the agency can also add, delete, or change the schedule of a drug. Schedule II substances also have a high potential for misuse, but they have an accepted medical use; these include methadone, morphine, and fentanyl. Drugs in Schedules III through V have progressively lower potential for misuse and accepted medical uses.[31] The CSA made it illegal for doctors to prescribe any opioid for the treatment of addiction, effectively removing the medical profession from this area of practice. It cemented the clinic as the sole source and provider of methadone.

Diversion Is a Diversion

It's not possible to talk about methadone and not talk about diversion. Drug diversion is a medical and legal concept involving the transfer of a legally prescribed substance from the person for whom it was prescribed to another for illicit use. Methadone and diversion are repeatedly paired, and that is deliberate. Since it was first piloted to treat addiction, the FBN and its successor, the DEA, have used diversion to ensure their power and control over methadone. The drug warriors have cynically promoted the threat of diversion to create fear and mistrust of people who take the medication, to whip up drug panics, and to design a clinic dispensing system that functions like a prison. The justification for controlling patients always goes back to diversion. In the DEA's view: "Methadone is an addictive, euphoria-producing drug with a high street value, and we believe it obvious that the dispensing of such a drug to an addict population, which by definition has shown itself to be more likely to abuse drugs than the general population, should be done only within a tightly regulated framework."[32] Here again, the drug warriors display their ignorance. Methadone doesn't create euphoria, nor does it have a high street value in comparison to substances like heroin, prescription opioids, or cocaine.[33] Methadone has never attained the status of a recreational drug precisely because it doesn't offer a heightened state of intoxication and its onset is significantly slower than injecting or smoking opioids.

Diversion of methadone has always occurred and will continue to occur to some extent as long as methadone is prescribed. But is this diversion dangerous and responsible for increases in overdose deaths, as the DEA has claimed? A study examining methadone overdoses in New York City in 1971 was inconclusive. The researchers noted, "As presently constituted, the Office of the Chief Medical Examiner system for ascertaining deaths in methadone users seems rather insensitive and nonspecific, since both history and toxicology methods demonstrate gross inadequacies. . . . The size and characteristics of the putative methadone user group are in question, as are the data concerning the number and characteristics of addict deaths in general."[34]

In 1995, the IoM Committee on Federal Regulation of Methadone Treatment published a report with an in-depth evaluation of studies on methadone diversion. A main source that the DEA relied on to document the extent of diversion in the 1970s was methadone "mentions" in the Drug Abuse Warning Network (DAWN). Committee researchers debunk the interpretation of the data, specifically reports of "methadone-related deaths" from medical examiners, and they cite surveys that show disparities in how toxicological findings were interpreted. The DAWN data didn't account for the variability of tolerance and how there is overlap between "therapeutic" and "toxic" blood methadone levels. According to the researchers, patients who are highly tolerant to methadone experience no toxic effects at blood levels that would be deadly to a person lacking tolerance. They concluded, "One cannot rely solely on blood methadone levels to determine if methadone toxicity is the cause of death. . . . DAWN data likely overcounted the number of drug-related deaths that are attributable only to methadone." Moreover, the report asserted that "methadone's involvement in drug-related deaths needs to include if the deceased was on methadone maintenance. Most of the time this information wasn't available."[35]

Nixon's War on Drugs created diversion. The crackdown on heroin suppliers and dealers opened up a market for methadone on the street:

"A number of cities, particularly those on the East Coast, experienced a decline in heroin supplies, owing to a combination of enforcement efforts and dock strikes. The relative scarcity of heroin stimulated market demand for illicit methadone as a substitute for heroin."[36]

Community Redistribution

Who is buying diverted methadone and why? It is not the opioid-naive general public looking to experiment with a narcotic. It is overwhelmingly people who are dependent on an opioid and are not in treatment.[37] One study showed that 34 percent of people who used diverted methadone were trying to stop using heroin, 10 percent to reduce a drug habit, 10 percent because no other narcotics were available, and 9 percent to avoid withdrawal.[38] Diversion is community redistribution. An IoM report explained how two clinic policies lead to patients buying the medication on the street: to supplement a low dose and when discharged for nonpayment of fees.[39] Use of diverted methadone is also related to losing take-home bottles, missing supervised doses, shortages of programs, and long waiting lists. The barriers to getting and staying in treatment guarantee that an illicit market will have customers. Methadone diversion is DEA- and clinic-generated.

The House Select Committee on Narcotics Abuse and Control held hearings where DEA agents testified that diversion was dangerously out of control. A report from the committee concluded: "From a public perspective, methadone diversion and illicit use represent a significant threat. . . . Illicit methadone must be minimized; that is why the committee has concluded that take-home dosage units represent a major threat. The benefits of methadone treatment are great but the social and public health costs of its widespread use are also great."[40] This is a great exaggeration.

The corporate media played a shameful role in whipping up a drug panic around methadone. They published dozens of newspaper articles with sensational headlines: "Methadone: Will It Spread Addiction?" "Study Finds

Black Market Developing in Methadone," "Curse or Cure? Controversy Balloons over Use of Methadone as a Heroin Substitute."[41] The widely watched TV program *60 Minutes* aired a segment on methadone, and Jaffe and SAODAP were targeted. "Every time someone sold a dose of methadone illegally, it was a front-page headline," he said. "We felt under siege all the time." He was dubbed "the methadone king."[42]

Narcotic Addict Treatment Act

The final piece of the legal framework for regulating methadone was the enactment of the Narcotic Addict Treatment Act (NATA) of 1974, which amended the CSA.[43] The NATA focused on eliminating patient diversion by implementing a host of rules to surveil patients inside the clinic. Dosing would always be observed by a nurse. Methadone was to be dispensed in liquid rather than pill form to obscure dosage size and reduce its attractiveness and ease of illicit use. [44] This puts people who use diverted liquid methadone at risk for overdose because it's difficult to tell what the dosage is, or even if it is methadone. The medication is diluted with water, and the patient must swallow it all and then either lift up their tongue or speak in order to prevent spit-back. Empty containers or beverage cups are not allowed in the dosing area or the waiting room, and dispensing windows are separated to better witness medication ingestion.[45] Urine is tested for methadone metabolites, and if there are none, diversion is suspected.

Patients who "earn" take-home medication are randomly contacted to bring in all bottles, empty or filled, for nurse inspection. Patients receiving greater than one hundred milligrams of methadone aren't allowed any take-homes. When doctors argued that there was no medical justification for this, federal agencies said that such doses "present a high risk of diversion" and that "concerns about the possibility of diversion must outweigh concerns about infringing on the clinical judgment of the program's physician."[46] The NATA also zoomed in on doctors. In order to prescribe any narcotic, they were required to register with the DEA, and only doctors who worked in methadone clinics could prescribe the medication to treat addiction.[47] The NATA reserved a dose of punishment for doctors who continued to dispense methadone for addiction: They faced suspension or criminal charges.

The medical community didn't push back against the over-regulation of methadone even though it took clinical decision-making away from doctors, monitored them via their DEA license number, and threatened them with prison if they were accused of diversion. In fact, the opposite happened: The American Medical Association (AMA) published "Narcotics and Medical Practice," a report that made a series of recommendations, including frequent urine testing, and "rigid controls of methods of dispensing methadone to prevent diversion to illicit sale or to possible intravenous use."[48] It stated that methadone should not be available in office-based settings because of the threat of diversion. The AMA welcomed the intervention of the police, asserting, "Responsible medical bodies should be developed in each state to promote coordination between law enforcement and medical treatment."[49] Ironically, the same report said that physicians must win the trust of patients who use illegal drugs and not threaten to inform police authorities. The AMA abandoned methadone patients and endorsed segregated and punitive treatment programs. Doctors have enormous power to enact change in how health care is delivered, but they have never used it to free methadone from the inhumane clinic system that inflicts great harm on patients.

The NATA, by focusing on the DEA's obsession with diversion, consolidated a closed system of dispensing. Methadone clinics offer DEA diversion-centered care, not patient-centered care. The primacy of diversion control shaped most clinic regulations, created hostile architecture, and turned staff into diversion enforcement cops. All the noise around diverting methadone reinforced the idea that patients were criminals and fueled yet more stigma and community opposition to clinics. Fifty years on, diversion remains at the core of OTP operations and still threatens patient access and retention. In 2025 a person sent me a take-home agreement form from her clinic:

> Methadone/Buprenorphine is a controlled medication and is under strict regulations from the DEA, federal and state governments, and accrediting organizations. Engaging in diversion or other illegal activity related to this medication may result in: Reduction in take-home status, termination from treatment, loss of Medicaid/Medicare benefits, legal fines, and other legal consequences.

The Executive Summary of the IoM Committee on Federal Regulation of Methadone Treatment report states that strict regulations put too much emphasis on protecting society *from* methadone. After convincingly cataloging problems that are foundational to the operation of OTPs, they concluded, "The committee is not recommending abolition of the methadone regulations."[50] They should have.

4

METHADONE IN BLACK AND BROWN COMMUNITIES:
Slavery and Social Control

Wake up, clean up, stand up.

—MALCOLM X

The images are designed to instill fear—of methadone. A flyer created by the Blackman's Development Center features a skull with vacant hollowed-out eyes. It warns "drug dependents" that "they are tools of the white-faced mafia and Cosa Nostra dogs who laugh while you suffer. When heroin is cut off you will be sick and alone!!!"[1] A sign outside one of their offices made their position crystal clear: "This is drug cure—*not* methadone maintenance."[2] The headline of a flyer, "Rocky Holds the Keys to the Methadone Jail," is embossed with a skeletal hand. "Rocky" refers to the notorious New York state governor Nelson Rockefeller. It hints at a conspiracy—the "Rockefeller family has been involved in methadone for some time. . . . It was at Rockefeller University that the theory of methadone maintenance was first concocted." The *Black News* published the article "The Myth of Methadone" with a graphic of men and women standing in line to get medicated. They are called "Methadone Slaves" and claim "Methadone is Slavery."[3]

From the start, there has been suspicion in Black and Latino communities and often a rejection of methadone as a modality to treat opioid addiction. Use of the medication became highly political and a symbol of racial oppression and social control. Taking methadone was seen as a chemical form of slavery and genocide. These ideas need to be viewed in the context of the radical politics and urban rebellions of the 1960s and early 1970s for Black and brown liberation. To understand the hostility toward methadone, it is also necessary to examine the intersection of medical apartheid and neglect in communities of color, the powerful influence of the drug-free abstinence-only rehabilitation industry, and the racist War on Drugs.

The struggles against racism in the United States were met with massive state violence and the assassination of beloved political leaders—Martin Luther King Jr., Malcolm X, and Fred Hampton. The Counterintelligence Program (COINTELPRO) unleashed by J. Edgar Hoover's FBI infiltrated, disrupted, and surveilled political organizations like the American Indian Movement, the Black Panther Party, and the Young Lords Party. The Nixon administration, known for its serial lying, was reviled by millions of Americans. Therefore, distrust and fear of the federal government as well as state and local authorities who cooperated with them was grounded in reality.

The leading proponents of methadone maintenance in the Nixon administration were all white men, and they consistently connected methadone and crime. In the early 1970s, methadone clinics were opened in Chicago, New York City, Oakland, and Washington, DC, which were hotbeds of Black Power and civil rights struggles. According to historian Dr. Samuel Kelton Roberts, "Cognizant of the long history of the popular White association of Black Americans with crime and deviant behavior, and suspicious of methadone maintenance as a convenient technological fix to inconveniently complex social problems, many White and Black

Americans have wondered which aspect of methadone—addiction recovery or crime reduction—was most attractive to its proponents."[4] Probably both, but activists were correct in pointing out that social control of poor people of color is foundational to the clinic system. A candid comment from Dr. Peter Bourne, a former drug czar, confirms this:

> Nixon was under a lot of pressure to show real evidence that he was cutting down Black street crime. . . . You get those people into a program they're getting methadone everyday they have no withdrawal symptoms and have no need to go out and steal or hold somebody up at gunpoint. There is a direct correlation; the more people on methadone, the lower the crime rate. It's then possible to get access to the person on a regular basis. . . . The very fact that [methadone] is addicting is one of its attributes. Once a person is on methadone, he has to come back every day.[5]

Tuskegee and Medical Racism

Adding to the mistrust of government agencies was the infamous Tuskegee syphilis study, brought to light in 1972. Researchers at the Public Health Service carried out the study for over forty years and knowingly let Black men die from the effects of untreated syphilis.[6] It was one of the most egregious medical ethics scandals in US history and exposed the deep-rooted racism of the white medical establishment. In 1973, congressional hearings were held, but no one involved was ever held accountable. The damaging effects of Tuskegee live on and can influence medical decisions, at times leading to rejection of interventions that actually save lives. During the AIDS crisis in the 1980s, harm reductionists gave sterile syringes to intravenous drug users to stop the spread of HIV. Leading members of the Black community opposed this, believing that giving out free needles was a "genocidal campaign against Black and Hispanic people."[7] Early in the COVID-19 pandemic, the vaccination rate in the Black community lagged well behind that of whites. Distrust of the medical establishment is one of the main reasons behind vaccine hesitancy.[8]

The American health care system is structurally racist.[9] Racial disparities exist in every area of medical care, from a greater prevalence of diseases like diabetes and cancer to greater numbers of uninsured to lower rates of accessing medication to treat opioid use disorder. The last major attempt to reform health care resulted in the Affordable Care Act in 2010. Yet over twenty-five million people are still uninsured and millions are underinsured.[10] The federal government forbade states from dropping Medicaid coverage during the pandemic, but once the COVID-19 public health emergency was declared over, the Biden administration dumped twenty million people from the program in what has been euphemistically called the "Medicaid unwinding."[11] Medicaid is the largest payer for addiction treatment.[12] Cost remains a serious challenge for people seeking addiction treatment, and millions of the uninsured and underinsured cannot pay for inpatient or outpatient drug treatment.[13] Only one in five US adults with opioid use disorder received medications to treat it in 2021.[14] Paying out-of-pocket for methadone can cost $300 per month or more.[15] It's routine to discharge patients for nonpayment of fees, nicknamed "feetox." This word is a combination of *fee* and *detoxification*.

Without access to health care and medication, people are at higher risk for dangerous health complications that could have been prevented: endocarditis, necrotizing soft tissue infections, xylazine wounds, and overdose death.

The Young Lords

The Young Lords Party (YLP) was a Puerto Rican civil and human rights organization founded in 1968. Activism around health issues was a priority. The South Bronx and East Harlem had some of the highest rates of preventable and curable diseases like lead poisoning and tuberculosis. The YLP initiated a campaign to get people tested and treated for TB.[16]

In 1970 the Young Lords "takeover" of the Lincoln Hospital, along with members of the Black Panther Party, led to the creation of a new drug treatment program and exposed the deplorable state of both health care and drug treatment at the time. It also revealed why the long-term use of methadone was rejected. Lincoln Hospital, located in the South Bronx, had a grim moniker: The Butcher Shop. The dilapidated building was created as a home for freed slaves in 1839.[17] It had been condemned but somehow remained open. Excrement backed up in the toilets.[18] The hospital was chronically understaffed and overcrowded with just 346 beds to serve an area of half a million people. In the emergency room, blood stained the walls and floors, and cockroaches could be found in medication cups.[19] Year after year, hospital grievances were ignored, so the Young Lords decided to occupy the hospital to force improvements. They had the support of progressive doctors who worked at the facility.[20] Among the seven demands were "Self-determination of all health services through a community-worker board to operate Lincoln Hospital" and "Door-to-door preventive care program emphasizing nutrition, drug addiction, child and senior citizen care." About two hundred activists were involved in the hospital takeover, which lasted for twelve hours. They quietly ended the occupation by putting on white coats or nurses' uniforms, donning stethoscopes, and walking out of an unguarded building exit, blending in with patients and staff. Five days later, a thirty-one-year-old mother of two, Carmen Rodriguez, died in the hospital from a routine abortion.[21]

The takeover of Lincoln Hospital and the tragic death of Rodriguez resulted in significant reforms. It took seven years, but a modern, bigger hospital was built. Activists won a Patient Bill of Rights that was eventually adopted at hospitals across the United States. It was a prescient document that called for patients to be treated with dignity and respect, the right to choose a doctor, and free health care.[22] The idea that health care was a human right for all was championed by the YLP long before other organizations.

Yet health care was still not widely accessible or affordable. "The South Bronx is a necropolis—a city of death," said Dr. Harold Wise, founder of the Martin Luther King Jr. Health Center. "There's a total breakdown of services, looting is rampant, fires are everywhere."[23] The 1970s was dubbed the "Decade of Fire" in the Bronx. Conflagrations decimated the area, destroyed 80 percent of the housing stock, and displaced a quarter million residents. Buildings in the South Bronx burned almost continuously from an estimated forty fires a day, while firefighting services were drastically cut.[24] The neighborhood had been gutted of jobs, and the vacuum of mass unemployment created a thriving drug economy. The Bronx had the highest rate of heroin addiction in the world and overdose deaths among the highest in the country.[25] There was virtually no drug treatment available in the borough. It took another direct action to win the opening of the Lincoln Detox People's Program. The Young Lords, hospital staff, and people who used drugs did a sit-in on the sixth floor of the Nurses Residence. The goal was to "implement a drug program that would serve the community effectively and be run by the community, provide an educational program that would teach the true nature of our oppression and the connection between capitalism, dope, and genocide, and demonstrate the need for a drug program at Lincoln since the South Bronx has a total of 40,000 drug addicts and Lincoln has facilities to deal with at the most 40."[26]

Capitalism, Addiction, and Acupuncture

The People's Program was run by volunteers, some of whom were former drug users, for the first few months, and then they secured city funding. On the first day, two hundred patients lined up for treatment. From the outset, the use of methadone as a maintenance medication was not part of the program. There was a strong belief that the US government was a "dope pusher" and was unleashing a "methadone plague."[27] A poster created by the People's Program declared, "We Will Fight Heroin and Methadone Addiction by Any Means Necessary." But in an interesting twist, initially the program did allow the use of methadone, but only for detoxification. Walter Bosque, an original staff member, said, "So we start with a 10-day detox cycle, first with 40 mg of methadone, and then every day we take away 5 mg, until we get down to 5 mg, and now they're detoxed."[28] In mandatory education classes, patients were given a copy of *The Opium Trail: Heroin and Imperialism*. The last chapter, "Kicking It: Methadone, Therapy or Revolution," advocated revolution because "by providing an alternative explanation and another focus for anger, as well as collective support and some sense of direction, the movement can be the best form of therapy."[29]

Through political education, the People's Program linked drug addiction to material conditions that were endemic to capitalism: poverty, state violence, trauma, racism, and other social inequities. From this point of view, methadone maintenance appeared to address only an individual's dependence on heroin and was swapping one drug for another.[30] The Young Lords focused on root causes, which they believed would cure drug dependence. This emphasis on dismantling the structural drivers of addiction was important because they are often ignored or dismissed by proponents who believe addiction is solely a brain disease. A system designed to keep heavily surveilled patients dependent on a synthetic opioid for a lifetime and supplied at government-run clinics that were outside community control was a nonstarter for the YLP. Adding even more suspicion were reports from patients that they were coerced to enroll in methadone programs as a requirement of parole or probation and in exchange for welfare benefits.[31]

Eventually the program phased out the use of methadone completely and started using acupuncture to taper patients off heroin.[32] With the leadership of Dr. Mutulu Shakur, a member of the Black Liberation Army who was a trained acupuncturist, and Dr. Michael O. Smith, who worked at the hospital, they developed five-point auricular acupuncture targeted at relieving withdrawal symptoms.[33] Bosque and other staff refined the technique called "acudetox" and became acupuncturists themselves. Open to all, the acupuncture program treated more than ten thousand people during the 1970s.[34] To be sure, auricular acupuncture helps some patients, but it doesn't work for everyone, and it doesn't cure opioid addiction. Research on acupuncture's ability to decrease drug cravings are mixed. One literature review concluded that acudetox isn't effective at all.[35]

The People's Program was a direct challenge to Nixon's support of and Jaffe's creation of methadone maintenance, which prided itself on the many ways it controlled patients. Bosque's observation is accurate: "Once on methadone, the client really can't travel. Let's say they want to go to Puerto Rico or to North Carolina to visit their grandma. Doctors won't give them the methadone to go. Methadone is a liquid handcuff."[36]

The Young Lords distrust of methadone, while understandable, was misdirected. The real problem was punitive methadone regulations and that patients could never exit the clinic system, not anything inherent to the medication itself. Instead of critiquing the carceral clinic system, they condemned the whole treatment modality. The Young Lords knew methadone successfully treated opioid withdrawal symptoms because they administered it at Lincoln Detox. And they had to know people who took the medication long-term and that their physical and mental health had improved. Taking methadone ended the relentless and risky "ripping and running" to score heroin of unknown purity and inject it with contaminated needles. Taking methadone allowed people to avoid the violence of the illegal drug trade, the police, arrest, and incarceration. Taking methadone made it possible to work, go to school, take care of home and family responsibilities, and be politically active in movements for social change. Taking methadone was life-enhancing.

In *Addicts Who Survived: An Oral History of Narcotic Use in America, 1923–1965*, people recall how taking methadone affected them. Amparo said, "The time I spent on heroin was hell. That's why I get emotional whenever anyone asks me about it. That's why I'm comfortable on methadone now." Dusty explained, "I've said it so many times. I wonder what I'd be doing if there wasn't any methadone program. I wonder if I'd still be alive." Jerry summed it up: "I entered the methadone program . . . I get up and I take a drink . . . I start to feel I'm coming to life. I go to work. I do whatever I have to do."[37]

In *Surviving Heroin: Interviews with Women in Methadone Clinics*, Liz, who is HIV-positive, said, "I went through this detox program, but when I got off of it, I just started shooting dope again. . . . I made this decision. I have to get on maintenance because it's important to me to be straight at this point in my life. . . . Primarily this is why I want to be on the methadone clinic. . . . I'm really afraid to die."[38]

I have to wonder: What if the YLP took over a methadone clinic and made demands to abolish all the regulations that control, punish, and disrespect patients? What would have happened if they organized a campaign to close clinics, and they created a system where methadone was dispensed in community-controlled health centers by trusted health care providers and people with lived experience? What if the activists and the acupuncturists had met with Dole, Nyswander, and Kreek for a debate about the nature of addiction? The YLP would have argued that capitalism creates the conditions for addiction and must be overthrown, and that methadone is slavery. The physicians would have asserted that addiction is a chronic relapsing brain disease that caused a permanent metabolic change that only long-term use of methadone could successfully treat and that it was liberation. The debate would have been electric, illuminating, and historic.

Blackman's Development Center

Like the South Bronx, Washington, DC, had a large heroin-using population. Over eighteen thousand people were addicted to the drug, and they were overwhelmingly young Black men.[39] The Narcotics Treatment Administration (NTA), under the leadership of Dr. Robert DuPont, Nixon's second drug czar, opened methadone clinics around the city where people could receive treatment for free. The NTA operated thirteen outpatient and three inpatient facilities and enrolled thousands in treatment. Opposition to methadone clinics in the capital came from the influential Black nationalist Hassan Jeru-Ahmed, the founder of the Blackman's Development Center (BDC). Jeru-Ahmed was a former heroin user. In a series of posters plastered around the capital, the group denounced heroin addiction as "Slavery 1969." The BDC warned, "Methadone maintenance, callously operated to end crime by creating dependence upon methadone without regard for the drug dependent's chance to rid himself fully from drugs, will fail in even the first objective."[40] But like the Young Lords, the BDC thought it was acceptable to use the medication in small doses for tapering.

The BDC opened a drug treatment center in 1969 that preceded the rollout of NTA clinics by nearly a year. Jeru-Ahmed collaborated with Dr. Claude Walker, an alumnus of Howard University, who had started writing methadone prescriptions in 1967. Walker explained: "There was no local drug treatment program. . . . I was doing it because heroin was crime-related and there was no adequate program to help these unfortunate people who want to help themselves."[41] Treatment consisted of rapid tapering using methadone combined with education, vocational training, and social rehabilitation. The BDC operated four treatment centers and over one hundred abstinence-based "halfway" houses that served thousands of Washingtonians.[42] The NTA supported and funded these programs.

Dr. DuPont was acutely aware of the racial politics of methadone in DC and said:

> It was being given out by the government for political purposes, to make docile the revolutionaries who were otherwise going to free themselves and change the society. . . . That methadone and its expansion was associated with Nixon, that was a tremendous problem. I was the agent of Richard Nixon and it was anti-black, anti-poor. . . . Ninety percent of the patients were black. The city was seventy-one percent black, and I was obviously white. There was a charge that this was racist, that this was a form of enslaving the black young men in the nation's cities.[43]

DuPont didn't acknowledge valid concerns from Black leaders and activists that clinics had too much power and control over the lives of patients.

Dr. Robert Newman was the rare physician who did acknowledge the toxic power differential in OTPs. He was a fierce and unapologetic advocate for methadone starting in the early 1970s, a contemporary of doctors

Dole and Nyswander, and a trailblazer in opening clinics in New York City. He was asked in an interview in 2011 about the evolution of methadone treatment, and with characteristic candor said:

> The current providers of methadone include some spectacularly wonderful methadone treatment programs, but there are also providers who do want to maintain the status quo and restrict availability and maintain total control over the lives of their patients. They have total control, and they like that. I think that's very sad. The power of the methadone maintenance provider over its patients is absolute under the current system.[44]

The BDC targeted drug dealers. Members of the group gave dealers one warning to cease, and if they didn't, the police were alerted and the drugs were confiscated. Drug users were also targeted. The BDC showed little empathy for users, especially those who committed crimes to fund their habit. They were told to stop and offered treatment. Those who declined were reported to the police or roughed up.[45] Jeru-Ahmed actively collaborated with law enforcement to arrest drug dealers and was a police informant.[46] The BDC made the same error that the Young Lords did in rejecting and vilifying methadone maintenance. That position abandoned so many to the dangerous and deadly illicit drug underground.

Dr. Primm and Methadone

Yet there were defenders of methadone in the Black community. Dr. Beny J. Primm was one of the few Black medical directors of a clinic and a fearless methadone pioneer. Primm was influenced by Black radical politics and was involved in takeovers of abandoned buildings in Harlem that were turned into a halfway house and a detox program. He took part in a sit-in at the New York State Department of Social Services to protest cuts to Medicaid.[47] In 1969, he opened the Addiction Research and Treatment Corporation (ARTC) in Brooklyn. The program was run "by and for blacks."[48] Still, Primm was conflicted, and described himself as "the black man who had been chosen by the white man to deliver a white man's poison to the community."[49] Despite the rough-and-tumble racial politics that attacked methadone and the doctors prescribing it, Primm understood that it worked. He made a commitment to the Black community to dispense it, saying, "I think this drug can help a lot of addicts—maybe thousands of them—who just aren't going to make it any other way."[50]

Right off, the existence of the ARTC clinic drew criticism and polarized the gentrifying Fort Greene neighborhood. In a 1970 *Black News* article, the ARTC was described as "one more of white Amerikkka's experiments in genocide against black people."[51] The clinic was targeted for harassment and closure by both politically connected white NIMBY groups and Black organizations. Dr. Primm was in the clinic when four men from Nat's Coming, a Black group named after the slave rebellion leader Nat Turner, forced their way into the building and confronted him. Two of the men carried machetes and threatened to cut his head off. He was able to talk them out of murder by listening to their complaints. After the incident, Mayor John Lindsay provided Primm with bodyguards from the NYPD.[52] The verbal attacks didn't stop, and he was slandered in the press: "Beny Primm isn't black. He's colored. He has sold out. He is only interested in making a dollar for himself."[53] Despite neighborhood opposition, Primm soldiered on and ARTC never closed. During the AIDS epidemic, Dr. Primm was a leading advocate for needle exchange programs and drug treatment on demand.

Another potent force that mobilized to discredit methadone as an effective treatment were therapeutic communities who saw their drug treatment programs in competition with methadone clinics. Most accounts of how TCs function ignore, omit, or minimize the cruelty and exploitation that participants endured. The centerpiece of "treatment" was attack therapy. A person was put on a "hot seat" and screamed and cursed at by dozens of participants for hours. A person who relapsed was told: "You're a dope fiend with an attitude—you ain't part of this house!" "Get real—or get the fuck out!" "You just a scumbag using this family!" "Ain't no dope fiend can't see through your bullshit! Get your ass out of here!"[54] It's astonishing that this brutality passed for treatment. And yet millions of dollars in government funding allowed thousands of TCs to open across the country. Research shows that confrontational approaches to break denial and defenses did the opposite. Studies have concluded that people are more likely to drop out of treatment early when exposed to attack therapy, and it's associated with higher rates of recidivism in drug users involved in the criminal-legal system.[55] Many survivors of TCs suffer from treatment trauma and are reluctant to reengage in treatment.

Logos, a TC in the South Bronx affiliated with Lincoln Hospital, was started by alumni of Synanon and used the same degrading methods, including forcing people to sit on a bench for hours in silence and to shave their heads. Some residents from Logos disagreed with these harsh methods, split off, and formed The Spirit of Logos. Members of this new group then divided along racial lines, with whites forming the organization White Lightening, with the goal of educating whites about drug addiction. White people also rejected the use of methadone. Their newspaper devoted an issue to disparaging it. One article warns, "Now . . . from the animals that brought us opium, morphine and heroin!! Methadone!!" Another page displays a poster with a skull and tombstone with "Capitalism and methadone equal chemical fascism" written on it. There is a White Lightening comic strip named *Methadone Maintenance Blues* with "methadone zombies" and a caricature of Richard Nixon admitting, "From our point of view, methadone is an ideal way to control poor and oppressed peoples."[56]

The pressure to stop taking methadone has always existed, and TCs fuel it. But there are real-world reasons to taper off methadone: the pervasive societal stigma, and the desperation to get out of the punishing clinic system. Tapering should be done slowly and with support, but often it's rushed. The vast majority of people relapse. Studies show return-to-use rates in the range of 80 to 90 percent within twelve months.[57] Just below the surface of the push to get off methadone is abstinence: the belief that "drug-free" is the only acceptable goal of treatment. It sets people up for grave harm. That was true during the heroin crisis in the 1970s and the

AIDS epidemic in the 1980s and 1990s, and it's even more true now in the era of fentanyl.

Treatment choices for people with an opioid addiction were limited to the methadone clinic system that controlled and humiliated them or a TC that did the same with a turn in the hot seat. Liquid handcuffs or cult: Which would you chose?

Free to Fee

During the Reagan administration, the "Just say no" to drugs mantra applied to methadone. The government-subsidized clinics that offered no- or low-cost methadone were defunded.[58] As the number of public slots available nationwide shrunk, private clinics opened and patients had to pay out of pocket. This transition from "free to fee" led to thousands of patients being involuntarily detoxed. A study of women in Alameda County, California, reveals the wide-reaching negative effects. When a county-funded program cut treatment slots, patients were given the choice of switching to a private clinic and paying full fees for methadone (then $200 a month) or detoxifying from the program. Researchers found that over 80 percent of those opting to leave treatment had resumed using heroin, and over half of those remaining in treatment resorted to criminal activities in order to pay clinic fees.[59]

Cutting off government support for methadone was catastrophic for patients. It pushed them back into the illicit drug market and increased their risk for overdose. Reaganomics signaled a political shift that "big government" was getting out of the business of funding methadone. Federal bureaucrats no longer cared about the high rates of heroin use and overdose deaths, or even the most touted reason for people to take methadone: to reduce crime.

Suboxone: The Rich Man's Methadone

In 2000 another medication to treat opioid addiction became available: buprenorphine, marketed under the trade name Suboxone. The backstory of how a new narcotic got approved by the FDA—no small feat in a country hostile to the maintenance use of narcotics and the people who take them—centers on the shrewd maneuvering of Reckitt Benckiser Pharmaceuticals (now named Indivior) and exposes how racial capitalism ranks and sorts access to legal opioids by color and class.

In the early 2000s the pharmaceutical company Purdue Pharma was claiming some of its first victims: White middle-class suburbanites as well as whites in rural parts of the United States who were addicted to and overdosing on their blockbuster opioid OxyContin.[60] This was the first wave of the overdose crisis. The reformulation of the narcotic that made it harder to crush and inject, along with a dramatic decrease in physician prescribing, led many to switch to heroin, which marked its second wave around 2007.[61] An even more deadly third wave was unleashed with the introduction of ultrapotent fentanyl beginning around 2013.[62] A new narrative was needed to understand and tackle the unending overdose crisis that was killing not only white adults but young adults as well. White people became the "new face of opioid addiction."

The opioid overdose crisis is more complicated than corporate villain and innocent victim. It is the latest iteration of a century of punitive and rehabilitative changes in drug policy and practice based on race and class.[63] The headline of a *New York Times* article sums up this color correction: "In Heroin Crisis, White Families Seek Gentler War on Drugs." Michael Botticelli, a former White House drug czar, explained how whiteness was a game changer: "Because the demographic of people affected are more white, more middle class, these are parents who are empowered. . . . They know how to call a legislator, they know how to get angry with their insurance company, they know how to advocate. They have been so instrumental in changing the conversation."[64]

The visual images in the corporate media changed too. Photos depicted white drug users in a sympathetic light highlighting family bonds, faith, rehab settings, and survivor grief that stood in stark contrast to unsympathetic and sinister images of Black and Latino drug users who were often shown on the ground and in handcuffs.[65] The racial bias wasn't lost on Kimberlé Williams Crenshaw, attorney and scholar of critical race theory: "This new turn to a more compassionate view of those addicted to heroin is welcome. But one cannot help notice that had this compassion existed for African-Americans caught up in addiction and the behaviors it produces, the devastating impact of mass incarceration upon entire communities would never have happened."[66]

Race and Class

The Drug Addiction Treatment Act of 2000 (DATA 2000) was championed through the federal legislative sausage-making process by Charles O'Keeffe, the former CEO of Reckitt Benckiser, with the assistance of Dr. Jerome Jaffe, who was wise to the ways Washington worked. From the outset, it was critical to differentiate buprenorphine from methadone. In an interview with Dr. Helena Hansen, one of the authors of *Whiteout: How Racial Capitalism Changed the Color of Opioids in America*, Jaffe explained, "[The manufacturers] were concerned that [buprenorphine] might become stigmatized the way methadone was . . . that if it were limited to clinics the way methadone was, that this would not be much of a breakthrough drug. . . . The real issue was, could this be something that any doctor could prescribe with some training, or would it be regulated in the same way [as methadone]."[67] Why didn't Jaffe fight for deregulating methadone? Why didn't he make the case that the medication should be available outside of clinics in office-based settings as was being proposed for buprenorphine? Instead, Jaffe worked with O'Keeffe to ensure buprenorphine didn't end up in a siloed carceral clinic system like methadone.

Congressional testimony on DATA 2000 centered the "new face of opioid users" and that methadone clinics were not the setting to treat their addiction. Alan Leshner, then director of NIDA, believed Suboxone was the medication for this new group because methadone, "which tends to concentrate in urban areas, is a poor fit for suburban spread of narcotic addiction."[68] Using his power as the head of NIDA, he could have called for the rapid opening of OTPs, mobile methadone vans, or for methadone to be picked up at the pharmacy, but he didn't. Leshner advocated for office-based prescribing of Suboxone as a "good fit" for this more affluent group of patients. Donna Shalala, Health and Human Services director at the time, testified that buprenorphine was needed to serve "a new kind of addict, including those who would not normally be associated with the term addiction."[69] All the coded language! Who is this "new" opioid user who needs buprenorphine, not methadone?

The promoters of DATA 2000 used copious amounts of euphemistic language to conceal that buprenorphine would be targeted mainly to a white demographic. O'Keeffe and Jaffe were acutely aware that methadone had long been associated with Black people and crime in urban areas. The segregated clinic system Jaffe designed along with the DEA was based on constant surveillance and punishment, mandated counseling, supervised urine tests, daily dosing, and random drug testing. That horrific level of control and humiliation wasn't acceptable for white middle-class soccer moms, wealthy business executives, celebrities, or famous actors.[70] Nor were these patients to be expected to drive into a Black neighborhood, where many methadone clinics are concentrated as a result of medical redlining. One white woman explained, "They had me certified with the Rockefeller Program. That was the worst thing. . . . It was all black . . . like I was never around so many black people in my life. And they were butchers and I was scared shit of them."[71] Dr. Edwin Salsitz, a leader in addiction medicine in New York City, explained that he encountered many middle-class white opioid users in his practice who refused to ever set foot in a methadone clinic: "Sometimes, a couple of years later, they'd be HIV positive, or something more catastrophic would have occurred. There's no way to explain what this meant to the addiction field to have another option [buprenorphine] besides the clinics."[72]

O'Keeffe and Jaffe needed two things to change to guarantee buprenorphine didn't end up stuck in opioid treatment prisons and stigmatized like methadone. The first was scrapping the sentence in the Controlled Substances Act that forbade doctors from prescribing opioids for maintenance in office-based settings, and the second was to ensure that buprenorphine was put in Schedule III, the category for drugs that have moderate addictive potential, low risk of abuse, and high therapeutic use. It was argued that Suboxone, which is a partial opioid agonist and contains naloxone, the overdose prevention drug, was safer than methadone, which is a full agonist and doesn't contain naloxone. Suboxone causes less respiratory depression than methadone due to its ceiling effect and therefore has lower overdose potential.[73] The medication comes in three forms: a tablet, a sublingual film that dissolves under the tongue, and a long-acting injection. There is no liquid formulation. Methadone is in Schedule II; drugs in this tier are considered highly addictive.[74] With the support of influential legislators, including Senator Joseph Biden, O'Keeffe and Jaffe got both changes.[75] DATA 2000 was slipped into a children's mental health bill with no rancor, no endless debate, no daily drug panic stories in the media.

With the passing of DATA 2000, cash-only Suboxone clinics opened for business, charging up to $7,200 a year per patient, and doctors in private practice could demand $1,000 for an initial half-hour induction visit with an average daily dose costing around $16. No wonder Suboxone was dubbed "the rich man's methadone."[76] Reckitt Benckiser was cashing in too; buprenorphine became a blockbuster drug, raking in over $1 billion a year in US sales by 2012.[77]

The DEA and DATA 2000

The interference of the DEA in medical practice one again ensured that there would be barriers to accessing an essential medication. Citing, wait for it, the threat of diversion, they devised special restrictions to limit doctors and pharmacies from prescribing and filling Suboxone prescriptions. As a result, DATA 2000 hasn't reversed the opioid overdose crisis. To prescribe, doctors had to complete an eight-hour SAMHSA-approved training to get an X-waiver from the DEA, which pharmacists used to validate prescriptions. The number of patients a physician could treat was capped at thirty.[78] No other prescription medication has been burdened with these non-evidence-based requirements, not even other opioids like OxyContin and Vicodin. And tellingly, an X-waiver isn't needed to prescribe buprenorphine for pain. Patients who take buprenorphine are less policed than those on methadone, but they can't completely escape discrimination—from difficulty finding doctors who will prescribe it to retail pharmacies that refuse to stock it.[79] Given the training requirement, the need to track how many patients were receiving buprenorphine so as not to go over the cap, and the DEA monitoring of physician prescribing, is it any wonder that only a small percentage have been certified to prescribe the medication?

Interviews with pharmaceutical executives and drug policy makers by the authors of *Whiteout* found that they "realized that the restrictions would limit access to buprenorphine and create inequalities in treatment, but stated that these restrictions were necessary to get office-based buprenorphine accepted by federal regulators."[80] The legislative handiwork of O'Keeffe, Jaffe, and the DEA did indeed result in racial inequalities, and they were enormous. In 2005 a national study showed that buprenorphine patients were 91 percent white.[81] Research conducted from 2012 to 2015 reveals: "After accounting for payment method, sex, and age, we found that black patients had statistically significantly lower odds of receiving a buprenorphine prescription. . . . Self-pay and private insurance were the most common payment methods."[82] This racist treatment gap remains. In 2023, a national study found whites were three to four times as likely to get buprenorphine as Blacks.[83] The lack of access has been disproportionately deadly. Between 1999 and 2022, the Black overdose death rate increased more than six-fold.[84]

X the X-Waiver

It didn't take long for physicians to complain about the DEA-generated obstacles to prescribing, and a *twenty-three-year-long* campaign to eliminate the X-waiver was launched. It was finally removed in 2023. Having an X-waiver put a target on the back of every doctor because it allowed the DEA to monitor the number of prescriptions written and filled. Agents showed up unannounced to inspect doctors' offices and to review medical records. Before one doctor even started prescribing, "DEA agents came into our office one day and said we want to audit all your Suboxone and charts. Well, we don't have any, but that's scary. I mean, you're under scrutiny and, am I going to be walked out of here in cuffs if you don't like what you see?"[85]

The creation of prescription drug monitoring programs (PDMPs) gave law enforcement a powerful new Big Brother tool to surveil and threaten physicians, pharmacists, and patients. In two states, PDMPs contain drug arrest and conviction data.[86] Pharmacies that fill what are erroneously considered to be a high volume of buprenorphine prescriptions are targeted for harassment by the DEA, leading to some independent pharmacies closing down, chain drugstores refusing to stock it, or pharmacies adding absurd restrictions.[87] The Oak Hill Hometown Pharmacy in West Virginia was targeted by the DEA for filling prescriptions from out of state, accepting cash payments, and dispensing "too much" Subutex, which they consider easier to "abuse" because this formulation doesn't contain naloxone. All of these are considered red flags for diversion. A patient in Florida couldn't get a prescription filled by a Walgreens that requires those taking any controlled substance to live within fifty miles of treatment providers. The patient lived sixty-nine miles away.[88]

The approval and marketing of buprenorphine exposed how structural racism in the US health care system ensured that white patients would have access to this medication outside the confines of opioid treatment prisons that were created for Black patients. It should be a national scandal that buprenorphine was *deliberately developed* for the white middle-class. It validates that medications for the treatment of opioid addiction are not color blind.

Racism is foundational to the methadone clinic system, though it is rarely acknowledged. Political activists in the 1970s understood this as a result of doctors, researchers, and the federal government consistently connecting crime in urban centers with the use of methadone. The carceral structure of OTPs, and the fact that most medical directors were white, reinforced the notion that clinics were designed to oppress people of color. Dr. Kelton Roberts noted, "This alienation of methadone from the communities it was supposed to serve contributed greatly to the perception that methadone easily could be weaponized as an agent of social control and even genocide."[89] The tragedy was the criticism and protest weren't directed toward the abolition of the clinic system, which is the real problem, not methadone.

5

"WOULD YOU WANT TO LIVE NEXT TO A METHADONE CLINIC?": NIMBY Movements

The speeches at the press conference in Harlem were a distillation of stigmatizing ideas about methadone, clinics, and patients that have existed since clinics opened in the 1970s. Communities engaged in NIMBY protests against OTPs from New York to North Dakota have a tried-and-true template: They are a threat to children and families, increase crime, attract drug dealers, and decrease quality of life. And always, this isn't the right location for an OTP; somewhere else is. Except there is no somewhere else. No neighborhood welcomes a methadone clinic, and nothing unites a community faster than when one tries to open its doors.

I met Fab 5 Freddy, the host of *Yo! MTV Raps*, hip-hop pioneer, artist, and filmmaker, at a press conference a few blocks from where I live in Harlem. He wore a black T-shirt that said "Harlem American" and a broad-brimmed porkpie hat. It was a sunny day in August 2018. A Who's Who group of local politicians wearing crisp light blue and brown suits and ties stood behind a podium. About twenty members of the neighborhood were arranged behind them on the sidewalk. The local media set up video cameras on tripods and clipped microphones to the podium. Everyone was assembled to celebrate that they had stopped a methadone clinic from opening in a historic brownstone.

A Black woman representing the Sugar Hill Concerned Neighbors Group described how they mobilized a hundred people within two days to attend a meeting with Argus, the corporation that planned to open the clinic and had paid $4.3 million for the property. She asked, "Who would want to live next to a methadone clinic?" Another speaker explained that Sugar Hill was a family community of brownstones and therefore it was the wrong location for a clinic. Speakers were mindful to say they cared about people struggling with an addiction and that it wasn't "pushing back at the lesser of us." Al Taylor, a reverend and state assembly member who represents Harlem said, "We're not anti the people who need these services. Just not here." Adriano Espaillat, a US representative whose congressional district includes Harlem, asserted, "This isn't a not-in-my-backyard thing. We need to have empathy." He added that the neighborhood wanted to keep its quality of life and that Argus should look for another location. Espaillat suggested the Upper East Side of Manhattan. Then he smiled and called everyone involved in the fight the "Sugar Hill Gang."[1] The crowd broke into laughter. Several speakers asserted Harlem was oversaturated with methadone clinics, and thousands of people were commuting in from other boroughs. It wasn't fair, they said. The press conference ended with another elected official commending everyone and cautioning, "We must stay united. One finger you do nothing. With a fist, you can win. We won!"

After the press conference, I approached Fab 5 Freddy. I wanted to ask him why he opposed the methadone clinic, and he agreed to an interview. In front of the Kingdom Hall Of Jehovah's Witnesses, Fab explained that for twenty years he has lived in a brownstone about a block from where Argus wanted to open the OTP. Over that time, he saw the neighborhood change for the better. He said that Sugar Hill was damaged by open drug dealing and drug use for decades: "The neighborhood has gone through a lot of trauma, and we don't want to see something that could take us back there." He's not a fan of methadone and said, "I'm not a doctor, but I don't think methadone is the best treatment. It keeps them caught up in an addictive state." During the conversation, Fab was easily convinced that methadone was a lifesaving maintenance medication and that the problem was the clinic system. I assured him that no one wanted to travel to a clinic in Harlem six days a week and stand in a line to get dosed. The solution was to shut down OTPs and let all patients pick up a prescription once a month at a pharmacy in their neighborhood. It was a light bulb moment for Fab.

NIMBYism Fuels the Culture of Cruelty

NIMBY movements use a number of strategies and tactics to keep clinics out. One of Dr. Beny Primm's greatest frustrations was the community opposition he encountered whenever he tried to open an OTP in Harlem or Brooklyn. Primm said, "It seemed that there were people who would use any means to block us. . . . We found a building at 145th Street and Eighth Avenue and began renovations for a clinic. The building was set on fire. We brought guard dogs to the location and they killed the dogs."[2] Primm suspected that a drug-free organization in Harlem was responsible. The clinic never opened.

Residents from the city of Lynnwood in Washington State launched a fight against Acadia Healthcare, the largest methadone provider in the state, to block a clinic from opening. They were angry that it was near the Boys & Girls Club building. They formed a group called Safe Lynnwood and organized a protest march to the site where the OTP would open. At a city council meeting, an elderly woman told a representative from Acadia that he should be ashamed to open a clinic near the Boys & Girls Club. A city council member said during a hearing, "We can't sacrifice the safety of our children," and another official added, "If a single child is injured as a result, what is the price for that single child being injured due to the location of this facility?"[3] The obsessive focus on "the children" and the perceived harm that a clinic could cause has no basis in reality. There is no evidence that OTPs make a neighborhood unsafe for children. Are the people who promote these hateful ideas aware that thousands of methadone patients are parents?

As is common when an OTP wants to open a clinic, Arcadia submitted a written response to address community safety concerns and to explain how an OTP operates. They clarified that the clinic would only be open six hours a day, about 140 patients per day would be medicated, and all dosing would be completed by 11:30 a.m.[4] Arcadia assured the community that patients receive counseling. For security, the OTP would employ guards during and after operating hours to deter loitering at the facility or surrounding areas. Patients would be told loitering would not be tolerated and any illegal activity would be immediately reported to the police.

To assuage community fears, OTPs promise to police and punish patients. They hype that security guards and video cameras will surveil them constantly inside and outside the clinic. They'll only provide narrow windows of time when people can get medicated to assure the community that "those" people will only be in the area for a short time. If caught lingering, patients will be penalized. These carceral concessions to NIMBY groups further criminalize patients, reinforce discrimination, and create hardships. For decades, patients have complained about the limited hours OTPs are open, which contributes to missing doses, being late for work or school, and not being able to take care of life responsibilities. Clinic owners focus on reducing and penalizing loitering because they believe that it triggers community complaints, so they want patients to get medicated and get out—dose and dash! It's an iteration of the sundown town. The Family Guidance Center in Chicago has a sign on the entrance door that threatens: "If you are seen loitering or lingering around the building or the surrounding area, you will immediately be placed on involuntary withdrawal." The clinic is in a Black neighborhood that has gentrified and it's a few blocks from Magnificent Mile, a luxury shopping district on Michigan Avenue.

Methadone Clinics: Bad For Business

Woe to established methadone clinics that find themselves in a neighborhood targeted by real estate developers. Many OTPs were forced to open in dangerous, desolate, and deindustrialized zones. There was usually little community opposition because no one lived there, so no one cared. But cities change, and what was once a blighted wasteland can be reinvented as a new upscale neighborhood. A methadone clinic won't be tolerated among million-dollar condominiums, museums, luxury shopping, boutique hotels, restaurants with Michelin stars, and espresso bars. Boston's Methadone Mile is facing that threat. Several clinics were established when the area was populated with warehouses, a homeless shelter, the Suffolk County House of Corrections, and the Boston Medical Center. Now expensive renovated brownstones dot Massachusetts Avenue, just a few blocks from the shelter and the OTPs. The South End–Roxbury Community Partnership, a NIMBY group, has held numerous protests and wants services for the unhoused and drug treatment programs to move out of the neighborhood.[5]

It doesn't matter where an OTP tries to open; there will be opposition. In West Baltimore, Charm City Medical Center opened a clinic in a former auto parts warehouse next to a funeral parlor and across from a strip of vacant and burned-out buildings. Jacqueline Caldwell, the president of the Whittier-Monroe Neighborhood Association, led an unsuccessful fight to keep the clinic out. It was a rare defeat. Caldwell said at a public planning commission meeting: "If it didn't have addiction services with it, we probably wouldn't have a problem with it. . . . If it's such a great idea, put it where your mother lives." Joseph Brown, the owner of the funeral home, told the commission he would install a chain-link fence and might need to hire private security. "I'm afraid I'm going to lose some business because

I'm right next door to—and I hate to say—a methadone clinic," Brown said.[6] A business that embalms dead bodies and provides burial and cremation services needs to protect itself against people who take methadone? Once again, the OTP owner assured the community that patients would be strictly monitored and controlled.

Dr. Devesh Kanjarpane, the owner of Charm City Medical Center, met with residents and explained how patients are medicated. He compared the space where the methadone would be dispensed to the cashier's counter at a casino. Facial recognition technology is used, there are four cameras at each of the five seats along a counter to ensure that the right person is taking the correct dose, a thick pane of glass separates patients from the nurses, the medication is stored in two large safes, and there will be security guards on-site.[7] I've never heard a more depressing and dystopian description of an OTP. What's next: autonomous, mobile robotic nurses dispensing methadone?

Even a makeshift temporary clinic floating on the Hudson River faced a NIMBY attack. A thousand patients got dosed on a ferryboat called the *Gold Star Mother*. It caused a major uproar from veterans organizations that said treating drug users on a boat with that moniker disgraced the memory of fallen heroes and their families.[8] Gold Star Mother was the designation for women who had lost sons in World War I. Perhaps these vets forgot how many soldiers have become dependent on opioids during America's many wars. It had a special name: soldiers disease. When the ferry was moved to a dock in the West Village, the community opposed it, but patients continued to swallow a daily dose of methadone on board.[9]

Clinics, Crime, and Cops

In Minot, North Dakota, population 47,373, Community Medical Services (CMS), a for-profit OTP chain, was set to open a methadone clinic. CMS was told that a one-year moratorium would be placed on the opening because of concerns about crime raised by the local police department.[10]

OTPs are often thought to be magnets for crime. A study by researchers at Johns Hopkins University debunks that notion. It found that convenience stores, corner stores, and liquor stores can attract violent crime, but drug treatment centers, including methadone clinics, did not.[11] When Minot police learned that crime would not increase, they gave the green light.

Powerful testimony at a town meeting by Minot resident Rebecca Schmaltz helped convince skeptics on the city council. Schmaltz was pregnant and using heroin. She wanted to take methadone but there were no clinics in North Dakota, with the nearest one almost 450 miles away in Billings, Montana. She moved in with a relative more than 700 miles away in northern Montana, where the drive to the closest methadone clinic was an hour and fifteen minutes. Her fiancé and six-year-old daughter stayed in Minot, and after Schmaltz gave birth, she moved back. The OTP in Billings helped her get federal permission to take home a two-week supply of methadone. But she had to travel nearly seven hours each way to Montana every two weeks to pick up her methadone. After she shared her story, the room was silent and the council unanimously approved the CMS clinic.[12] In 2016, it was the first ever to open in North Dakota. This story is a maddening illustration of how access to methadone derails patient's lives and proof that the clinic system is wildly outdated. Why couldn't a pregnant Schmaltz simply get a prescription from her obstetrician, pick up methadone at a pharmacy in Minot, and get on with her life?

OTPs have also been targeted by local law enforcement. Susan Staats-Combs, the director of the Chilton County Treatment Center in Clanton, Alabama, said police harassment started around the time the city decided to tear down a nearby hotel and build a new one. This NIMBY action was triggered by commercial interests that believed an OTP is bad for business. Police parked beside the clinic to surveil people entering and leaving. Officers threatened patients with a DUI simply because they had dosed, confronted passengers at traffic stops to ask if they take methadone, and even threatened clinic staff.[13]

The police presence at or near an OTP sends an unmistakable message to patients that they are not safe. It will deter some from entering treatment, especially those with prior contact with the criminal-legal system. A patient in an East Harlem clinic told me he was stopped and frisked by the police on his way to the OTP: "On Saturdays, we would see a police van parked near the clinic. You never knew if you would get your dose because an officer would stop you and ask for ID for no probable cause, just because you were going to the clinic."

Regulatory Hell

Rigid and nonsensical federal regulations combined with those at the state and local level are another major detriment to opening an OTP. They make it an expensive and bureaucratic nightmare for new clinics. As a result, 80 percent of counties in the United States had no OTP in 2018.[14] Pew published "Overview of Opioid Treatment Program Regulations by State" and documents how moratoriums, capping the numbers of clinics, restrictive zoning rules, and requirements for a certificate of need create barriers.[15] It's notable that these restrictions don't apply to other health care facilities. Nineteen states and the District of Columbia require a certificate before a new OTP can open. It's a legal document that demonstrates the need for a new facility, and it's a long byzantine process that allows a community time to mobilize. A certificate of need should be irrelevant in the midst of an ongoing opioid overdose crisis. West Virginia is the most restrictive state, with a legal moratorium banning the opening of new clinics.

Another set of regulatory barriers is oddly pharmacy-based. Sixteen states require that OTPs be licensed or registered as pharmacies; five require clinics to follow general pharmacy regulations that apply to neighborhood drugstores; and 15 states require OTPs to hire a pharmacist or a consultant pharmacist.[16] Why? Methadone clinics are not pharmacies and in no way do they operate like a CVS or Walgreens. According to the Pew report, these requirements limit access to methadone.[17] A combination of state, federal, and local regulations as well as NIMBY campaigns drive up operating costs. Nick Stavros, the CEO of CMS, a large clinic chain, estimates that it costs a million dollars to open a new OTP.[18]

Street Scenes

It's important to acknowledge that OTPs can have a negative impact on communities. Peter Vanderkloot writes:

> The communities in which clinics are located suffer, and it is wrong to dismiss their complaints as knee-jerk "NIMBY-ism." By requiring daily attendance by their patients, the clinics serve as the nexus for a variety of street scenes. Patients who are frustrated in their attempts to leave "The Life" by clinic-generated roadblocks are often forced to make their clinic visits the centerpiece of their days. Friendships are maintained, drugs exchanged, goods boosted, all in the immediate vicinity of the clinic. This system ensures that the community only sees those patients who don't care about being seen: those with the least investment in the straight world. Those fearful of the stigma attached to methadone impacting on their jobs or families do their best to remain invisible as they rush in and out of the clinics. Those who have little to lose and few ways to express their hatred of the clinics provide the public with their image of a typical methadone patient.[19]

Vanderkloot's truthful observations come from his lived experience taking methadone for decades. OTPs require hundreds of patients to go to the same clinic daily in perpetuity, unless take-homes are earned. That invariably creates a community of people who know one another. The positives are that patients offer one another emotional support and camaraderie and share resources. When I made my first documentary about methadone, I met with patients in a McDonald's a few blocks from the clinic. After they got medicated, a small group would meet at the restaurant for coffee and Egg McMuffin sandwiches. The conversation was a mix of clinic complaints, family updates, gossip, and information about housing and employment opportunities. There was a lot of sarcasm and laughter. Elvin, who attends an OTP in the Bronx, told me, "A community of people is formed at the clinic who care about one another, that love one another—it might be the only person to visit you in the hospital or show up at your funeral. That's real!"

The problem of bringing hundreds of methadone patients together in a centralized location seven days a week is drug dealers. They know where potential customers are. In San Francisco, I saw dealers selling fentanyl around the corner from an OTP on Market Street, a busy commercial district. In numerous interviews, patients told me they were furious that dealers were selling close the clinic because it made them vulnerable to relapse. Jenna said: "I don't like to deal with people at the program because a lot of them are still getting high, and the drug dealers. How does that help me in my recovery? I'm there to get my methadone. I'm doing good for myself and I have to be surrounded by addicts who are not in that same mind frame? It messes things up for me. Being around that all the time if you're not strong, you'll fall."[20]

Another problem with forcing so many people to attend clinic on a daily basis is that it sets the stage for a street scene to develop. People who are unemployed or unhoused, or have no income and nowhere to go after getting medicated as many shelters close during the day, stay in the neighborhood. Some use drugs out in the open, nod off, or overdose. Others panhandle for money in front of businesses or work in the illicit street economy. These are the patients that Vanderkloot describes as having the least investment in the straight world, and they experience multiple oppressions. Because their behavior is clearly visible to the community, it triggers yet more complaints by NIMBY groups. This is where the issue of safety is often brought up. But walking by people on the street who are unhoused, asking for money, using drugs, or experiencing the effects of drugs isn't about safety as much as it is about feeling uncomfortable. It's painful to see people in the throes of addiction who have nowhere to live. An obvious solution to this problem is to move people into affordable housing, and the street scenes that cause so much community discomfort would largely disappear.

To be sure, fear and hatred of people who take methadone drives most NIMBYism, but there are other reasons OTPs are opposed, particularly in communities of color. In East Harlem, a predominately Black and Latino neighborhood, there is a dense concentration of methadone clinics, outpatient drug and mental health treatment programs, and homeless shelters. The Greater Harlem Coalition (GHC), a NIMBY organization composed of block associations and businesses, was founded to prevent the location of more OTPs and other services for vulnerable populations in the neighborhood. The group believes that "Harlem is the Black Cultural Capital, but decades of structural racism has relegated it as New York City's containment zone."[21] The coalition isn't wrong, and in a series of color-coded maps, they document pervasive medical redlining. According to data from the New York State Office of Addiction Services and Supports, Harlem has 18 percent of New York City's total OTP capacity, about 5,700 patients. There are eight methadone clinics in a five-block radius of 125th Street and Park Avenue.[22] This hyperconcentration of methadone clinics in East Harlem isn't an accident; it's the result of the power of white NIMBYism. Wealthy white neighborhoods have the power, political connections, and lawyers to block OTPs from opening in a way that low-income communities of color historically have not. A study found that African American and Latino communities have more methadone clinics per capita than white communities.[23]

Medical Redlining in Harlem

I met with Syderia Asberry-Chresfield, a cofounder of the GHC. She is a former vice president for JP Morgan Chase and the owner of a beautiful brownstone that has landmark preservation status. We had coffee at Ginjan Café in East Harlem to discuss why her organization is opposed to OTPs. She said, "It's just not fair dumping on Harlem, which is systemically what has been done for the decades since I've lived here. . . . We don't need any more clinics. Go to a hospital, go to a doctor's office for methadone." Other reasons were ending medical redlining and preventing drug dealing. Asberry-Chresfield said, "The drug dealers are here because this is where you sell to your customer base. . . . We have the methadone folks trying to sell their methadone to get other drugs, and you have all of the dealers saying this is the place to be." She is aware of the hardships methadone patients experience. One day she met a person from Brooklyn who came to Harlem to get medicated: "I think it took him an hour and a half because he had to take a bus to the train, which was ridiculous, just to come uptown to get his medication and then go back. That's not fair." The GHC obtained data showing the zip codes of patients attending clinics and found that most did not live in or near Harlem.[24] Toward the end of our meeting, Asberry-Chresfield shared a personal story with me. Years ago, she saw a relative standing in line at a clinic: "He was on his way to work. No one knew he took methadone. And I just turned my head, you know, and pretended like I didn't see him. I know he contributed to his family, that he paid the rent."

Shawn Hill, another cofounder of GHC, is also concerned about the number of OTPs in the neighborhood. He works for Fordham University as an instructional technologist for digital scholarship and pedagogy. Hill is also the garden coordinator for Lydia's Magic Garden in East Harlem. In addition to their concerns about OTPs, the GHC organized a protest against OnPoint NYC, the organization that opened an overdose prevention center (OPC) in East Harlem.[25] At OnPoint NYC, people can use opioids they bring in to the building, and trained staff provide sterile supplies and intervene if an overdose occurs. They have reversed over 1,700 overdoses since opening in 2021.[26] The OPC is also a drop-in center where buprenorphine induction, case management, and holistic services like acupuncture and meditation are offered. There are outreach and public safety teams that clean up hazardous waste like discarded needles, and they operate a public safety hotline for syringe cleanup. OnPoint NYC is trying to be a good neighbor while keeping people who use drugs alive.

Swallow This and Clinic Abolition

Marilena, my co-filmmaker, and I asked Hill to show our film *Swallow THIS: A Documentary About Methadone and COVID-19* to members of the GHC. NIMBY groups don't realize how their efforts to block clinics strengthen the culture of cruelty and contribute to stigma. We wanted them to see and hear people who take methadone to help them understand how their activism can cause harm. Hill agreed to organize a screening. On a rainy Saturday in the community room of a modern high-rise apartment building in East Harlem, about thirty people, mostly African American, watched our short documentary.

The discussion afterward was revealing. Most were not aware how clinic regulations punished patients, and some expressed shock. There were questions about how people pay for methadone and why it was dispensed in liquid form. One woman was hesitant to use the word *racism* when reflecting on buprenorphine and how more white people had access to the medication, and that it was dispensed in a pharmacy. Why couldn't methadone be picked up in a pharmacy, she wondered? Another woman in the audience replied that it was definitely racism. There was nodding all around. It gave us an opportunity to talk about the racist roots of methadone clinics.

Terrell Jones and Hiawatha Collins, codirectors of the Peer Network of New York, attended the screening. Drug dealing was brought up, and Jones explained that Harlem had a long history of people buying and selling drugs that predated the arrival of OTPs. Collins talked about harm reduction and urged people to have empathy for those struggling with addiction who were unhoused. Jones revealed that he worked at OnPoint NYC, and that the overdose prevention center not only helped people stay alive, it brought public drug use indoors. It was a win-win. A respectful conversation, with some disagreements, followed. Members of the GHC were invited to take a tour of OnPoint NYC and meet with staff. The discussion then turned to the solution to the concentration of so many methadone programs in East Harlem. We made the case for clinic abolition, and not surprisingly, there were no disagreements.

NIMBYism stalks every methadone clinic that tries to open in the United States, whether in urban or rural areas. The racism, medical redlining, byzantine state regulations, and destructive community organizing to keep OTPs out using stigma and hatred combine to make it clear that clinic closure is long overdue. It makes no sense to continue dispensing methadone in community clinics in the face of this decades-long and unrelenting opposition, some of which is warranted. Shutting down OTPs and permitting pharmacy pickup liberates patients and communities. It will end NIMBY campaigns once and for all.

6

THE RISE OF FOR-PROFIT
METHADONE CLINIC CHAINS

Jason Kletter was angry. Kletter is the president of BayMark Health Services and has a PhD in organizational psychology. He was feeling threatened by the widespread criticism of OTPs and the growing national chorus calling for reform. It was 2022, and I attended the panel he was speaking on, "MAT Policy, Advocacy, and Reform: Being a Voice in a Time of Change," at the AATOD conference. AATOD is the industry trade association that represents the interests of methadone clinics. Kletter is also on the board of directors and serves as the legislative chair.

The petulant president of a for-profit methadone clinic chain came out swinging in his PowerPoint presentation, and he attempted to discredit and belittle the voices for change. It was a master class in minimizing and outright denial of the copious harms that clinics inflict on patients. Kletter made me angry. It was sickening to listen to him defend the clinic system and act like he wasn't responsible for the suffering that he profits from. He opened the presentation with slides that documented the horrendous death toll of the opioid-related overdose crisis. He didn't acknowledge a key reason so many people have died: They couldn't access methadone, or if they did, humiliating dispensing regulations drove them out of treatment and back to fentanyl.[1]

His next set of slides were a series of contradictory claims about harm reduction—an approach that he called "extreme"—and a condescending rebuke to people who want real clinic reform. One slide said, "Confusing Harm Reduction With Treatment. Smart, well-intentioned people are conflating harm reduction and treatment and suggesting things like: Medication alone is treatment, counseling is ineffective/unimportant, drug testing is a barrier to access, and supervised dosing is oppressive." All those things are true. Another slide criticized a two-day workshop examining methadone regulations convened by the National Academies of Sciences, Engineering and Medicine.[2] Kletter was apoplectic that speakers— including people who take methadone—dared to call out OTPs and advocate for deregulation and pharmacy dispensing. He's opposed to these changes because they would end the methadone monopoly and that would hurt BayMark's bottom line. The workshop featured dozens of speakers, with Mark Parrino, the president of AATOD, presenting on the first day.[3] Kenneth B. Stoller, a board member of AATOD, was on the workshop planning committee, so their views were well represented.

The Power of the Pandemic

COVID-19 exposed how the dysfunctional, patchwork, and for-profit American health care system fails millions of people and needs fundamental reform.[4] The pandemic did the same thing for OTPs. It was a long overdue gut punch that revealed their prison-like practices in a way they never had been before. From their inception, clinics have existed in the shadows, have garnered little mainstream media attention outside of NIMBY campaigns, have been immune from criticism, and have been resistant to change. It's as if every clinic was preserved in amber circa the Nixonian 1970s.

No more: With the onset of the pandemic, calls for reform have come from federal and state agencies involved in methadone regulation as well as from patient advocacy organizations, legislators, and addiction experts. Even

Nora Volkow, the director of the NIDA, came out for reform: "Although more research would be of value, the initial evidence suggests that providing methadone outside of OTPs is feasible, acceptable, and leads to good outcomes."[5] Those words probably infuriated Kletter and Parrino. They're not used to being criticized by their biggest government backers and politicians. They don't like media stories that are sympathetic to the plight of patients and that expose the culture of cruelty. An article in *STAT* pulled no punches: "Patients at methadone clinics go to extraordinary lengths to receive their medication, complying with rules and suffering indignities that would be unthinkable in any other health care setting. . . . In interviews, several patients, across multiple clinics, reported that they were admonished by clinic staff for not saying 'please' or 'thank you.'"[6]

The pandemic also revealed the way OTP funding has shifted since their inception. The Nixon administration created and financed a national network of methadone clinics that were free. Over the next few decades, especially during the eight-year presidency of Ronald Reagan, the federal government cut funding for clinics and transferred their operation to state and local nonprofit organizations. For-profit corporations begin buying up nonprofit OTPs and opening new ones. Now, according to federal data, 65 percent are operated by for-profit companies.[7] It is the era of mergers and mega methadone chains owned by profit-seeking private equity investors like Waud Capital Partners and Bain Capital Ventures.

Private Equity and Profits

In twenty-one states, at least 50 percent of all OTPs are owned either by private equity firms or by Acadia Healthcare, and in Louisiana, Montana, Nebraska, and New Hampshire, 100 percent are owned either by Acadia or by private equity firms.[8] New York is an outlier in not having any OTP chains because it's the birthplace of methadone treatment. The academic medical centers Mount Sinai and Montefiore Einstein are two of the largest providers of methadone in New York City, and there are dozens of community-based nonprofit legacy OTPs—Acacia Network, Greenwich House, and START Recovery. Another legacy holdout is Ward 93, the methadone clinic at San Francisco General Hospital that opened in the 1970s.

The rise of private equity–owned methadone clinic chains was inevitable in a health care system that is privatized and for-profit. As the number of people addicted to opioids skyrocketed and the federal government started requiring Medicaid and Medicare to cover methadone treatment, private equity investors saw an expanding market for methadone and an opportunity to bill large government insurance programs.

Drug treatment in the United States is a Wild West, and there is no national coordination. In most states, the drug rehab industry is unregulated, and many programs don't have licensed professionals on staff.[9] The "Florida shuffle" is a cautionary tale of what happens when there is little regulation and profit, not patient care, is the motive. This is how it works: Drug treatment facilities in Florida paid brokers to find and book patients into treatment; the facilities would pay brokers by charging the patients' insurance. The going rate to direct an insured patient to a particular facility at one point was $7,000.[10] *Reveal*, an investigative radio show and podcast, documented that at hundreds of "sober homes," patients were forced to work as the main form of addiction treatment—and the participants rarely got paid.[11] Patients relapsed and shuffled from rehab to rehab until their insurance coverage ran out. These relapse cycles are financially lucrative for treatment providers. Many of these sober homes reject the use of evidence-based medications like methadone and buprenorphine, and that puts patients at great risk for overdose.[12]

Anyone with enough capital can open an OTP; no experience or training in addiction medicine is required. Nick Stavros, a board member of AATOD, operates over eighty clinics. He spent eight years in the US Army as an intelligence analyst, and upon discharge, pursued an MBA.[13] Acadia Healthcare, the country's largest for-profit chain, owns over 180 methadone clinics. In his past career, Acadia's CEO, Christopher H. Hunter, was president for military and specialty businesses at Humana, one of the largest for-profit health insurance companies. Acadia has generated more than $1.3 billion in revenue since 2022, and Hunter told investors it is "a business that we continue to feel great about."[14] Kletter's BayMark operates over a hundred methadone clinics across the United States. It is the parent company of BAART, MedMark, and Health Care Resource Centers. The company also operates over seventy OTPs in Canada.[15] Two private equity firms, BPEA Private Equity and Webster Equity Partners, bought BayMark in 2015.[16]

BayMark's tagline, "Leading Positive Change," is a rip-off of the slogan "Any Positive Change" coined by the naloxone pioneer Dan Bigg.[17] The positive change is more profits for investors. Bigg would not approve.

Bill, Baby, Bill

OTPs are highly overregulated. Private equity investors got into the business of methadone despite this because the strict regulations often work in their favor. The DEA gives OTPs the exclusive right to dispense methadone, and the SAMHSA guidelines, plus state regulations, guarantee them patients for life, unless they drop out of treatment. The methadone monopoly has several strategies to boost profits. Bruce Trigg, a former OTP medical director in New Mexico, explained to me:

> One way of increasing profits is to have doctors come in for a few hours a week to mainly sign paperwork and to spend little time with patients. [Clinic owners] really didn't like having to pay me to spend time working with patients because doctors cost money—$200 an hour or more. The clinics were only open until 1 p.m., minimizing costs even further. They also pay counselors, nurses, pharmacists, and security staff as little as possible, and as a result have huge turnover that really lowers the quality of care. Many staff had second or third jobs. At one place I worked at in Albuquerque for two years, I was the only person on the entire staff, including administrators, who was still there after two years. This is what I call low-quality, high-profit care.

OTPs generally make money when patients come to the clinic and receive numerous billable services. Those services are easiest to provide when patients attend their clinics frequently—regardless of whether it is medically necessary. In 2019, a CMS clinic in Arizona began to operate 24-7, and while this around-the-clock availability makes methadone more accessible, it also allows for more billing. The expansion of hours was made possible by a grant from the federal 21st Century Cures Act.[18] The legislation includes funding for state grants to support prevention and treatment to address the opioid overdose crisis and for the development of new drugs and medical devices.

Michael Hegarty, a former counselor at a BAART clinic in San Francisco, told me, "BAART is only about what's billable. The only reason anybody gets counseling or sees a nurse practitioner or a doctor is the intake, the checkups; it's all billable. Checking the boxes to get paid. That's all they care about. Why did you see this person for forty minutes when you were supposed to see them for sixty minutes? The incentive is to bill the absolute maximum, primarily to public insurance sources like Medi-Cal." A job responsibility for the methadone counselor position at a Montefiore OTP in the Bronx states: "Ensure all counselor specific billable services are billed and perform follow-ups to billing delinquent payments, obtaining information required to bill, confirming and updating billing information, etc."[19] Counselor involvement in billing sets up yet another adversarial dynamic, especially for patients who pay out-of-pocket for methadone and are late paying fees. It can lead to a feetox.

BayMark receives funding from numerous public sources. They were awarded grants from the Department of Health Care Services California MAT Expansion Project to offer 24-7 access at a BAART clinic in Los Angeles. The San Francisco Department of Public Health provided funding to increase hours for treatment at BAART's Market Street program and at their buprenorphine clinic.[20] Why does a for-profit, private OTP chain receive money from public sources to expand access? Why doesn't BayMark pay? Most OTPs use a fee-for-service model and charge for nurse-observed dosing, individual and group counseling, urine toxicologies, physical exams, and other tests. Older SAMHSA guidelines mandated that within the first three months of treatment patients had to attend six days a week and could only get one take-home bottle—on Sunday when the clinic was closed. In some states clinics are open seven days a week and patients get zero take-home medication. Because OTPs only get paid when patients are on-site, there is a financial incentive to keep them on daily witnessed dosing.

I learned how profit margins related directly to patient attendance during an interview with Janet Urdahl, a licensed clinical social worker and a former executive director of a methadone clinic in Delaware. She ended Saturday dosing so patients could get a full weekend of freedom. The clinic lost $16,000 a month.[21] Massachusetts, New York, and Connecticut have instituted a weekly or daily bundled payment scheme that provides a set fee to cover a defined range of services. Under this payment model, methadone clinics shouldn't lose money by allowing patients more take-home medication.[22] But why should Medicaid or Medicare, taxpayer-funded insurance programs, even care if for-profit clinics lose money? Hegarty said, "There is a massive transfer of wealth from public coffers into private hands. This is looting the public treasury to put my tax dollars into some schlub's pocket in Texas."[23]

Private equity–owned methadone clinics have been charged with defrauding Medicaid. In 2019, federal prosecutors in West Virginia accused Acadia of overbilling Medicaid for medical tests, and the company paid $17 million to resolve the allegations. Counselors at Acadia have accused their employer of billing for therapy sessions that never took place.[24] Crossroads is a chain with over one hundred clinics owned by the private equity firm Revelstoke Capital. Crossroads paid close to $1 million to settle charges by the State of Virginia and the US Department of Justice that from 2016 through mid-2023 the clinics defrauded Medicaid. A whistleblower tipped off the Department of Justice that the clinics were submitting claims that patient-provider visits involved comprehensive assessments, but an investigation found that the visits were just regular check-ins.[25] Even nonprofit programs have scammed Medicaid. Apt Foundation, founded in 1970 by members of the Yale University Department of Psychiatry, was investigated by the Connecticut Attorney General for double-billing Medicaid and paid over $800,000 to settle the case.[26]

Mega methadone chains are lining up for opioid settlement slush fund handouts. Opioid manufacturers, distributors, and retailers have put over $50 billion dollars in the settlement funds for restitution to settle lawsuits over their role in the overdose crisis.[27] Acadia successfully lobbied the Kansas Legislature to allow for-profit companies to receive grants from the funds, and CEO Hunter told investors that the money will be "a really nice tailwind" for the company.[28]

Policing for Profit with Tech

The pandemic in 2020 caused the fossilized world of the methadone clinic to crack open and forced innovations in operations for the first time in fifty years. OTPs pivoted to providing counseling via telemedicine, and in an unprecedented move, the DEA and SAMHSA allowed all patients to be screened for fourteen to twenty-eight days of take-home medication. For those who got them, it was liberation from daily dosing.[29] The shift to a new business model that uses surveillance technologies to provide services remotely—while maintaining or increasing profitability—suddenly became possible.

Unsupervised dosing is a financial loss for most OTPs. Enter a group of tech bros whose goal is to ensure that doesn't happen. Back at the booths inside the exhibition hall at the AATOD conference, there were displays of the products from the corporations that make up the methadone surveillance state: DEA-compliant safes, high-density urine collection cups, pilfer-resistant plastic bottles, computerized liquid methadone dispensers, GPS-enabled lockboxes.[30] That's where I met Dr. Michael Giles, the founder and CEO of Sonara Health, and where I saw the future of policing patients for profit with remote technology.[31] His company, founded in 2020, makes a web-based application called Virtual Dosing Window. This is how the app works: Patients are given bottles with QR codes with labels that state "Do not open until instructed." At a time designated by the clinic, the patient logs on to Sonara's web app to scan the QR code. Once scanned and opened, the code is voided and the label indicates that it has been opened. Then they record themselves drinking the methadone with their cell phone camera—a video "selfie." To ensure the liquid is fully swallowed, the app instructs the patient to say: "The quick brown fox jumps over the lazy dog."[32] The video and dosing data is then uploaded to Sonara's platform and reviewed by staff.

Giles got this authoritarian idea during a psychiatry residency rotation in the methadone clinic at the Veterans Administration in Dallas. He saw how strict clinic rules harmed patients, but instead of advocating for them to be treated as adults and trusted with more take-home medication, he decided to develop an app to surveil them—with hopes of cashing in. Sonara raised $5 million, with billionaire Mark Cuban investing $2.3 million in the company.[33] Cuban said, "I think Sonara can have a major impact on this problem [rigid clinic regulations] and I wanted to be a small part of it. That simple."[34]

Mistrust

Sonara's tagline is "Empowering Recovery, Fostering Trust." But everything about the app is rooted in mistrust and reinforces the power differential between staff and patients. Staff instructing a person when to take their dose and receiving an alert when a bottle with a "tamper-aware" label has been opened, filming ingestion, forcing the person to recite a ridiculous and infantilizing sentence, and approval that the medication has been taken correctly—all that is the opposite of trust.

Company vice president of operations Sheeba Ibidunni said, "Sonara, by offering remote observation of take-home methadone, creates this layer of supervision to what was previously unsupervised, and that is able to build trust between the provider and the patient."[35] Ibidunni is wrong. It makes no difference if the person is dosing at the clinic window with a nurse watching or if they are using Sonara's trademarked Virtual Dosing Window app in an offsite location. Both systems are rooted in deep distrust and are built around invasive monitoring.

Sonara's remote observation moves the surveillance from the clinic into the home. What the company is cynically betting on to get their high-tech spying app into more of them is patient desperation to avoid the major inconvenience and humiliation of daily in-person dosing. Who wouldn't chose dosing at home with a Big Brother app versus the expense, travel time, waiting in lines, and often unpredictable circumstances of getting medicated at an OTP? It's akin to people desperate to get out of jail and agreeing to wear a GPS ankle monitor, referred to as "digital shackles," that tracks their every move.[36] Sonara's app is a form of video shackles, and it contributes to the culture of cruelty. Since the creation of the methadone clinic system, if a patient has take-home medication, they have not been monitored. Trust has been established in the sense that they've followed clinic rules, often for years, and earned the privilege to take methadone in the privacy of their home. When a person takes their medication, or even if they skip or split a dose, it's their own business. If adopted widely, Sonara's technology has the potential to end all unsupervised dosing, and the financial incentive for that model shift is enormous. As well as rewarding some patients, teledosing will punish patients who don't take their medication as prescribed. It's inevitable that staff will use the information from recordings to force some patients back to daily dosing. Hegarty said:

> Sonara is about making profits. The company doesn't care if you pick up your methadone at an OTP or a pharmacy. It shifts the brick-and-mortar clinic system into a fully virtual telemedicine model. The technology lowers expenses by moving everything virtual. If you can do telemedicine

for intake, counseling, and monitoring ingestion and bill for it, then at a certain point you can lower your costs, either by eliminating or reducing your real estate and operational expenses.

There is nothing inherently wrong with telemedicine. If a video platform is designed to surveil patients while they ingest methadone, it should be rejected. If health care providers utilize it to do assessments to get patients started on methadone and check in with them around dosing issues or side effects, it should be supported.

Sonara has partnered with BayMark to pilot the app.[37] The company got funding from the National Center for Advancing Translational Sciences and NIDA to conduct research.[38] The "Remotely Observed Methadone Evaluation" study that they conducted was designed with the aim of "developing and integrating machine learning features such as facial recognition and methadone vial position tracking for automated dosing event interpretation."[39] *What?* In 2024, Sonara received $250,000 from the state of New Jersey—yet more public tax dollars—for a pilot study.[40] "We really want to help modernize the treatment experience and establish a new standard of care in the state of New Jersey," Giles said. "These opioid treatment programs haven't had the opportunity to do anything new since their inception until very recently."[41] Sonara is now in use at OTPs in more than a dozen states.

The other thing Sonara is banking on to get its product into more homes is Medicaid spending on transportation. Many patients insured through this public insurance program are transported to their OTP six or seven days a week. That's expensive. Remote dosing could save Medicaid money, which in turn could expand the use of Sonara's surveillance app.

Opioid Settlement Funds for Policing Patients

Not to be left out, the tech bros are working hard to get millions from the opioid settlement funds. In the webinar "Using Opioid Settlement Funds to Support OTP Innovation," moderated by Phil Beck, Sonara's vice president of growth, it was noted that they frequently partner with OTPs to draft settlement fund applications to finance their Virtual Dosing Window app.[42] The company received money from the settlement to implement their spy tool in MedMark clinics in Pennsylvania. Giles stated, "We hope OTPs will continue to leverage opioid settlement funds strategically to support innovative, evidence-based treatments."[43]

I asked Giles about the name of his company. He said it comes from the Spanish word *soñara*, which means "will dream." No doubt Dr. Giles is dreaming about all the profits he hopes to rake in from recording patients swallowing methadone.

Sonara isn't the only company using remote technology to police patients for profit. Verinetics makes DispenSecur, a heavy, bulky lockbox that can hold up fourteen bottles of methadone. It is markedly different from the traditional medication lockbox patients are currently mandated to store take-home bottles in but equally stigmatizing. The DispenSecur device needs to be charged, features GPS location monitoring, a real-time view to a dispensing activity log, and inventory tracking. An online map shows the "last known location" of the lockbox.

I visited the Verinetics booth, and a sales representative showed me how the product works.[44] Plastic bottles of liquid methadone are loaded into a carousel by OTP staff, and a metal cover then locks into place so patients can't see or take out all the bottles. A small green door opens at a predetermined time, and only one bottle can be removed. This is a diversion control measure. The person consumes the medication, puts the empty bottle back, and presses a button to confirm they've taken the dose. OTP staff log into a dashboard that displays if the dose was taken as scheduled, skipped, or if a bottle is missing. The most insidious Big Brother feature is that it can be locked remotely by clinic staff at any moment, cutting off access. DispenSecur can go into lockdown mode if it detects signs of medication theft or tampering. A digital screen displays a message to the patient, "Device locked by OTP," and gives the clinic phone number. An information brochure states, "Locking may be invoked if a provider has concerns about the patient or medication. . . . It can be used to encourage a telemedicine session." This feature of the lockbox called autonomous dispensing deactivation, lets patients know that they are not in control of their medication, not even in their own home.

Verinetics asserts that remote supervision builds trust—that word again—between patients and OTP staff. But how does a device that enables "providers to monitor medications from the time patients leave the clinic to the moment they access each of their daily doses of methadone" build trust? Constant surveillance is the opposite of trust. The company believes that DispenSecur fosters autonomy: "Monitoring is strictly based on data analytics and not observing dose administration, allowing preservation of individual independence."[45] But the high-tech lockbox *is* observing patients when they take their medication: not with a video app but with GPS location tracking and dosing data. And like Sonara, Verinetics technology has the ability to punish patients and force them back to in-person daily dosing. To make the case for the use of DispenSecur, clinic-generated barriers patients have endured for decades are criticized. A video at their booth showed patients, umbrellas in hand, standing in line in the rain. The caption read, "Every day individuals wait in OTP lines like this one to receive their methadone dose. . . . How do you get your kids to school or get yourself to a job?"

The company also recognizes thousands of patients in rural areas struggle to get to a clinic hundreds of miles away. "We are committed to improving the lives of the country's most stigmatized people who simply need convenient yet controlled access to their lifesaving medications," said Tom Mercolino, the founder and former CEO of Verinetics. "We believe DispenSecur will be a groundbreaking tool to enable individuals to receive take-home doses in earlier phases of treatment. Dosing at home means these individuals have more time for work and their families." And it means more money for Mercolino. Verinetics has also received taxpayer dollars to develop their spy tool. It was awarded $1.5 million from NIDA to develop the dystopian DispenSecur.[46]

Next up is MedMinder, a venture capitalist–funded company that makes a variety of pillbox organizers to monitor medication adherence.[47] Researchers at Johns Hopkins University School of Medicine conducted a study using a MedMinder electronic and Wi-Fi-enabled pillbox called "Jon" that monitored patients with take-home doses of methadone during the pandemic.[48] Jon contains twenty-eight individually programmed and remotely activated cells that are unlocked automatically for a short dosing window. At a designated time, patients remove a medication cup containing methadone in pill form and swallow it. Each cell in the pillbox locks independently to deter diversion or the taking of additional doses. Jon tracks everything from missed doses to attempts to open a locked cell, then notifies staff in real time. The pillbox can be remotely reprogrammed at any time to unlock or lock a cell. The words *locking* and *unlocking* cells won't be lost on methadone patients, who often compare clinics to jails. It turns out Jon is a "virtual correctional officer." The language these corporations use is Orwellian. Trust is location tracking. Remote observation is autonomy. Dispensing deactivation is independence.

These remote supervision, tracking, and recording devices are the brave new world of the methadone surveillance state. The technology was developed to maintain control of dosing outside the confines of OTPs, and it retains the power imbalance between staff and patients. These corporations are extracting profits from structurally disempowered patients despite all the fake happy talk about how their tech promotes trust, autonomy, privacy, and personal dignity. They dangle a Faustian bargain and offer the fiction of freedom, but at a price. You can take methadone at home and avoid the commute and the hassles at the clinic, but in return you must submit to constant monitoring and can be cut off at any time.

It has always been wrong that methadone patients have to prove they can be trusted to take their medication without being observed, but thousands who got additional take-home bottles actually did during the pandemic. "If the evidence from COVID wasn't enough to show that people who use drugs deserve less, rather than more, monitoring, then I'm not sure what would be," Aaron Ferguson, the methadone liaison for the National Survivors Union, told me.[49]

Kletter and the tech-savvy capitalists at Sonara, Verinetics, and Med-Minder understand that there needs to be change in order for things to stay the same. Their remote-dosing surveillance tools do just that. And the methadone monopoly continues to make money for private equity investors while a bottle with a tamper-aware QR code is scanned, Jon unlocks cells, dispensing is deactivated, and patients recite "The quick brown fox jumps over the lazy dog."

7

JUST SAY NO TO METHADONE IN DRUG TREATMENT COURT, JAIL, OR PRISON

You Americans have a court for everything.

—NUNO CAPAZ, sociologist and
member of the Portuguese Ministry
of Health's Dissuasion Commissions

The torn white paper taped to the black metal door of the drug treatment court in Manhattan revealed the race of the people who were expected to be passing through: "No hats, hoods, doo rags, skullys." I've sat in drug treatment court on hard benches in Manhattan over a dozen times and witnessed the proceedings. The court system was a microcosm of all of the ways people who use drugs are discriminated against and punished for having an addiction. The anecdotes below are only a small fraction of the interactions I've observed.

The drug treatment court judge was angry as she spoke to a young Black man with locs and tattooed arms sitting at the defense table, hands uncomfortably shackled behind his back. He was surrounded by four armed and unsmiling court officers wearing dark-blue uniforms and bullet-proof vests. The judge's comments came quickly: "This is a bad report. You've had six unexcused absences from the outpatient program. You've got to go when you are told, and now you have to make up all the meetings you missed. And you had two positive urine screenings for THC. You can't smoke marijuana. You have to abstain from all drugs. I'm going to give you one more chance, but if you don't follow the rules, you're going back to jail."

Next defendant. A middle-aged Latina from Washington Heights tested positive for alcohol. The judge had made her write an essay on why she drank, and the judge now praises her for admitting the reasons she had a couple of beers (it was her birthday) and how it was a serious violation of her court contract.

Next defendant. A young Black woman with box braids from the Bronx is met with a smile from the judge. "You are doing great. All negative urine screenings." He gives her a certificate of achievement for six months clean time, the court erupts into applause, the judge blows a kazoo-like whistle, and staff ring bells. The loud celebratory noise ricocheted around the huge high-ceilinged courtroom that is normally silent.

Next defendant. The judge informs the lawyer from Legal Aid that her client failed the program after being given three opportunities to succeed. The last straw was that he "absconded" from the inpatient facility and had an unauthorized cell phone. The thirty-two-year-old Black man would be sentenced to two to four years in prison. The only words the judge spoke as the man was ushered out in handcuffs was, "I wish you good luck, sir."

Next defendant. A thirty-seven-year-old Latino man is admonished for missing five drug tests at the treatment court office in Manhattan. He explained that he worked in the Bronx and had to pick his toddler up in Queens, and it was hard to make it to the office every week. Twice he arrived a few minutes late and was turned away. As a sanction, he was "flash incarcerated" for ten days.

Next defendant. A heavyset Black man is sitting in the back of the court room and is agitated—he's mumbling under his breath and is occasionally slamming his backpack onto the hard wooden bench. He's been waiting all morning for his case to be called, and when it finally is, he expresses his frustration to the judge. The man hates the inpatient facility. He is constantly searched, there is a nine o'clock curfew, the staff are aggressive and disrespectful, and it took over a month to have an individual session with a counselor. The man wondered why the court sent him to this program because—he emphatically stressed the last word—it was bullshit! The judge was livid: "You treat me with respect!" The arguing escalated, and she ordered him to leave the courtroom and wait outside.

Next defendant. A handcuffed sixty-year-old Black man is brought into the courtroom from Rikers Island jail. The judge is smiling and asks him how he feels. Then she tells him that a staffer from the Fortune Society is ready to escort him to a program. The judge says she wants to see a good first report, gently warns him not to leave the facility without permission, and to start "living your best life." The shackles are taken off, and the man, beaming with relief, sprints out of the courtroom with the escort.

The Drug War and Drug Courts

How did access to drug treatment end up in courtrooms that operate like assembly lines where people who use drugs are alternately praised or punished by a judge who doesn't understand the complexity of addiction? The escalation of the war on drugs in the 1980s and 1990s led to the creation of drug courts. Hundreds of thousands of newly hired cops enforced low-level drug laws and criminal penalties for the possession and sale of small amounts of illicit substances. In turn, millions of petty cases overwhelmed the court system, and people charged with minor drug law violations received mandatory minimum sentences that exploded the number of people in jails and prisons. Frustrated judges spoke out about high rates of recidivism. This pattern of mass incarceration and prison overcrowding in turn created drug courts tasked with diverting people away from prisons and jails.

Drug courts are specialized court programs that address substance use problems by offering an alternative to incarceration. Because drug courts are developed locally, they tend to vary significantly in their rules and structure. No two are exactly alike. Judges are not required to have training in substance use. Drug treatment courts are primarily for justice-involved individuals who are accused of a nonviolent felony crime and have a documented substance use disorder. Individuals can be referred to drug court either before pleading guilty (pre-trial diversion) or after a guilty plea, with sentencing deferred while they are enrolled in the program (post-adjudication). They must plead guilty.

Drug courts involve close monitoring of participants, with frequent court appearances and regular check-ins with case managers. Failure to appear in court can result in a bench warrant being issued for arrest. A case manager creates a participant treatment plan, arranges for them to enter a court-approved inpatient or outpatient program, and provides linkages to medical, employment, and educational resources that are crucial for success in graduating from drug court. Total abstinence from all substances, including alcohol and cannabis, is required, even though alcohol is legal, medical use of cannabis is legal in forty states, and recreational use is legal in twenty-four states plus the District of Columbia. Participants are usually drug tested weekly in both their treatment program and by the court. Positive urine screenings can trigger sanctions like jail time, sitting in drug court all day, verbal reprimands, or termination. The court rewards progress with verbal praise from the judge, noisemakers, applause, certificates of achievement, or less frequent court appearances.

The requirements to graduate from the Manhattan Drug Court (MDC) are numerous. Participants must maintain abstinence from all substances, reach all drug treatment program goals, complete the three phases of the MDC, participate in community service, demonstrate progress toward

vocational and educational goals, have a verifiable means of financial support, and show good faith efforts to get full-time employment.[1] A drug
court judge was honest and told me, "Drug court is a lot, and it's not for
everybody." Successful completion can have a life-changing impact—the
dismissal of charges, reduced sentences, and having records expunged or
sealed. On the other hand, if a participant is terminated, they are sentenced
to the prison time agreed on when they pleaded guilty. Ironically, "failing"
drug treatment court can result in harsher penalties than if the person had
not participated.[2]

Coerced Drug Treatment

Substance use programs are vital partners with drug courts. The criminal-
legal system is the single largest source of referrals to publicly funded drug
treatment for adults.[3] Without court-mandated clients, many would go
out of business. Staff wield enormous power, and with one call or email to
the judge, they can have a person jailed for the smallest infraction. Drug
treatment programs' insistence on abstinence from all drugs, even alcohol
and cannabis, is a set up for failure. Forcing people who have a lifetime of
drug use, especially those with a mental health diagnosis, to abstain from
all drugs doesn't work.

The US Department of Justice's Drug Courts Program Office was clear
on the mission: "Drug courts leverage the coercive power of the criminal
justice system to achieve abstinence and alter criminal behavior through
the combination of judicial supervision, treatment, drug testing, incentives, sanctions, and case management."[4] Funding and expanding community supports and services for voluntary drug treatment programs based
on the principles of harm reduction and human rights weren't on offer,
nor was the solution of legalization and regulation of all drugs. Instead,
bipartisan advocates for reform did the opposite.[5] Over thirty years, a drug
court industrial complex was built with powerful for-profit players who
have a vested interest in maintaining the status quo. US drug treatment

courts exist within a sprawling prison industrial complex that incarcer-
ates more people than any other country: 1.9 million were incarcerated,
803,000 were on parole, and 2.9 million were on probation in 2023. Black
people are overrepresented in carceral settings and make up 38 percent
of the prison and jail population; Black people are only 12 percent of the
US population.[6]

The National Association of Drug Court Professionals, renamed All
Rise, is a powerful advocacy organization for drug court personnel. They
believe that treatment courts are the most successful justice intervention
for individuals with substance use and mental health disorders.[7] Arrest-
ing, punishing, and incarcerating people for drug use is the antithesis
of harm reduction, and yet All Rise has curated the fiction that drug
courts use a harm reduction approach. In the webinar "Navigating Harm
Reduction in Treatment Courts," Aaron Arnold, chief development officer at All Rise, cites the preamble to the Principles of Harm Reduction
from the National Harm Reduction Coalition.[8] Arnold didn't mention
the core harm reduction principles that are in direct opposition to drug
court rules: The provision of noncoercive services and the cessation of all
drug use isn't the only criteria for success; the realities of poverty, class,
racism, social isolation, past trauma, sex-based discrimination, and other
social inequalities affect both people's vulnerability to and capacity for
effectively dealing with drug-related harm; and people who use drugs
have a real voice in the creation of programs and policies designed to
serve them.[9] All Rise doesn't accept that participants can show improvement by working, parenting, and attending classes even if they are not
completely abstinent. As long as the threat of punishment remains, these
so-called alternatives to incarceration are not harm reduction, they are
just harm. They only end up delaying incarceration.[10] Drug courts need
to be seen as a part of what the civil rights lawyer Alec Karakatsanis calls
the "punishment bureaucracy."[11]

It is a big gamble to choose drug court, but many roll the dice because
certain incarceration is a terrifying prospect. Violence, rape, solitary

confinement, suicide, and medical neglect are central features of imprisonment in the United States. Given that reality, mandated drug treatment in the community appears to be a much better option—except that approximately half of all participants don't complete treatment and go to prison, often with a sentence that is much longer than if they had been conventionally sentenced in the first place. Black people are at least 30 percent more likely than whites to be expelled from drug treatment court, in part as a result of socioeconomic disadvantages.[12] Studies have found that graduation rates for white participants are much higher than for Black participants.[13]

Urinetown

For judges, like OTPs, a negative urine screen is the most important measure of progress. From observing the MDC, I've noted that positive drug tests are often hotly contested by participants and lead to bitter arguments with the judge and prosecutor, and then more confirmatory testing. In the MDC, participants are tested weekly. A week without a drug test is considered to be a positive. A section in the MDC Handbook contains a series of warnings. Consumption of food that contains poppy seeds is forbidden, and a positive test with a claim it was poppy seeds is regarded as positive for opioids. Do not eat everything bagels or poppy seed salad dressing![14] Cough syrup with any alcohol content could produce a positive urine and a sanction. Participants are told not to drink large amounts of water three hours before a drug test. This is called "water-loading" and is considered tampering with the urine. The "lab will identify that the sample is diluted and it will be reported to the judge."[15]

There is an entire All Rise document devoted to the minutia of drug and alcohol testing that argues it's necessary because the more frequently a person is drug tested the better the outcomes in terms of graduation rates.[16] All collection of urine is witnessed by staff trained to prevent tampering. With all that urine sloshing around, it's no wonder that a key stakeholder in the drug treatment court ecosystem is drug testing corporations, whose profits depend on thousands of case managers from Connecticut to California watching people pee in cups weekly for years.

The perverse fixation on urine is another form of surveillance and control that leads to punishment. A positive toxicology actually tells us very little about a person, and it shifts the focus away from viewing them wholistically. It privileges urine over any positive change. Nothing else a participant does has the same weight or is reviewed more than the results of a urine test: not finding employment or housing or improved mental and physical health.

Judging Methadone

People who take methadone probably won't be shocked by how rigid drug courts are. The control, constant drug testing, punishment, and power imbalance that is foundational to methadone clinics is foundational to drug courts. People who take methadone are in grave danger in drug treatment courts. For decades, there was a blanket prohibition against methadone in drug courts, and OTPs weren't considered an appropriate referral for outpatient drug treatment. Courts argued that a person wasn't abstinent if they took methadone. In New York, judges routinely ordered people to stop taking the medication.[17] It didn't matter if the participant was pregnant.

Dr. Robert Newman spent the latter half of his career as an expert witness testifying in courts across the country for women who were in danger of being incarcerated or losing their children simply because they took prescribed methadone. In many courtrooms he argued with judges that the medication was vital to protect the health of the fetus, that it was the standard of care, and that it was wrong to overrule a doctor's medical judgment. Newman, a thin, wiry man with a great sense of humor, told me in an interview at his home in 2015 that he was frustrated that the stigma of methadone endured. He found it intolerable that courts weren't allowing people to take methadone:

> Most judges are not justifying their opinions with any evidence, and they overrule the physician who has prescribed methadone. If you say, "Your honor, what is the basis for that decision? Where is the evidence for your demand that a patient stop getting a prescribed treatment?" the judge says, "No, I don't have to give you any evidence. I just don't believe in it." They threaten the mother by saying if you take methadone and anything happens [to the fetus], it could be considered a homicide. You murdered your baby. We are going to sanction you with prison or a loss of child custody. What is the logic there? It's completely irrational. It's incomprehensible. It will drive you nuts!

He worked closely with the National Advocates for Pregnant Women, renamed Pregnancy Justice, and was fearless in his advocacy for people who took methadone. Newman was held in contempt of court and sentenced to thirty days in jail for refusing to turn over medical records from a methadone clinic to the Manhattan District Attorney's office. He went to court to defend patient privacy rights and won.[18] Newman set the bar high for doctors who worked in methadone clinics.

The abstinence-based inpatient drug treatment programs and sober recovery houses that drug court participants are referred to do not like methadone either. They have a long track record of denying services to people who take the medication. When these facilities do allow methadone, they often pressure people to taper off.[19] Discrimination in the drug treatment community is so universal that even twelve-step groups don't want methadone users in meetings because they're not considered drug-free. Medication-Assisted Recovery Anonymous (MARA) was formed to welcome everyone who takes prescribed medication for addiction.[20]

For many years the MDC had a policy that in order to participate, a person had to agree to transition from methadone to abstinence. According to the court handbook guidelines, in Phase I, a participant had to follow all OTP rules and reduce their methadone dose in half; Phase II was detoxification from methadone; and in Phase III, complete abstinence in order to graduate.[21] The "get off methadone" mantra is an example of how drug court judges play doctor, and the consequences can be dire. People denied methadone have overdosed and died.[22]

Drug treatment courts don't have a great track record of graduating participants with an opioid addiction. An Indiana study found that people who use opioids were 80 percent less likely to complete the program than others, and a study in Massachusetts found that one-third of participants with an opioid dependence relapsed *on the day of program completion*, and 50 percent two months after completion.[23]

The most updated handbook permits people to take methadone: "Participants who, with professional medical advice, voluntarily elect medication-assisted treatment . . . will be evaluated by a multidisciplinary team to determine eligibility."[24] Since 2011, All Rise has had a position that under no circumstances should a court have a blanket prohibition against methadone, and requests to take the medication should be evaluated on a case-by-case basis.[25] A study in 2013 found that only 47 percent of treatment courts permitted the use of methadone and buprenorphine.[26] Judges still have the power to decide if a person can take medication. There is no mandate that courts follow the recommendations of All Rise.

Drug courts have strict rules for taking methadone. The All Rise Best Practice Standards regarding medication monitoring could have been written by the DEA. There is an excessive fixation on diversion and witnessed ingestion. To ensure medication compliance, drug courts recommend that a member of the treatment court team or a sober trustworthy family member or friend directly supervise a person who has earned take-home bottles. In addition, they endorse the use of electronic devices with GPS that record when and how many bottles of liquid or pills are taken from a medication container and observe medication using facial recognition and smart phone technology, random pill counts, and "abuse-deterrence" formulations such as Suboxone sublingual films, liquid methadone, and long-acting injections.[27]

Curiously, there is one medication to treat addiction that drug courts have embraced without reservation: Vivitrol. It is a long-acting injectable form of naltrexone manufactured by Alkermes. Vivitrol is favored by drug courts because it's not a synthetic opioid like methadone and blocks the euphoric effects of opioids. It is given by injection once a month. Drug courts and correctional facilities are a major source of customers and profits for Alkermes. Vivitrol can cost as much as $1,000 per shot and is the company's highest-grossing drug; it generated up to $410 million in sales in 2023.[28] Alkermes has become a key player in the for-profit drug treatment court industrial complex. Company sales representatives have lobbied judges directly to allow use of the medication as an alternative to methadone and Suboxone. The lobbying has paid off. In some drug treatment courts, judges only allow Vivitrol, and getting the injection is a condition of participation.[29] The hope of courts—and of carceral institutions, where people who "fail" their treatment are often sent—is that the medication will prevent overdose once the person is back in the community, when they are at the highest risk. But studies have shown that Vivitrol doesn't reduce overdose, frequently increases it, and fatal overdoses have been undercounted.[30]

The Punishment Bureaucracy

Drug courts are part of the continued criminalization of drug users: Treatment is offered only when a person has been arrested. They are an example of how entrenched the idea is that illicit drug users are criminals that need to be controlled, penalized, and locked up, even when offered supports and services. All Rise asserts that drug treatment courts are trauma-informed, but what could be more traumatizing for participants than living with the constant threat of going to prison if you "fail?" Cognitive dissonance kicks in every time a prisoner shuffles into a courtroom shackled and surrounded by court officers with guns. Drug treatment courts are the worst possible setting to connect people who use substances to treatment because they create a dangerous illusion that a criminal courtroom—where a judge and prosecutors have all the power and little knowledge of addiction—can be a site for color-blind therapeutic interventions. The need for drug treatment should never be the reason that people enter the criminal-legal system.[31]

That drug courts have helped some participants struggling with addiction to get their lives back and avoid incarceration is true. They offer support and access to resources that can make a huge difference. Judges and staff have a genuine interest in participants graduating and becoming healthy and happy. I've personally witnessed that. The problem is the drug treatment court paradigm. There are more effective approaches to help people with a drug dependence that are located outside courtrooms and inside harm reduction–based drug treatment programs. The Harm Reduction Therapy Center (HRTC) in San Francisco is an example of what that looks like in practice. The center was created by Patt Denning and Jeannie Little to offer a completely different way of working with people who use drugs. HRTC's model offers low-barrier, integrated mental health care and substance use treatment in a friendly, respectful drop-in setting where people who are actively using drugs are welcome.[32] Clinically trained and supervised therapists provide free group and individual therapy. And snacks! The HRTC motto—grounded in the noncoercive and voluntary nature of their treatment model—simply states: "Come as you are, take what you need, leave when you want."

Torture in Jails and Prisons

I went into jail and wrote down all my medications. Staff told me flat out I'm not going to get methadone and they were putting me on an opiate protocol, which basically means you're going to the hole. You're going to be on twenty-three-hour lockdown, you'll be on suicide watch, and someone will come by your cell every fifteen minutes to check on you. To combat withdrawal symptoms, I was given Bentyl, ibuprofen, and trazodone to sleep. It was impossible to sleep with a guard shining a flashlight in my face every fifteen minutes to make sure I didn't off myself. But being in that situation made me the most suicidal that I had ever been in my life. Every joint in your body hurts, you're cold but you're sweating profusely, you're throwing up, diarrhea nonstop. I think the only reason that I got through it was not wanting to disappoint my family. I didn't want them to bury me coming out of jail. It was one of lowest points of my life.

When I got out, I shot a bag of dope and overdosed. My tolerance had gone way down. If my sister hadn't found me in the bathroom and called 911, I would have died. They make you feel like you're the biggest piece of shit and they want you to suffer every second of every day till you're done detoxing. I was so far down that I didn't want to live. Another time I did fourteen days. I have a prosthetic leg. On my previous trips to jail, I'd seen how they searched it, and what they missed. I took a baggie full of methadone pills, and stuffed it inside the pole connecting the socket to the foot. They didn't find it. I didn't want to go through detox again. I took the risk even knowing if they caught me I could get other charges. I didn't care because the only thing that really went through my mind was not wanting to go through that amount of pain.

Ryan Montague, who lives in the Northeast, shared this harrowing story of state-sanctioned torture with me. As his experience shows, incarceration poses unique risks to people who have an opioid dependence. Unfortunately, the torture he endured happens every day in jails and prisons across the United States of Addiction.

A report on the availability of medications for opioid use disorder found that less than 1 percent of the Federal Bureau of Prisons population received them in 2021.[33] A review by the Jail & Prison Opioid Project in the same year found that just 632 of the approximately 5,000 correctional facilities, 12 percent, offer any medication to treat opioid use disorder.[34] These abysmal numbers haven't changed despite an ongoing opioid overdose crisis where access to medication is a matter of life and death. Drug use among justice-involved populations is prevalent. SAMHSA reports that approximately 17 percent of people incarcerated in state prisons and 19 percent incarcerated in jails report regular opioid use.[35] The chances of dying from an overdose are significantly higher for newly released individuals who are not receiving addiction treatment in the first two weeks following release from jail.[36]

So why is there a prohibition on medications to treat opioid use disorders in most carceral settings? Prison and jail administrators—wait for it—often cite diversion as the primary reason for restricting access. Dr. Kelly Ramsey, an expert in addiction and a consultant to jails and prisons explained to me:

> I think there is a little bit of an overemphasis on diversion. What is going to reduce it more than anything is making medication easily available to all who need it. That means not having criteria of who can and who cannot get the medication and not having a zero-tolerance policy around diversion because people divert for many different reasons. Maybe it's to help another person who wasn't given access to the program.

Thousands of lawsuits have been filed on behalf of those who take methadone or buprenorphine while behind bars. Prohibition is why there is an illicit drug economy for Suboxone and methadone in carceral settings. Suboxone is often dispensed as a sublingual film strip, but shrewd prison dealers cut a single strip into dozens of pieces and sell them for $20 each.[37] Those trying desperately to avoid the agony of withdrawal are caught in a dilemma, because if they buy contraband drugs and are caught, the consequences are severe. Federal law treats the use of any narcotics without a prescription in federal prisons as a "greatest severity level prohibited act," allowing the punishment of prisoners by delaying release dates, the confiscation of property, taking away visiting or phone privileges, and the use of solitary confinement.[38] This is the upside-down world of addiction in prison—a fellow inmate will supply medication to treat addiction but not the medical staff.

But carceral institutions love naltrexone. They promote it for the same reasons drug courts do, and for a few more: It's almost impossible to divert the medication, it's not a DEA controlled substance, and it's often supplied for free. All prisons and jails in Massachusetts get free samples from Alkermes for the first Vivitrol injection before release.[39]

The Federal Bureau of Prisons has fought for years to prevent people entering jails and prisons from staying on addiction medications. Lawyers have argued that prohibiting the use of medication for opioid use disorder violates Title II of the Americans with Disabilities Act because it discriminates against those individuals, while other cases invoked the Eighth Amendment, which states people should be free from cruel and unusual punishment.[40] Stephanie DiPierro is one of those people. She was sentenced to a year in federal prison after pleading guilty to theft of public funds; she received disability benefits and food stamps without reporting income from a job. DiPierro, who takes methadone, sued the prison over its policy prohibiting use of the medication. She wrote in a statement, "I am afraid of what it will mean to lose my methadone treatment at the exact moment when I am put in the most anxiety-producing situation of my life. I am afraid for my life and my safety if the Bureau of Prisons withholds medicine that I know I need."[41] Despite all the litigation, the overdose deaths and suicides, jails and prisons across the country are still denying access. Methadone availability in jails and prisons is much lower than for buprenorphine because of strict methadone dispensing regulations, and that it is only available in OTPs. DEA regulations have created barriers that make providing methadone in correctional settings time-consuming and costly. There is no reason for this, as jails and prisons stock opioid pain relievers and comply with DEA oversight requirements for these controlled substances.[42]

Four Bad DEA Options

To get more methadone into penal institutions, the DEA has created four options. The first is to become an OTP and comply with all the regulations that OTPs do. This option is ridiculous because many regulations don't make sense in a correctional environment. For example, there are strict rules involving surveillance cameras, the number of security personnel, and safes to store methadone. The safe has to be a certain size and weight, and every time it's opened, an alarm must go off at a police station.[43] These regulations are redundant because jails and prisons are highly surveilled environments where staff and prisoner movement are monitored 24-7.

The second option is to register with the DEA as a "hospital/clinic." Inexplicably, though, in order to take methadone, the person has to have a primary diagnosis other than addiction. There are no federal guidelines for what qualifies as a primary condition under the DEA's regulations and that permit the use of methadone.[44]

The third possibility is to contract with an OTP to provide methadone. Patients could be transported to the clinic, or the medication delivered to the correctional facility. This option is expensive, labor intensive, and logistically complex, especially in rural areas where an OTP could be several hours away. Many jails and prisons don't have enough guards to accompany inmates to routine medical appointments, let alone to a clinic seven days a week.

The fourth option is for a medication unit—a van—to visit daily, but it depends on an OTP being willing to establish a mobile site and having sufficient staff. The DEA overregulates these vans too, making them costly to operate.[45] "The physical units must have a dispensary approved by the DEA," Linda Hurley, the CEO of CODAC Behavioral Healthcare explained: "These vans weren't designed for the hard work that mobile methadone entails. They're not designed to go out all day every day of the year. . . . The generator system breaks. The hydraulics break."[46] Methadone vans are a pricey boondoggle. The uncomplicated, cheap solution is to let all correctional facilities stock methadone and have nurses dispense it as they do all other medications.

In one Pennsylvania jail that allows methadone, there is a cruel and unusual restraint protocol. A cape or smock is placed over a prisoner and they are handcuffed behind their back while seated.[47] Then a nurse instructs the person to open their mouth and the medication is placed inside. Monitored by guards, they have to stay seated and handcuffed for several minutes to ensure that it has been ingested. This is to stop diversion. In this sick scenario, it's easy to see why penal institutions enjoy Vivitrol. A shot once a month in the buttock and it's right back to the cell.

The availability of medications to treat addiction to all who need it is critical. Ramsey said:

> To treat people for opioid use disorder in jails and prisons is not only for the benefit of that individual, but actually for better outcomes in the jail or prison. You get a better environment inside, and because people are more comfortable, you're likely to have less conflict going on. There is a decrease in overdoses and complications due to withdrawal. Some people commit suicide when they have untreated withdrawal, and those rates go down when they have access to medication.

Denying people methadone, whether it's in a drug treatment court or a correctional facility, is a form of torture, and for some, a death sentence.

8

"IF THE CHEMIST LIKES YOU": Methadone Dispensing in Australia, Canada, and Britain

Tragically, the US methadone clinic system has been exported around the globe. From Afghanistan to Vietnam, the carceral, stigmatizing, and surveillance features that are foundational to American OTPs have been adopted by most countries.[1] Even Portugal, which has led the world in expanding drug treatment while decriminalizing all drugs, strictly controls access to methadone. Magda Ferreira, a drug user activist in Lisbon who takes methadone, told me, "The system treats us like children. We have to dose at a clinic every day, and even with the van, you have to go daily, weekends too. And we are punished for telling the truth if we are still using drugs."

Australia, Canada, and Britain share a model of providing methadone that varies in important ways from the US clinic system but still monitors, controls, and discriminates against methadone patients. In these countries, the surveillance and punishment of patients has been transferred to doctors and pharmacists. There are four significant ways that these nations differ that impact the dispensing of methadone.

First, each has a national health program that guarantees medical care, including drug treatment, to everyone. No one ever loses access to coverage, whereas in the United States health care isn't guaranteed to anyone, and millions are uninsured. Universal provision of health care from birth to death allows for the prevention of disease and access to prescription medication and an array of medical tests and services that are vital for the maintenance of mental health and physical well-being. This is particularly important for people who inject illicit drugs because they are at greater risk of acquiring HIV and hepatitis C, vein damage, and overdose as well as other health conditions related to drug use. Accessibility and affordability, including copays for medication and waiting lists, vary in each country and have worsened in recent years due to underfunding, understaffing, and privatization.

Second, all physicians can write a prescription for methadone to treat addiction, which increases the pool of providers. Third, pharmacists play a key role in dispensing the medication, and community pharmacies are the setting where most patients are dosed. The fourth major difference is the absence of involvement of a policing organization like the DEA in regulating methadone.

In Australia, It's a Lottery

Australia—a country of wide-open spaces, sugar-white beaches, deserts, the Outback, and grilled shrimp on the barbie—is divided into six states and ten territories. Australia's universal health insurance scheme is called Medicare. Since the 1960s, heroin has been available in Australia and is imported from the nearby Golden Triangle. Laos, Myanmar, and Thailand compose the Golden Triangle, and those three countries are the major producers of heroin for the illicit market. Interestingly, the Australian state of Tasmania is the world's largest producer of opium alkaloids for the pharmaceutical market. The small island grows about 85 percent of the world's thebaine, an opium poppy extract used to make OxyContin, and also produces a quarter of the world's morphine and codeine.[2]

There is no shortage of opioids in the land Down Under. In the 1990s there was a sharp increase in heroin use: The price was low and the purity was high. Researchers estimate that over one hundred thousand Australians meet the criteria for opioid dependency, which includes pharmaceutical opioids, but only about fifty-five thousand are currently in treatment.[3]

In Australia, the states of New South Wales (NSW), Victoria, and Queensland have the highest number of people on medication for opioid use disorder, and together these jurisdictions account for about 86 percent of all people in the country receiving methadone or buprenorphine.[4] The "National Guidelines for Medication-Assisted Treatment of Opioid Dependence," published by the federal government in 2014, provides a national framework for opioid pharmacotherapy treatment (OPT) in Australia.[5] Though they are not binding, state and territory governments use the national guidelines as the basis for their own versions. Despite common features across jurisdictions, regulations governing the prescribing and dispensing of medications vary greatly. The lack of regulatory uniformity across the country causes problems if a patient moves to another state or travels.

"Good luck trying to understand how it all works," John Ryan, the CEO of Penington Institute in Melbourne, told me. "It's incredibly complex and contradictory, and OPT is divided up between the states, the territories, and the commonwealth. It's not an integrated system. It's a mess." There is a general consensus in Australia that there are too many barriers to accessing treatment and they must be eliminated.

"Our population is expanding dramatically, and there's a massive shortage of prescribers. We have people who travel unbelievable distances to get to their doctor and dispensing pharmacist. . . . The systems are a lottery in terms of which prescriber you get, and it's a geographical lottery in terms of how convenient or accessible services are," Ryan said. The shortage of prescribers is in part because Australian doctors don't have to prescribe methadone, and the majority refuse to. Likewise, pharmacies are not required to dispense methadone.

"I just think it's outrageous that doctors and chemists can choose to prescribe or not prescribe for you. Imagine if they said, 'Oh, I'm not going to treat gay people or women.' People would be up in arms," Leah McLeod, who is the communications specialist for the International Network for People Who Use Drugs, told me.

Dispensing Down Under

Across Australia, OPT is dispensed in three settings: public clinics, private clinics, and at community chemists (pharmacies). Doctors rank and sort methadone patients by stability criteria, which determines where they'll get medicated, but it's possible to move between the three settings. Public clinics receive funding from state and territory governments to provide treatment, generally at no cost. These clinics are for patients evaluated as "unstable," and they are subjected to witnessed daily dosing and staff-observed urination. Publicly funded clinics are found in every state and territory, with the overwhelming majority in Queensland, NSW, and Victoria.

Methadone has been prescribed in the state of Victoria since the mid-1980s, but the way the medication is dispensed has changed over the decades. "Originally, there were two or three hospital-based clinics, and it was an incredibly punitive delivery system," Sarah Lord, the program manager for Pharmacotherapy Advocacy, Mediation, and Support at Harm Reduction Victoria, said to me during a phone interview.[6] "There was heaps of drug testing, and if any test was positive for opioids, they would reduce your dose, and you could be thrown off the program. HIV changed everything in Australia, and GPs were encouraged to get onboard to tackle the HIV epidemic, and that is when methadone really became widely available."

Most patients receive daily, or near daily, supervised dosing at community pharmacies. Some of these pharmacies have a separate counter where the chemist (pharmacist) watches the patient ingest methadone, but many don't offer any privacy.[7] In some jurisdictions, community pharmacies are limited in the number of patients they can dose at a given time. In NSW, for example, community pharmacies can only treat sixty-five people.[8] Private methadone clinics were created as a result of long waiting lists in the public system. These clinics offer both prescribing, on-site dosing, and more generous take-home medication. Despite being called "private," the doctors in these clinics are reimbursed by the Australian government on a fee-for-service basis.

Access to take-home doses of methadone is strictly controlled in Australia. During the first three months of treatment in any jurisdiction, and during the first six months in Western Australia, take-home doses are not allowed. Public clinics are the most miserly and generally don't allow any take-home medication. In order to get take-homes, patients are forced to transfer to private clinics or community pharmacies, which disrupts continuity of care and can result in longer commutes. Doctors decide how many take-homes a patient can get based on urine screenings and a risk assessment.[9]

"It's usually around four [doses] a week; that's the recommended ceiling a doctor can give, and more as long as they justify it in their clinical notes," McLeod said. "But if they give more takeaways on a regular basis, they'll be investigated by the Australian Health Practitioners Regulation Authority." The mercurial nature of the Australian system allows a minority of model methadone patients to escape the clinics with stingy take-home rules and get fourteen days of take-homes. Patients have to meet "stability" criteria and find doctors and chemists who trust them.[10] After many years of daily dosing, McLeod gets two weeks of take-home bottles. It's like winning the methadone lottery.

Pharmacy Fee Exploitation

Australian methadone patients have faced debilitating discrimination in another way. For decades they had to pay exorbitant pharmacy dispensing fees, which were identified as a primary reason for discontinuing treatment.[11] That's because, unlike any other medications on the Pharmaceutical Benefits Scheme (PBS)—Australia's subsidized medicine program—they were required to pay a private chemist dispensing fee that was determined by the individual pharmacy and varied from person to person. It could be between $5 and $15 a day. For other PBS medications, the government covers pharmacy dispensing fees, and there's a maximum $30 copayment for prescriptions.

Gino Vumbaca, a board member of Harm Reduction Australia, said, "It's something we have never understood—with all the documented issues that happen with people who become opioid dependent, why would you make treatment harder to reach? There's no economic justification for that." McLeod estimates that over two decades, she and her partner spent $180,000 on methadone dispensing fees. "The stuff we're balancing that money against is money for our kids. What if I had been able to put that money into housing, or a future for her?"[12] The inability to pay dispensing fees sets up an adversarial relationship between patients and chemists.[13] The "good" ones would allow patients to accrue debt and pay it over time, the "bad" ones would refuse to dispense until payment was received, putting people at risk to use illicit opioids to avoid withdrawal. It's another lottery. Lord said, "If a patient didn't have the dispensing fee, in a lot of cases, the pharmacist wouldn't dose them, and once you've missed four days in a row, your prescription becomes invalid. There is so much stupidity in that."

This cruel and unconscionable financial exploitation, coupled with the expense of travel and the extraction of their time to get dosed six or seven days a week, should have provoked national outrage. Excluding lifesaving medications that opioid dependent patients need from the PBS was pure prejudice against Australia's most vulnerable and low-income populations. Access to methadone is a matter of life and death. In 2022, there were 2,356 drug-induced deaths in Australia; 80 percent involved an opioid. Among Indigenous Australians, the rate of unintentional drug-induced death is far higher than for non-Indigenous Australians.[14]

In 2023, in a huge win for people who take methadone, the national government finally added pharmacotherapy drugs to the PBS. The new system replaces the unjust, uncapped, private dosing fees that caused enormous hardship and impoverished and drove patients out of treatment.[15] Lord was elated at the elimination of private dispensing fees and told me, "Now if you are employed, you pay $30 a month for your prescription, and if unemployed, it's $7.30." Still, this long overdue victory doesn't mean that the Australian OPT system isn't in need of more fundamental reforms.

Methadone patients are disempowered, according to a Penington Institute report, "Pharmacotherapy at the Crossroads: Enduring Barriers and New Opportunities": "Dosing points are a site of acute vulnerability; whether at community pharmacies or in public clinics, people on pharmacotherapy routinely experience mistreatment and feel judged. . . . Pharmacists and pharmacy assistants are frequently perceived as suspicious and begrudging, while clinicians are sometimes viewed as controlling and paternalistic."[16] This massive power imbalance has created a deep-rooted culture of cruelty where patients are denied take-home medication, positive urine screenings are used to punish, and the pharmacist might not dispense your methadone. McLeod told me that when she was pregnant, she had morning sickness throughout the pregnancy. McLeod was dosing at a private clinic then because there was no waiting list: "Even if I vomited my dose in front of them, they wouldn't let me take another dose, nor would they give me a split dose or let me take it at home."

In Canada, Nobody Trusts You

In the land of ice hockey, maple syrup, and poutine, the publicly funded, universal health insurance program is known as Medicare. Canada is divided into ten provinces and three territories, and each has a separate single-payer health insurance scheme. The Canadian system of methadone dispensing is similar to that of Australia and shares many of the same structural problems: variability in dispensing regulations in each province, strict take-home medication regulations (in Canada they are called "carries"), witnessed dosing, high dispensing fees, and a shortage of prescribers.

It's no fun sharing a border with the United States. In key ways, the evolution of methadone treatment in Canada was influenced by developments in the United States, most importantly by incorporating surveillance, control, and punishment into prescribing and dispensing. Like the United States, Canada is experiencing an opioid overdose crisis where fentanyl dominates the illicit drug supply. An average of twenty-one lives were lost each day in Canada because of opioid-related overdoses in 2022.[17]

The Le Dain Commission

The late 1960s and early 1970s saw methadone treatment expand rapidly in response to increasing rates of heroin addiction. The medication was prescribed in doctors' offices. A medical model to treat addiction received a strong endorsement from the landmark Commission of Inquiry into the Non-Medical Use of Drugs, also referred to as the Le Dain Commission. Their two reports—1972 "Treatment" and 1973 "Final Report"—advocated for methadone availability in all areas of the country and stated, "Methadone maintenance provides to date the cheapest and most effective weapon we have for dealing with large scale opiate dependence. . . . The overall proportion of those who can be kept out of the illicit heroin market and usefully employed is impressive." In a prescient acknowledgment, both reports included a recommendation to establish heroin maintenance for patients who didn't respond to methadone.[18]

The call to make methadone widely accessible, with some restrictions, by the Le Dain Commission coincided with the beginning of fierce opposition to methadone treatment in Canada. The federal Department of Health started to warn of physician overprescribing, increased diversion, and overdose deaths. A special joint committee of health officials, law enforcement officers, and members of the Canadian Medical Association was created to investigate these alleged problems. With no conclusive evidence, the committee decided that doctors didn't have the requisite expertise to prescribe methadone. Their report reveals pervasive stigma: "Doctors are frequently unable to establish a therapeutic relationship with their patients because of their apparent interest only in obtaining drugs, their lack of sufficient motivation for treatment, and the well-known manipulative behavior of the addict." Instead of physicians prescribing in their private offices, the committee wanted highly structured clinics, oral and liquid forms of methadone only, witnessed consumption, special authorization from the federal health department to prescribe methadone, and the threat of criminal sanctions for violations.[19]

The Committee's recommendations were accepted by the federal government and became effective as law via amendments to the Narcotic Control Act in 1972. These changes paralleled US regulations introduced by the FDA in 1972 and the Narcotic Addict Treatment Act in 1974. After the adoption of these treatment restrictions, the number of patients in methadone treatment dropped dramatically, as did the number of physician prescribers.[20] Once again, without any regard for patient safety, instead of expanding access to a lifesaving medication, it was reduced. The special joint committee's recommendations produced the carceral Canadian clinic and pharmacy dispensing systems that exist today. More draconian restrictions were added in 1992 that diminished the power of doctors to make treatment decisions and increased control over patients. The revised guidelines imposed a maximum dosage of one hundred milligrams per day—a federal exemption was needed to prescribe a larger dose—as well as patient caps, supervised urine screenings, and mandated psychosocial treatment.[21] Tragically, changes in the Canadian methadone dispensing system evolved and mirrored those just across the border.

Liz Evans, the former director of PHS Community Services Society and a cofounder of North America's first sanctioned supervised-injection facility in Vancouver, explained, "There has been a longstanding belief that delivering methadone to people with opioid use disorder requires a disproportionate level of control. I believe this perception has largely been driven by bigotry and animus, rooted in the belief that people who use drugs are inherently untrustworthy and prone to deceit."[22]

Loosening the Liquid Handcuffs

Beginning in 1996 the regulation of methadone was transferred to the provincial level, and a long, uneven process of easing some restrictions across the ten provinces began. In 2018, in response to increasing opioid-related overdose deaths, the requirement to obtain a federal exemption from Health Canada to prescribe methadone was eliminated and nurse practitioners were allowed to prescribe the drug.[23] Methadone is now prescribed and dispensed in hospitals, private for-profit clinics, public provincially funded addiction clinics, pharmacies, or outpatient physician offices.

Trained in addiction medicine, Dr. Joshua Fletcher works in Toronto. "Back in the day, you had to find a specific provider who prescribed methadone. Now, at least in major cities, there are a ton of prescribers and we have a clinic called the Rapid Access Addiction Medicine Clinic." But there are still access issues, Fletcher told me. "It can be a problem for people, especially in remote and rural Ontario. Transportation is always a problem. . . . Methadone helps you feel better, but it's like your handcuffed to the treatment, and you have to go so often. We're trying to improve and be more patient centered."

Garth Mullins is the host of the *Crackdown* podcast and an organizer with the Vancouver Area Network of Drug Users (VANDU). He started taking methadone in 2002 in British Columbia, one of the provinces that has greatly expanded access to the medication. In his book, *Crackdown: Surviving and Resisting the War on Drugs*, Mullins devotes an entire chapter to methadone and describes how it changed the trajectory of his life for the better, but also how the clinic system controlled and put him in liquid handcuffs.

Mullins went to the pharmacy inside a Safeway grocery store to get medicated for the first time. An employee handed him a sheet of paper with the pharmacy rules for methadone patients. It read, "Any instance of deceitful practice or communication, physical or verbal abuse, or theft will not be tolerated."[24] He drank a dose of Tang-flavored methadone while the pharmacy technician watched to make sure he didn't "cheek" the liquid. It was degrading. As Mullins left Safeway, he had the awful realization that he would have to do this every day: "Methadone was going to be a lot of work. There would be piss tests every time I went to the clinic. Other times they would call me randomly to demand I present myself for urine analysis within twenty-four hours. If I failed to comply, it'd be recorded as a blown test. I knew people who got kicked off the program for too many blown tests. I also had to attend mandatory group counseling once a week."[25] He also had to pay a $15 dispensing fee for every witnessed dose, and he missed several for lack of money.

Once inside the methadone machine, Mullins had another awful realization: He would have to code-switch in the clinic and pharmacy to avoid conflict to ensure he got medicated. He created a fake, friendly, compliant persona, not only to follow all the rules but to "appear to like them."[26] There is a derogatory American term for this persona: Methadonian. This is one of the most soul-destroying aspects of taking methadone: having to smile and pretend you like being humiliated in order to get medicated. Eventually, Mullins earned take-home bottles: "Dr. M stopped writing 'daily witness' on my scrips. Instead, I got carries. I was beaming with pride on the way to the pharmacy. . . . I wouldn't have to come back to the pharmacy for a full week. I could just pull a bottle from my fridge in the morning. My liquid handcuffs felt looser."[27]

It's not easy to get carries in any Canadian province. Patients can request more, but the decision is made by the prescriber. Dr. Fletcher explained, "You look at clinical stability in terms of substance use, mental and physical health, social stability, employment status, housing status, their relationships, and so on. Drug screenings play a role, but it's not the be-all and end-all." Canadian stability criteria for carries parallels that in the United States.[28] Mullins estimates that about 80 percent of people in BC have to go to the pharmacy every day for supervised dosing.

Pay to Play

The cost of methadone and dispensing fees vary across the country, but each provincial and territorial government offers a drug benefit plan for eligible groups. Some are income-based universal programs, and most have specific programs for seniors, recipients of social assistance, and people who have chronic health problems that are associated with high drug costs.[29] The Ontario program, for example, covers those over age sixty-five and under twenty-four without private insurance, people who collect disability benefits, and those who are on Ontario Works, a government financial assistance program.[30] Other people fall through the cracks of Medicare and end up paying dispensing fees out of pocket, which can lead to missed doses or dropping out of treatment.

Far from refusing to dispense methadone to patients or capping their number, BC pharmacies are competing to fill their scrips because it is lucrative. Some drugstores pay patients cash incentives that can range $100 to $200 per month, depending on the number of visits.[31] Mullins said, "A lot of them are set up just to do methadone because it's so profitable. We have a lot of crooked pharmacists here, and they are paying people cash kickbacks to come in every day." One investigation alleged that sixty pharmacies in BC were offering kickbacks.[32]

For eligible low-income patients whose prescription fees are subsidized, pharmacies can charge PharmaCare, the provincial medication-cost assistance program, a daily $10 fee for up to three different medications, and a $7.70 "interaction fee" for every time a pharmacist witnesses methadone ingestion. Pharmacies can bill more than $1,000 a month per patient.[33] It's a methadone money machine. Who knew that hundreds of patients would suddenly be welcomed into drug stores every day (good-bye, stigma!) to dose and dash, as long as it guaranteed large profits?

But for the poorest patients, the cash payments can create a perverse incentive *not* to ask for more carries and continue to dose daily because they need the money. The BC kickback scam is another way that both profit and time is extracted from methadone patients, and it makes a mockery of the pharmacy rule that warns not to engage in "deceitful practices."

Safer Supply

Canada doesn't always follow the drug treatment policies of their obnoxious neighbor. Government-sanctioned overdose prevention centers have existed since 2003, and in some provinces, there are safer supply programs that offer prescription heroin, also called diamorphine, as well as fentanyl patches and hydromorphone. The website of Health Canada defines safer supply: "It refers to providing prescribed medications as a safer alternative to the toxic illegal drug supply to people who are at high risk of overdose."[34]

The province of British Columbia is the pioneer in North America in implementing safer supply, where medically prescribed heroin has been offered to a small group of patients since 2014. Laura Shaver receives injectable heroin and transdermal fentanyl patches at the Crosstown Clinic in Vancouver. She is a drug user activist and a leader in the BC Association of People on Opiate Maintenance. Shaver said, "I'm not on these drugs to get high. I just want to wake up in the morning and go to work."[35] The PHS Community Services Society offers both injectable and smokable fentanyl. The Enhanced Access program allows participants to purchase their prescriptions at an on-site pharmacy and take them home. "The patient decides what that dose is for them. There is no maximum dose for the program," PHS medical director Christy Sutherland said.[36]

Vending machines aren't just for soda and snacks anymore. There is a high-tech vending kiosk in Vancouver called MySafe that dispenses doses of hydromorphone. Dr. Mark Tyndall, an addiction specialist, created this innovative drug delivery machine to reduce the number of overdose deaths. Tyndall said, "I think ethically we need to offer people a safer source. The idea is that instead of buying unknown fentanyl from an alley, we can get people pharmaceutical-grade drugs."[37]

The first pilot machine was installed in the Downtown East Side and began distributing hydromorphone in December 2019. Tyndall collaborated with the tech company Dispension to create the eight-hundred-pound dispensing kiosk. It uses a biometric authentication system that reads the palm's internal vein pattern to verify that a patient has been prescribed hydromorphone.[38] Participants get their dose from the machine at a day and time they choose. A MySafe machine is available next door to an overdose prevention site and in three supportive housing programs.[39] Tyndall said, "It is time to build on lessons from this program and move to unwitnessed, flexible, and low-barrier models that are scalable."[40]

The province of Nova Scotia also provides safer supply. Fentanyl patches are available via the Mobile Outreach Street Health Safer Supply Project in Halifax. Matthew Bonn started in the project in 2023 and said that having access to transdermal fentanyl patches saved his life. "You go in every three days. You and your prescriber decide which days of the week fit you best. Then you need to find a pharmacy willing to take you on. . . . A pharmacist will put the patch on you, often on your arm . . . then they'll sign and date it. Three days later you'll go do it again."[41]

Crackdown Across Canada

Post COVID-19, a backlash against harm reduction–based programs across Canada is growing.[42] Safer supply and overdose prevention centers, which have saved thousands of lives, are under attack. In February 2025 it was announced that effective immediately, British Columbia would move to a witness-only model of dispensing safer supply opioids, starting with new clients and eventually expanding to existing ones.[43] Health minister Josie Osborne stated, "These medications will be taken under the supervision of a health-care worker. . . . This helps guarantee that the patient receives care in a safe, supportive environment and significantly reduces the likelihood of diversion." But it's not about patient safety at all. Diversion is a scare tactic that has always been used to crack down on people who use prescribed opioids. In this instance, the BC government is alleging that pharmacies are diverting opioids, but instead of addressing that, patients will be collectively punished.[44] Mullins wrote on social media, "A witness-only safe supply program in BC is a mistake. This is essentially how methadone is dispensed and amounts to a huge, well-documented barrier that keeps thousands from accessing lifesaving meds. BC will have still more corpses."[45]

The Respectable Addict in Britain

Marie Nyswander's book *The Drug Addict as a Patient* contains an appendix titled "The British Approach," about Britain's opioid dispensing system. She looked with envy across the Atlantic at how her counterparts were able to prescribe them to patients with minimal interference from the government and policing authorities. Nyswander quotes approvingly from a report by Scotland Yard: "Most doctors prescribing drugs were all right. . . . Addicts are able to get their drugs from doctors and there is little traffic."[46] She preferred this approach, having endured harassment from Harry Anslinger's agents at the FBN and losing patients to overdose from illicit heroin.

British history is inseparable from the sale and use of opioids. Britain fought two wars with China to ensure that opium was available at home and abroad. Throughout the nineteenth century the drug was sold legally in all sorts of places, from Soho pharmacies to Harrods to rural food shops. Physicians and pharmacists were able to prescribe and dispense narcotics with few restrictions.[47] The use of laudanum, a tincture of morphine and codeine, was widely used to treat pain and a host of other ailments. At the time, the number of people addicted to narcotics was very small, skewed white and upper and middle class, and included doctors, dentists, and other professionals. It was a common and accepted practice for doctors to write narcotics prescriptions for addicted patients and even for themselves. There were no national narcotics controls. Gradually that began to change after World War I with the creation of an international narcotic control regime that declared the use of opioids was only for "legitimate medical purposes."[48] Those purposes were open to wide interpretation.

Rolleston Report

From 1921 to 1924, doctors, pharmacists, and other groups battled attempts by the Home Office to impose strict controls over the prescribing and dispensing of narcotics, end medical maintenance, and imprison drug law violators.[49] Doctors opposed government intrusion into their relationships with patients and believed addiction was a treatable disease, not a crime. Where American doctors abandoned their patients, British doctors did not. In 1923, Professor W. E. Dixon wrote a letter to a newspaper lambasting the government: "We do not seem to have learnt anything from the experience of our American brethren. . . . Cannot our legislators understand that our only hope of stamping out the drug addict is through the doctors, that legislation above the doctors' heads is likely to prove our undoing and that we can no more stamp out addiction by prohibition than we can stamp out insanity?"[50]

The Home Office's attempt to exclude doctors from formulating narcotics policies failed, and the Rolleston Committee was formed in 1924 to hash out new regulations. Sir Humphry Davy Rolleston, the president of the Royal College of Physicians, was appointed to chair the group, composed of nine doctors. The committee was to "consider and advise as to the circumstances, if any, in which the supply of morphine and heroin to persons suffering from addiction to these drugs may be regarded as medically advisable."[51] Their conclusions created the system that Dr. Nyswander so admired. The "Report of the Departmental Committee on Morphine and Heroin Addiction," published in 1926, established addiction as a medical matter and that patients could be maintained on opioids. It noted that there are people who "are capable of leading a fairly normal and useful life so long as they take a certain quantity, usually small, of their drug of addiction."[52]

The British System carried on for forty years. During that time, the United States, a rising economic and political power, worked to enforce drug prohibition around the world. Part of that crusade was to end medical maintenance, and Harry Anslinger used his influential position to relentlessly attack and discredit it.[53] But there were also forces within Britain that would organize to undermine narcotic maintenance.

Swinging Sixties

There was a massive cultural and social upheaval in the country during the Swinging Sixties that celebrated drug use. The number of people who became dependent on opioids increased dramatically, and their demographics were different from those of users in the Rolleston era. Now they were working class, people of color, beatniks, and many identified with the counterculture.[54] A bohemian and "junkie" subculture was created that glamorized injecting heroin and believed it aided creativity. Think Keith Richards, the lead guitarist of the Rolling Stones, who was addicted to the drug for decades while creating some of the most memorable rock and roll music ever.[55] Against this backdrop, there was a move toward a more restrictive system that no longer allowed general practitioners to prescribe opioids, the establishment of drug dependency clinics, the substitution of methadone for heroin, a greater emphasis on curing addiction through abstinence, and the meddling of the Home Office.[56]

The race and class of the new opioid users was a major factor in drug treatment reforms that increasingly controlled and policed patients. The idea that certain kinds of drugs and drug use are intrinsically linked to criminality was promoted by the government.[57] There was little opposition from the medical establishment to the criminalizing of drug users. From 1968 to 1997, doctors were legally mandated to notify the Home Office of patients who, in their judgment, were addicted to cocaine, heroin, or methadone.[58]

One of the ironies is that the US methadone maintenance system created by Dr. Nyswander ended up replacing the British system of heroin maintenance.[59] As the pool of heroin prescribers dwindled as a result of laws limiting it to those with a special license from the Home Office, fewer patients were able to get it. At the same time, methadone became the preferred opioid to maintain patients, and any physician could prescribe it.

Clinic doctors wrote prescriptions and patients collected the medication at the pharmacy. From the 1960s until the early 1990s there was no witnessed daily dosing, and patients could get a supply of methadone for up to a month in liquid, tablets, or vials to inject. Injectable methadone could be prescribed by doctors without a special license, in contrast to injectable heroin, which required a license.[60] The AIDS crisis accelerated the number of people receiving methadone, and it was established as a vital harm reduction tool that saved the lives of people who injected drugs, along with syringe exchange.[61] Today there are a few legacy patients who continue to inject diamorphine, and it's still possible for new patients to get a prescription, but there are a number of barriers, including "failing" a trial of methadone.

Keep Calm and Carry On the Cruelty

In the 1990s, an increase in overdose deaths from methadone led to the gradual introduction of supervised consumption. Pharmacists began to monitor patients while they ingested methadone. Eventually it became standard practice in every pharmacy. Patients had to be supervised for the first three months of treatment and then it increased to six months.[62] There is no limit to how long observed dosing lasts. "It was around 2002 when I first came across supervised consumption, and over time the system has become more punitive," April Wareham, an independent consultant at Working with Everyone and a former methadone user, told me.[63] Wareham questioned the studies conducted in the 1990s that led to enacting witnessed dosing and said, "A cynical part of me says the way drug treatment was funded changed around that time. Before that, we couldn't afford supervised consumption because it's not cheap. And then we could." The British System devolved into a carceral system and created a culture of cruelty that mirrored the one across the pond: witnessed daily dosing but at the pharmacy, observed urination, bottle recalls, and "earning" take-homes.[64]

Mark Gilman, an opioid ethnographer based in Blackpool, explained how methadone prescribing and dispensing currently works in England. "People are referred to a local community drug team, and after an assessment by a doctor, it might be a psychiatrist, they get a prescription. You would go on to supervised consumption in most places with daily pickups. The medication is free." Each patient is assigned a "key worker" who functions like a counselor in US clinics. This is where the authority and coercion in the system lies—the key worker in collaboration with the physician has the power to make treatment decisions for the patient, for example, the number of drug tests and how many take-homes they can get. Gilman said a patient's experience taking methadone depends on whether they get a "good key worker."

I interviewed Erin O'Mara in 2018 for my documentary *Liquid Hand-cuffs: A Documentary to Free Methadone*.[65] She lives in London and is the founder and editor of *Black Poppy*, a magazine by and for drug users, and is a member of the European Network of People Who Use Drugs. She told me that the pharmacy dispensing system works well if the chemist likes you, but if they do not, interactions can be degrading. O'Mara shared this incident:

> To avoid diversion, they make you bring back the empty bottles. If you don't, you won't get your scrip for the day. I came to the clinic by car, and somewhere between parking and going inside, I lost my returns. Staff told me I wouldn't get my methadone. It was pouring rain and I remember walking up and down that street looking in the gutters, in the rubbish, looking under cars and crying. I spent two hours out there looking. It didn't matter.

O'Mara has heard hundreds of heartbreaking and outrageous stories from people who take methadone. One man told her that he needed an extra day's methadone scrip because he had to go to the dentist to have a tooth pulled at the same time he had to pick up his medication. The clinic told him that he could only get it after he brought his extracted tooth to the clinic as proof. Another was late to the clinic and the glass door was locked. He watched as a staff member waved his scrip at him before tearing it up.[66] In Britain, like in the United States, the cruelty is the point. O'Mara recalls, "Nobody knew what was going on in methadone treatment: the anguish, the horrific power imbalance."

Parked on Methadone

In 2010, a major paradigm shift occurred in British drug policy with the launch of the strategy "Reducing Demand, Restricting Supply, Building Recovery: Supporting People to Live a Drug-Free Life." The strategy promoted the idea that people were "parked" on methadone and needed to taper off. Scottish politician Annabel Goldie summed up this new attitude, saying, "It is a well-known fact that methadone is more addictive than heroin, yet this is virtually the only option open to many drug addicts across Scotland. Every pound spent on this so-called harm reduction route is a pound not spent on rehabilitation and the real fight against drugs."[67]

Gilman told me this policy change away from medical maintenance means the drug teams focus on three things: "Maximize the number of people in treatment, retain them for a minimum of ninety days, and sadly and tragically, the third one is to get them out. That often defaults to twelve-step and total abstinence. It's considered a successful recovery."

Wareham met a woman who had been on methadone for twenty-five years, and every time she tried to taper off, everything went horribly wrong. Now when she sees her key worker, the first thing she is asked is, "Do you want to reduce?" Wareham noted, "The power imbalance is often quite large. You want to please your key worker and show you are willing to reduce because you're worried they're going to take it away from you. People get cornered, and they're scared they'll lose the whole lot if they don't say yes. . . . Methadone is now seen as a stop on the way to abstinence."

The Future of Methadone: Burn It to the Ground

In Australia, Canada, and Britain, harm reduction advocates want the ability to access life-saving medications without surveillance, to have methadone treated like any other medication, and to have access to an array of opioids for maintenance.

The reform in Australia that Leah McLeod strongly endorses is that all doctors prescribe and all chemists dispense methadone and other opioids, including diamorphine. No opting out. She added, "I really just want to see decisions made based on clinical grounds, not on personality. I want them to make it feasible for your medication to fit into your lifestyle and to have the amount of takeaways that are suitable."

Sarah Lord wants methadone available in pill form to make travel easier. "Taking liquid methadone is really difficult. The bottles can explode and leak, then part of the dose is lost." She also thinks prescription parity is necessary and asked, "Why can't we have equality with everybody else who goes to their doctor and gets a prescription for opioids and picks it up at the pharmacy?"

Harm reductionists in Canada advocate for radical change. For Garth Mullins, it's a no-brainer: "I think the system needs to be burned to the ground and rebuilt by people who use drugs, by people on methadone." Mullins also wants a wider suite of medications to treat opioid addiction: "I just don't know how people are managing to substitute poor old methadone for the fucking rocket fuel of fentanyl and benzo dope. We need fentanyl to substitute for fentanyl, or diamorphine."

Liz Evans created a humane system to access methadone that could be implemented today. "Years ago, I was fortunate to oversee a program where we provided methadone in a truly low-barrier housing setting. People could pick it up from the front desk staff at any time without being required to provide urine samples or pay fees." Evans said the administration of methadone was simple and normalized, and there was no distinction between people getting methadone and those receiving other medications.

In Britain, April Wareham wants everyone to be able to get a prescription for methadone on the day they want it and to be titrated up to a stable dose on that day. She added, "I would like supervised consumption to be used intelligently for the people who need it instead of making it a blanket one-size-fits-all."

Mark Gilman doesn't want people to go to a pharmacy for daily pickups because he believes it's impractical and makes a normal life impossible. He warned, "People drop out of treatment, and that increases the risk of death. It's not as bad as in the United States, but it's getting worse." Gilman wants diamorphine to be a first-line treatment medication. "I just think so many people would do much better if they got diamorphine. I'm absolutely convinced. I've seen it all my professional and personal life as well."

Fundamental reforms are needed in how methadone is prescribed and dispensed in Australia, Canada, and Britain. People who take methadone in these countries cannot be free until there is prescription parity and supervised daily dosing is eliminated.

Many of us in the United States have looked to the dispensing models in these countries and argued that we should emulate them. We should not. Some of us believed that they were more humane. They are not.

9

"IT TOOK A PANDEMIC TO GET MORE TAKE-HOMES": Methadone and COVID-19

Not everything that is faced can be changed. But nothing can be changed until it is faced.

—JAMES BALDWIN

The arrival of COVID-19 in 2020 was a moment of truth for methadone in the United States. Methadone, the lifesaving medication that has been trapped inside clinics for over fifty years. Methadone, the gold standard of treatment that vast numbers of people need but cannot get and as a result die. *Yes. That methadone.*

Opioid treatment programs that are purposely invisible suddenly became visible, and methadone had a moment. Because in-person dosing was deemed unsafe, SAMHSA revised the rules and allowed patients to get fourteen to twenty-eight days of take-home doses. It was an unprecedented rule change. In many clinics, urine testing stopped, and counseling sessions were canceled. Thousands of patients felt free from the control of the clinic in a way they never had been.

The moment didn't last. Within months, OTPs reverted to standard operating procedures and put patients right back into liquid handcuffs. Fortunately, this "natural experiment" in freedom triggered calls for methadone reform. This is when the violence of organized forgetting, denial, minimization, and erasure of the cruel history of methadone clinics began. Systematic erasure is essential for the perpetrators responsible for so much human suffering.

The opening salvo for organized forgetting occurred in 2022. Dr. Alan Leshner, the former director of the NIDA, chaired a historic two-day webinar examining federal methadone regulations sponsored by the National Academies of Sciences, Engineering, and Medicine (NASEM). In opening remarks he said: "The focus is on what to do next, not lamenting the past so much as how to solve these terrible problems for the country. . . . The main goal is what to do next."[1] So move on, nothing to see here, don't waste time bemoaning the brutal treatment methadone patients have endured for over five decades. Leshner didn't acknowledge that during his seven years as the director of NIDA he didn't advocate to remove strict OTP regulations; instead he helped to make buprenorphine available in office-based settings with few restrictions.[2] It's a past he wants to forget.

Just a few speakers out of over thirty named and directly called out the culture of cruelty. Joy Rucker, a cofounder of the Black Harm Reduction Network, called methadone "liquid handcuffs" and said that waiting in line to get dosed creates tremendous stigma. Walter Ginter and Abby Coulter described in painful detail how losing take-home bottles upended their lives. Those powerful stories and their implications faded into the background as a parade of doctors, researchers, lawyers, and federal bureaucrats got hopelessly lost in slide presentations about the complexity of reforming the clinic system.

In her presentation, Kristi O'Malley, a senior adviser of the Diversion Control Division at the DEA, said that the agency was committed to expanding access to methadone in carceral settings and breaking down barriers. O'Malley said her organization is targeting pharmacies "in a positive way to make sure they get information and know DEA supports them supplying medication to those who need it." In reality, her agents have harassed pharmacies with high buprenorphine dispensing rates, suspecting them of diversion.

In the chat, people challenged the DEA. Dr. Erin Fanning Madden commented: "With all due respect, the DEA should not have a role in methadone treatment. What other areas of medicine are patients mistrusted and treated as criminals upon entering care?" Dr. Ruth Potee shared: "One of the hardest things I have ever done in my life was to get our full OTP license in our county jail. Our biggest problem was the DEA. The level of security they demanded in a highly secure environment was absurd. The DEA should not be involved in getting an OTP in a jail or prison." O'Malley erased the real role that the DEA drug warriors play: policing the methadone clinic system and threatening doctors and pharmacists who prescribe and dispense controlled substances. This intimidation is nothing new, and goes all the way back to doctors Dole and Nyswander.

The most progressive policy proposal in the NASEM report was to expand the availability of methadone outside OTPs into primary care settings, harm reduction programs, and mobile vans.[3] Allowing health care providers to prescribe methadone in primary care clinics and overdose prevention centers could bring thousands of new patients into treatment. The report didn't recommend clinic abolition.

The Methadone Mafia

AATOD is a powerful and influential national trade industry organization that represents hundreds of methadone clinics. Mark Parrino is the irascible president and founded the group in 1984.[4] More than anyone, Parrino has worked relentlessly to ensure the survival and expansion of opioid treatment prisons. His career started in the 1970s, and he graduated from counselor to become the director of a methadone clinic. For over forty years, Parrino has navigated choppy political waters, from Mayor Rudy

Giuliani's audacious attempt to shut down all methadone programs in New York City in 1998, to NIMBY campaigns, the rise of private equity–owned methadone chains, and the COVID-19 pandemic. AATOD's officers and board of directors is a Who's Who of proprietors of for-profit OTP chains.[5] Under his leadership, the group collaborates closely with federal and state agencies to guarantee that no reforms are enacted to free patients from clinic control.

AATOD's long history is one of defending the Nixonian 1970s status quo. A Reagan administration review in 1983 concluded that clinic regulations "have not kept pace with the state of the art and are too inflexible to allow adequate treatment." A National Academies of Sciences review in 1995 noted the same problems.[6] Parrino's organization has consistently ignored calls for OTP reform.

The pandemic shined a much-needed spotlight on methadone clinics, and the mainstream media has increasingly published articles that are critical of punitive OTP practices and that are sympathetic to the plight of patients.[7] For Parrino, this negative media attention is most unwelcome, but, like SAMHSA, he has been willing to make a rhetorical concession to "completely reexamine how treatment is offered to patients. . . . I think this is a good time to readjust." But he wasn't ready to completely readjust the liquid handcuffs, saying, "I don't think the dominant interest is just giving lots more take-homes to patients. There's more to treatment than that."[8] Parrino is minimizing and denying what patients want: more take-home medication to escape the humiliating and expensive grind of daily dosing.

It was at the AATOD conference in Baltimore in 2023 that I first heard Parrino speak and saw how his trade group has deep connections to the federal agencies that regulate methadone. I watched him suck up to the drug warriors and couldn't believe when he said, "The DEA is a wonderful partner." In the closing plenary, Parrino shared the stage with a spokesperson from SAMHSA and O'Malley. He stated emphatically, while glancing approvingly at her, "We work with the DEA, and we don't have a problem with regulation. . . . The DEA is not in the way of people getting care."[9] No one in the audience challenged Parrino or O'Malley. AATOD benefits from the carceral clinic structure that the DEA and SAMHSA created and control. Clinics need their harsh regulations to stay in business—they guarantee a captive group of disempowered hostages dosing daily in perpetuity and a lucrative methadone monopoly for private equity firms.

The only thing that was challenged was the Modernizing Opioid Treatment Access Act (MOTAA). The bill would allow board-certified addiction doctors to prescribe methadone in office-based settings. Members of the methadone mafia were both furious and running scared that some patients might bypass the clinic system entirely and pick up their medication from a pharmacy. They unleashed a lobbying campaign to oppose the legislation using fear-based messaging and misinformation that was straight out of the DEA playbook.[10] And though MOTAA is fatally flawed, the legislation recognizes that clinic-generated barriers limit access to methadone in the midst of an ongoing overdose crisis.

The conference took place after the Biden administration declared that the pandemic was over. Notably, there was no discussion about the impact of the unprecedented COVID-19 rule relaxations. Studies showed that allowing more take-home medication didn't increase overdose deaths or diversion, the two reasons always given to limit or deny them.[11] Why it wasn't celebrated was obvious—AATOD doesn't want to acknowledge the evidence because it exposes their lies about the need for strict regulations. It was erasure.

SAMHSA Isn't Coming to Save Us

Leshner, O'Malley, and Parrino aren't alone in trying to delete and deny the long history of oppression of methadone patients. SAMHSA too is having selective amnesia. The federal agency has been involved in creating methadone regulations since 2001, when the responsibility and oversight of OTPs switched from the FDA to them. Title 42 of the Code of Federal Regulations (42 CFR), Part 8, is where methadone and buprenorphine are listed, and it contains the rules that structure OTPs.[12] All other medications are listed under 21 CFR. It is an extraordinary intrusion into the doctor-patient relationship and dictates everything from starting doses to clinic attendance, split dosing, and the number of take-home bottles.

Dr. Ruth Potee admitted a rare truth: "42 CFR shouldn't exist at all. The fact that buprenorphine and methadone were extracted from the American pharmacopoeia and [are] not sitting in 21 CFR with every other drug is the basic problem."[13] The original, highly restrictive regulations created during the Nixon presidency have remained mostly unchanged for fifty years, during both the AIDS crisis and the ongoing opioid overdose crisis. Deaths from HIV skyrocketed among intravenous drug users who shared syringes in the 1980s and 1990s. Throughout the three waves of the overdose crisis, it has always been easier to buy illicit opioids on the street than to get methadone from a clinic. Why didn't SAMHSA revise regulations in all that time when methadone cuts the risk of overdose death by over 50 percent?[14] How many people would still be alive today if they had? For the agency to budge even an inch, a lethal global pandemic was required; without that, nothing would have changed. And those changes were temporary: Clinics scaled back the new more generous take-home medication rule within months, or rarely implemented it.[15]

The 2024 updates to 42 CFR Part 8 are spelled out in the *Federal Guidelines for Opioid Treatment Programs* Final Rule. It is a dense document full of jargon that micromanages almost every aspect of OTP operations. It is also a historic record detailing the myriad ways that patients have been disempowered and harmed by clinic rules. The easing of some of the harshest ones reveals what came before but minimizes the sheer brutality of them. Post-pandemic, the updated federal guidelines are full of language that views patients as *almost* equal partners in their treatment, assessed "in the full context of their lives," and that services will meet them "where they're at" and be culturally responsive and trauma-informed.[16] Now it's all about "shared decision making" and "patient-centered care." It never was before. Now clinic staff need to convey empathy and support patient autonomy. They never did before.

Getting more take-home medication has always been a top priority for patients, and the schedule to earn them has been radically restructured. The new rules permanently allows up to seven days of take-home doses during the first fourteen days of treatment; up to fourteen from day fifteen of treatment; and up to twenty-eight from day thirty-one.[17] Previously, a person had to be in treatment for three months in order to get a second take-home dose, and it took up to two years in treatment to be eligible for twenty-eight take-homes.[18] The new guidelines explain that, "Rather than imposing rigid, one-size-fits-all dosing schedules, the rule gives practitioners the authority and responsibility to work with patients to determine the appropriate level of patient medication visits based on each patient's individual needs, progress, and stability."[19] This is a partial acknowledgment that OTP rules have never been patient-centered. The numbers have changed, which is a huge improvement, but take-home bottles are still not guaranteed.

The DEA detests unsupervised dosing, believing it facilitates diversion. SAMHSA has consistently endorsed that position, and 42 CFR Part 8 contains a diversion control plan.[20] A stringent set of criteria is used to determine if a person is "stable" enough to be trusted with take-home bottles. The updated 2024 criteria:

1. Absence of active substance use disorders, other physical or behavioral health conditions that increase the risk of patient harm as it relates to the potential for overdose, or the ability to function safely.

2. Regularity of attendance for supervised medication administration.

3. Absence of serious behavioral problems that endanger the patient, the public, or others.

4. Absence of known recent diversion activity.

5. Whether take-home medication can be safely transported and stored.

6. Any other criteria that the medical director or medical practitioner considers relevant to the patient's safety and the public's health.[21]

The updated six-point criteria is almost identical to the eight-point criteria in the 2015 federal guidelines. Only the "stability of the patient's home environment and social relationships" was removed.[22] The benchmarks are not evidence-based and continue to give staff wide discretion. They effectively have unlimited reasons to deny take-homes or to snatch them back. Even Allegra Schorr, the owner of an OTP in Manhattan, believes they are too harsh: "Few people meet those criteria. It's just not human. It's so cut and dried."[23] Moreover, the criteria ignore the structural drivers of inequality, racism, and poverty that only let "model methadone patients" dose at home.[24]

It's notable that SAMHSA, up until the new revisions, used the phrase "take-homes privileges." No other medication is viewed this way, as a privilege, not even other prescription opioids. The agency's default position has continually erred on the side of keeping the liquid handcuffs on, and if there was a difference between state and federal polices, they recommended adhering to the take-home schedule that was the most restrictive.[25] But the 2024 guidelines warn: "OTP practitioners should not reserve take-home doses as a reward for perceived good behavior, nor should take-home doses be reduced or removed in a punitive manner."[26] That's quite an admission! It is exactly what clinic staff have been doing all along, and there is no reason to believe they will stop.

To make the revised regulations trickle down to the patient level, SAMHSA is calling for a transformation in the culture of care and treatment provision in OTPs.[27] This is yet another admission that a culture of cruelty, not care, exists in every clinic. That change isn't possible because the power differential between staff and patients hasn't been eliminated, and it can't be.

Updated and Unenforceable

Some of the 2024 updated guidelines sound liberating, but there's a big catch. None of them can be enforced by SAMHSA. There are several sections of 42 CFR Part 8 that state SAMHSA has no enforcement power: "This document is intended to be used only for guidance purposes and does not have the force or effect of law," and "It is important to note that these guidelines are not requirements."[28]

Dr. Neeraj Gandotra, SAMHSA's chief medical officer, made it clear in a webinar, "We are limited in our scope. While we can draft these federal regulations, it is up to the individual OTPs to exercise some of these options. . . . State restrictions still hold. It's all left to the discretion of the provider and the state opioid treatment authority."[29] What is the point of creating regulations that clinics and states don't have to follow?

There is another, even bigger catch. SAMHSA has always had the statutory authority to remove patient care regulations.[30] But with the 2024 update, they chose instead to amend the regulations. It's a choice that reveals the agency is committed to the maintenance of a clinic system that harms patients, despite all the happy talk of healing environments, harm reduction, trust, shared decision-making, and low-barrier care.[31] SAMHSA supports "carceral humanitarianism," where the surveillance, control, and punishment of patients is cynically reframed as patient-centered care.

When the revised treatment standards were released in 2024, Parrino was pleased. "These enlightened and thoughtful regulations have been in preparation for over one year and we appreciate the fact that these regulations have been reviewed by the DEA. . . . We extend our gratitude to SAMHSA for hearing our concerns so that we can improve our ability to care for our patients."[32] When the forever president of AATOD says the updated regulations are "thoughtful" and "enlightened" and have the seal of approval from the drug warriors, you can be sure they don't threaten clinic power. Parrino knows that the updated regulations are a SAMHSA dog and pony show, and the methadone mafia is still in charge. Patients like Melissa understand that most post-COVID changes in federal regulations won't reach the clinic level:

> Those of us on methadone see this for what it is, another blatant attempt to undermine our cries for humane medical care, free from the abuse of OTPs. The only people praising SAMHSA and acting as if these new rules are going to improve methadone access are either completely ignorant

to how these carceral clinics operate or they're blatantly misleading the public. . . . It's no mistake that SAMHSA doesn't mention that the clinics are free to ignore the updated rules entirely. And we know that they will.

How Not to Modernize Methadone Treatment

The pandemic exposed the numerous barriers to getting and staying on methadone. Politicians finally noticed and wrote a bill to make methadone more accessible. The Modernizing Opioid Treatment Access Act (MOTAA) was introduced in the US House by Representatives Donald Norcross and Don Bacon in 2023.[33] It is the first piece of legislation to be proposed that would allow doctors outside the clinic system to prescribe methadone and for patients to pick it up in a pharmacy. Norcross called out the clinic capitalists: "We must end the monopoly on this life-saving medicine that only serves to enrich a cartel of for-profit clinics and stigmatize patients."[34]

Senator Edward J. Markey introduced the legislation into the Senate. He vilified OTPs too: "Ultimately, tethering methadone exclusively to OTPs is less about access, or health and safety, but about control, and for many investors in those programs, it is about profit. The longer we leave this antiquated system in place, the more lives we lose."[35]

Norcross's and Markey's criticisms are refreshing and right, but their landmark legislation won't curb the control clinics have over patients because it doesn't offer a root cause solution. The problems start with the provision that only board-certified addiction doctors can prescribe the medication. There simply aren't enough to meet the demand. ASAM estimates that there are 7,000 physicians specializing in addiction who would be eligible to prescribe methadone under the current version of the bill, but another estimate puts it lower, at 5,517.[36] By not allowing all health care providers, including nurse practitioners and physician assistants, to prescribe the medication, MOTAA can only help a small number of patients.

Even worse, limiting prescribing to addiction specialists reinforces structural racism. "The way that it works in this country is the better insured and the more money you have, the more access you have to hyperspecialists like board-certified addiction psychiatrists," Dr. Helena Hansen, one of the authors of *Whiteout*, told me. "So if you're a hyperspecialist, you know who your clientele is going to be: rich and largely white. If we rely on this same small group that does buprenorphine prescribing to do methadone prescribing, if you look at who gets served by them, it's the same exclusive group that currently gets buprenorphine."[37] MOTAA is a new iteration of DATA 2000 for methadone.

Insurance coverage is another issue. Medicaid is the largest payer for methadone treatment, so patients will need to find an addiction specialist who accepts it and whose practice is taking on new patients. Finding doctors who accept Medicaid is a widespread problem, and doctors, especially psychiatrists, are less likely to accept Medicaid than Medicare or commercial insurance.[38] Other provisions that spell doom for the bill involve the DEA. The bill requires the DEA to register doctors. Most don't welcome diversion investigator oversight, and many physicians will refuse to prescribe the medication to avoid that, which will result in even fewer prescribers.

There is another poison pill provision in the bill: "A state may request that the DEA stop registering such practitioners in its jurisdiction."[39] State opioid treatment authorities work closely with clinics, so expect many of them to request this opt-out, and the DEA to grant it. This will further winnow down the numbers of patients able to escape the clinic system.

The bill doesn't threaten the power of the methadone monopoly, despite their loud protestations. Dr. Stephen M. Taylor, the president-elect of ASAM, revealed when he testified to a US Senate committee: "To be clear, MOTAA is not methadone for everyone, prescribed by anyone. It represents a responsible expansion in methadone access for [opioid use disorder]."[40] What a travesty that a medical society committed to the treatment of addiction doesn't believe, amidst the greatest loss of life from drug overdoses in the recorded history of the United States, that methadone is for everyone and should be prescribed by anyone. Surely ASAM knows that opioid-related overdoses are the leading cause of death among Americans age forty and younger, accounting for more deaths than homicide, suicide, motor vehicle accidents, gun violence, and cancer.[41]

Dr. Robert Newman was in favor of the integration of care for patients with an opioid use disorder into mainstream medical care. In 2011 he criticized ASAM: "But of course, when you have specialty societies like the American Society of Addiction Medicine, it makes it that much more difficult to foster the notion that [addiction] is a condition that all physicians should be treating within the limits of their training. It's terrific that we have specialists, but I've never heard an endocrinology society, or an endocrinologist as an individual, say, 'Gee, it's really appalling that those family practitioners are prescribing insulin to diabetics.'"[42]

MOTAA is a compromised bill that repeats the mistakes of DATA 2000. It is office-based opioid treatment, but worse. The OBOT programs that were launched in the 1980s allowed any physician to prescribe methadone, and it was an effort to end the siloing of addiction treatment. At a panel about expanding access to methadone that both Norcross and I spoke on at the Cato Institute in Washington, DC, in 2023, he admitted that MOTAA doesn't go far enough and agreed that the clinic system should be eliminated, but that only incremental change was possible. Norcross also said that once the bill was passed, legislators would go back and amend it.[43] Dr. Bruce Trigg, a former medical director of an OTP, warned against incrementalism: "It is vital that they get the legislation right from the start. It will not be easy to fix once all the problems are widely recognized. We have seen from the buprenorphine regulatory experience that it will take many years and even decades to modify the federal regulations. The Norcross bill must be amended to allow any licensed medical provider to prescribe methadone."[44]

A root cause solution to the disastrous methadone clinic system is needed. A comprehensive bill to do that would: integrate methadone into the health care system, allow all doctors, physician assistants, and nurse practitioners to prescribe, create a peer navigator program to support patients, and increase

Medicaid reimbursement rates. Money would be allocated to fund a national network of community pharmacies and a dedicated network of pharmacists to dispense the medication.

Post pandemic, there was a historic opportunity to pass legislation to end this antiquated system and build a new one that finally liberated patients from fifty years of clinic oppression. Instead, we got erasure, denial, updated and unenforceable guidelines from SAMHSA, the mobilization of the methadone mafia to block any fundamental change, and a terrible bill that would reinforce racial disparities in access to methadone.

10

METHADONE PATIENT ADVOCACY GROUPS, UNHOLY ALLIANCES, AND THE FUTURE OF METHADONE

We must act now to get the safe supply and resources that we need. We must not be silent, ashamed or scared. We must talk, even if we are hated. We must scream, if that is what it takes.

—LOUISE VINCENT, drug user activist

The systematic erasure and minimization of harm that the clinic system engages in must be resisted and remembered in order to guarantee a future where people who take methadone are finally free. Past is prologue. The future is abolition.

While the clinic system remains in existence, methadone patients need a militant, independent political organization. There are formidable, well-endowed enemies to fight: the DEA, SAMHSA, state opioid treatment authorities, and AATOD. The combined institutional power of these organizations creates a multilevel maze of arcane regulations that lock in the oppression of people who take methadone and make reform nearly impossible. There are simply too many cooks in the methadone kitchen.

Two legacy groups—the National Alliance for Medication Assisted Recovery (NAMA-R) and Stop Stigma Now (SSN)—have advocated for the rights of methadone patients for decades. But neither of these organizations opposes the clinic system nor is in favor of abolition. Curiously, they don't view the federal or state agencies that regulate methadone or AATOD as enemies. In fact, they collaborate with and rarely criticize them. NAMA-R and SSN are directly invested in the continuation of the clinic system, albeit with some reforms.

National Alliance for Methadone Advocates

The National Alliance for Methadone Advocates (NAMA) was founded in 1988 in New York City by methadone patients and professionals who worked in the field of addiction.[1] The name was changed in 2009 to NAMA-R. At one time, the group had approximately fourteen thousand members representing the fifty states, Puerto Rico, and fourteen countries.[2] Their website states, "NAMA Recovery works to correct the misconceptions about methadone and buprenorphine treatment and overcome the prejudice directed against patients and medications to treat opioid use disorder. . . . Patients are mistreated and misinformed and considered as social outcasts. They are victims of discrimination in health care, the job market, education, insurance, and housing."[3]

The leadership was concerned about how methadone users were studied by researchers and academics. Joycelyn Sue Woods, the executive vice president of the group, wrote an editorial for the *Journal of Maintenance in the Addictions*: "Successful patients are rarely discussed in scientific journals, with researchers preferring to study the dysfunctional patients. This focus has contributed to the stigma that patients endure."[4]

MARS, MAT, and Gripes

In 2002, NAMA member Walter Ginter became the founding director of the Medication Assisted Recovery Services (MARS) project. It was the first national peer support program in the United States for methadone patients.[5] The much needed project offered peer leader training and mentoring. In an interview, he explained, "The idea for the MARS project was for methadone patients to consider themselves in recovery. We were the ones who said if you take methadone, you can be in recovery. It was something patients had never heard before. They were told, if you're taking methadone, you're still using drugs. We changed that." In addition to educating patients, support groups were offered. Ginter said: "MARS is support for people on methadone in recovery. . . . It's like twelve-step, but without any of the rules." With a grant from SAMHSA, he traveled around the country and internationally to promote the peer model. Ginter had a prior passion project related to methadone. He created and moderated a website called Bitch & Gripe. Ginter said: "The purpose of Bitch & Gripe is exactly what it sounds like. There were about nineteen Beth Israel methadone clinics. You could send in complaints and compliments about them and I would put everything online. It made people laugh."

In 2012, NAMA-R launched the Medication Assisted Treatment Advocate course to train people to become a Certified MAT Advocate.[6] In the half-day training, participants learn about the science of opioid use disorder, the medications to treat it, and how federal and state law structure OTPs. They are taught basic communication skills and strategies to use in patient advocacy. The training is offered every year at the AATOD conference.

Another advocacy effort focuses on filing grievances against clinics. Patients fill out a complaint form that has a "category of incident" check box that tellingly summarizes many of the problems in OTPs: Punitive staff, threat of termination or discharge, urine testing, pickup schedule problems, medication hours, and dosage policies.[7] Brenda Davis, a member of the group since the 1990s and the former treasurer, worked with people to submit and resolve grievances. She is also the patient advocate manager for a Mount Sinai clinic in New York City. Davis told me, "Back in those days, we handled grievances from all over the place. Some of the things that you heard were so unbelievable. For example, a woman was pregnant, and when her program found out, they immediately forced her to taper off methadone, and said once she had the baby, she could come back into treatment." This is medical malpractice. Methadone is the standard of care for treating pregnant patients.[8]

To be sure, these projects have helped patients grappling with internalized stigma and have empowered peers, and lodging grievances has provided relief to some. But they have not decreased the stigma of taking methadone or ended punitive clinic practices. NAMA-R focuses on systems *outside* the clinic that discriminate against patients. They don't locate the foundational source of harm against people who take methadone in the DEA-designed clinic structure itself or acknowledge that the greatest harms occur *inside* clinics. With a few exceptions—the bottle recall memorandum being an important one—their advocacy efforts are not targeted at the culture of cruelty, and they don't use that term. Moreover, many members support the strict clinic structure as necessary, especially for patients at the start of treatment and for those deemed "unstable."[9]

During the COVID-19 pandemic, NAMA-R was inundated with grievances from patients and staff across the country who reported that their clinics were putting them at risk for infection. They provided video evidence and documented it on social media. In an urgent letter to Mark Parrino, the group detailed "potentially abusive practices." Clinics were still demanding in-person bottle recalls and group counseling, patients weren't given increases in take-home medication, those who tested positive for the coronavirus were forced to attend clinic daily, and there was no social distancing or infection control protocols inside or outside buildings.[10] It's astonishing that even during a deadly pandemic, clinics were loath to loosen the liquid handcuffs. NAMA-R was justifiably angry, and this was one of the few times they openly criticized OTP practices. Yet more often, the organization is content to work within the clinic system.

Conflicts of Interest

The advocacy work of NAMA-R is further compromised by members who work in clinics or own them. Zachary Talbott, the former president of

NAMA-R, is guilty of both. Talbott was an employee of BayMark and in 2018 he sold two of his for-profit clinics to BayMark. Talbott explained the acquisition: "What BayMark brings to the table is a commitment to quality treatment. It's the only large corporate chain where the CEO is a PhD clinician. I wanted to be in a company that had a similar philosophy to care."[11] That "clinician" is Jason Kletter and his "commitment to quality treatment" is debatable. When asked about private equity investing in OTPs, Talbot said: "I think the jury is still out on what private equity means for our field. I hope it means something positive."[12]

Talbott got back into the business of methadone. In 2021 he opened the Talbott Legacy Centers in Maryville, Tennessee.[13] I interviewed him for one of my documentaries about methadone.[14] When I told Talbott it was a conflict of interest to be both an OTP owner and the president of a methadone patient advocacy organization, he vehemently disagreed. He resigned from the presidency of NAMA-R in 2024. The president who succeeded him, Anita Kennedy, is employed by a Mount Sinai methadone program in New York City as a peer engagement specialist. In an interview with Kennedy, the collaboration between NAMA-R and the methadone mafia was clear: "We have an excellent relationship with AATOD and there is much respect between both organizations. Recently, Mark Parrino met with the group, and he gave us some ideas about how we can move forward and a little bit of history to motivate us. But we do butt heads every now and then." Under Talbott's leadership, the group did indeed butt heads. They endorsed and lobbied for the passage of MOTAA.[15] Parrino was not pleased.

There is significant overlap of members between the two organizations. In 2020, Jason Kletter and Allegra Schorr were on the advisory board of NAMA-R.[16] Kletter is a board member and Schorr is the first vice president of AATOD. The overlap goes even deeper. Megan A. Marx was a member of the NAMA-R board of directors, was formerly director of OTP accreditation at the joint commission, and is currently a director of a methadone clinic chain based in Oregon.[17]

The AATOD annual conference is where the cozy connections among all the organizations involved in opioid treatment are on full display. At the 2024 conference in Las Vegas, Talbott was a speaker on a panel about patient advocacy along with Marx and Dr. Yngvild K. Olsen, the director of the Center for Substance Abuse Treatment. Kennedy and Talbott spoke alongside two SAMHSA staff at the Certified MAT Advocate training in 2022 in Baltimore. Then there is the Richard Lane/Robert Holden Patient Advocacy Award that is presented to the winner at every AATOD conference. Several members of NAMA-R have won the award, including Davis, Ginter, Kennedy, Talbott, and Woods.[18]

The strategy of constant collaboration with the forces committed to a carceral clinic system has been a disaster for patient's rights and explains why there has been no fundamental change in OTPs. The interests of clinic owners, their industry trade cartel, and the federal agencies that create punitive program regulations are in direct opposition to the interests of people who take methadone. NAMA-R's unholy alliance with these groups ensures that advocacy projects steer clear of exposing or confronting the power dynamic between patients and staff. They haven't challenged these powerful organizations because if they had, their leadership wouldn't be winning patient advocacy awards, and Jason Kletter wouldn't be on their advisory board.

Even though they don't talk about it publicly, NAMA-R members know that a culture of cruelty exists in OTPs. They have been its victims. When Walter Ginter spoke at a webinar on methadone clinic reform, he explained how for over twenty years he was a patient in one of the few OBOT programs in the United States. He picked up a bottle of pills once a month at a pharmacy. The program closed, and he was forced back into the clinic system. Now Ginter believes that methadone should be regulated like buprenorphine.[19] He told me: "I would rather see methadone prescribed in doctor's offices. Now I have to go once a month to a clinic, and I get twenty-eight bottles of methadone, and it sucks. In the old days of OBOT, I could just go to Vietnam to do a MARS training. If I went today, I'd have to get a letter from somebody because I'll be carrying all this liquid medication." And he knows those precious twenty-eight bottles could be snatched away from him with the snap of a nurse's finger. Ginter misses his freedom.

Stop Stigma Now

Stop Stigma Now (SSN) operates in a similar fashion to NAMA-R. Their mission is "to inform the general public, the court systems, medical, nursing and counseling professions, public officials, and the media about the overwhelming scientific evidence supporting the success of medication treatment for opioid use disorder."[20] It's a worthy goal, but it's a failed strategy because it doesn't target the foundational source of stigma—methadone clinics. SSN focuses on ways to reduce stigma in order to get more people into treatment, which dovetails with the interests of OTP owners; more patients daily dosing equals more profits. There is also overlap between clinic owners, staff, and AATOD on SSN's executive committee.[21]

The genial co-president of SSN was Sy Demsky, a longtime passionate advocate of methadone. Demsky knew Dr. Dole, and in 1994, he received the Nyswander/Dole "Marie" Award from AATOD. For thirty-one years Demsky was the director of Mount Sinai Hospital's Narcotics Rehabilitation Center.[22] After he retired, it was shut down, and six hundred patients scrambled to find treatment. That made Demsky furious. He told me in an interview a few months before he died, "I love the field very much and so I started this organization in 2007. It brought together professional people who had been retired, and I convinced them to give something back to society."

One area of SSN's work that Demsky was proud of focuses on drug courts. Members attend the yearly conference of All Rise. They set up a booth in the exhibition hall and provide information about methadone and buprenorphine to dispel myths and to convince those who work in drug courts to allow participants to start or remain on these medications.

Demsky said that when the group first started going to the conference, most court staff were completely opposed to the use of medication to treat addiction. After a few years, there was a shift, and he believes more drug courts now approve of the use of evidence-based medications in part because of SSN advocacy efforts.

Demsky was honest about what SSN was up against when it comes to reform, and he offered a cautious mix of praise and criticism of the methadone mafia: "You have organizations in New York like the Coalition of Medication-Assisted Treatment Providers and Advocates (COMPA) and AATOD. They're doing a very good job, but they're in business to protect methadone programs and to make certain that Medicaid reimbursement increases take place. It's a political issue, so one has to be careful in my field not to antagonize the people I need to work with." Demsky is in favor of pharmacy pickup, but said, "It's a tremendous political battle. . . . It's a different ball game now, and AATOD has created many, many problems. They are against pharmacy dispensing, and Jason Kletter, who runs one of the largest programs in California, is absolutely against the pharmacies because it's going to destroy his business."

Fight the Powers That Be

Rather than relying on advocacy organizations that don't challenge regulatory agencies and don't oppose the methadone mafia, patients need an independent organization that fights for their rights that is modeled on the AIDS Coalition to Unleash Power (ACT UP). The group was created in the 1980s to respond to the AIDS crisis. Their membership comprised people who were HIV positive and their allies. The group won huge victories because they correctly identified and confronted the forces in US society that oppressed them. ACT UP attacked pharmaceutical corporations, Wall Street, health care systems, and state, federal, and local government agencies. AIDS activists confronted the people in power who ignored or discriminated against them and didn't care one iota that they were dying in unprecedented numbers. These are the same institutions that oppress and profit off people who take methadone and have done almost nothing to end the hundreds of thousands of overdose deaths. Schulman calls AIDS a "mass death experience."[23] The opioid overdose crisis is also a mass death experience.

The group deployed a number of strategies that disrupted business as usual. Activists fought with the FDA—they called it the Federal Death Administration—with a direct action called "Seize Control of the FDA."[24] Over a thousand activists descended on their headquarters and shut down the facility by blocking doors, walkways, and a road. They demanded that the government speed up the research, development, and approval of drugs for HIV.

In another direct action, a small group of ACT UP members pulled off a protest inside the New York Stock Exchange. The target was the drug company Burroughs Wellcome, which was charging an outrageous $10,000 per year for the medication AZT.[25] Once inside the Stock Exchange, the activists dropped a banner over a balcony that said "Sell Wellcome." They threw fake hundred-dollar bills onto the trading floor that said "Fuck your profiteering, we die while you make money." These angry protests won real reforms. The federal government poured millions of dollars into fast-tracking the development of drugs to treat HIV, and Burroughs Wellcome lowered the price of AZT by 20 percent.[26]

ACT UP was also centrally involved in creating needle exchange programs. Sharing needles was a leading cause of virus transmission. They engaged in civil disobedience with other organizations and got arrested for distributing syringes, which was against the law. At the time there was almost no support for this vital harm reduction intervention. Eight activists dubbed the "Needle Eight" went to trial in New York City.[27] Their lawyers made the argument that they had to break the law in order to save lives during the unprecedented AIDS crisis. The activists were found not guilty, and syringe exchange programs were legalized. It was one of ACT UP's most important victories because the lives of countless people who inject drugs were saved.

ACT UP's in-your-face political activism radically transformed the lives of people with HIV/AIDS for the better along with the vile American society that hated, stigmatized, and left them for dead. It wasn't easy, and there were setbacks, but they refused to give up because the suffering was so enormous, and too many lives were at stake. ACT UP was successful because they strategically targeted the institutions and policymakers who had the power to enact reforms that would save lives.

A popular and powerful ACT UP slogan is "Silence Equals Death." It was a direct response to the lack of public awareness and action surrounding the AIDS crisis. It aimed to rally LGBTQ people and anyone affected by AIDS to speak out, disclose their status, and engage in collective action. It was as difficult for people to reveal that they were HIV-positive as it was to come out of the gay closet. The reactions could be dire: rejection by family and friends, job loss, violence, and a host of other negative consequences. The discrimination that people with HIV/AIDS faced was everywhere and is similar to the discrimination that methadone patients endure. A hard-fought ACT UP victory was the virtual elimination of stigma against people living with HIV/AIDS in the United States, from Silence Equals Death to out and proud.

Dr. Edwin Salsitz witnessed how this stigma affected his patients: "In the '80s, when gay rights became an issue, my patients who were gay, they didn't have any problem marching in the gay pride parade. And then when HIV came along, which was stigmatized initially, they also marched. But methadone is different. They keep it the closest-guarded secret that they have."[28] It's time for more people who take methadone to come out of the closet. To be sure, there are risks, but there are also enormous benefits. As Harvey Milk, the indefatigable gay rights leader in San Francisco said about coming out, "How can people change their minds about us if they don't know who we are?"

OTPs Must Go

To end the oppression of people who take methadone, to truly be free, the clinic system must be abolished. It is neither possible nor desirable to reform a system that never should have been created in the first place. It is the original sin that a lifesaving medication was locked inside a structurally racist, carceral clinic system created by doctors and the DEA. Opioid treatment programs are a stain on humanity. As Peter Vanderkloot wrote over twenty-five years ago:

> The methadone clinic system must go. Thankfully, we don't need to search far for the means to replace it. All that is needed is parity with other medications. If the regulations unique to methadone are repealed, if the laws prohibiting maintenance of addicts are rewritten, then methadone becomes just another medication, prescribable by private physicians, dispensable in clinics—in short, available in whatever venues users and prescribers deem appropriate.[29]

But there is more. People who take methadone are *owed*. They are owed for all the fuckery they have endured. For the years they've waited in line in the freezing rain, hail, heat, and snow to drink one tiny cup of pink liquid. For all the pancake breakfasts they didn't cook for their kids, and for not being able to take them to school because they had to be at the clinic at 5 a.m. For all the weddings, funerals, conferences, and birthday parties they missed and the vacations they never took because they couldn't get take-home medication. For never being able to sleep in. For all the jobs they lost because the program was a two-hour commute and the old Ford Explorer kept breaking down, making them late for work. For all the bullshit bottle recalls. For the terror of eating a poppy-seed bagel. For the indignity of having their mouth inspected day after day, year after year. For the trauma of having their genitals watched as they urinated. For all the times they were told by a drug court judge to stop taking methadone. For wanting to die on the floor of a jail cell while vomiting through withdrawal because methadone is banned. For the constant gut-churning anxiety of never knowing if they'll get dosed when they approach the bullet-proof plexiglass window. People who take methadone are owed for being forced out of treatment and driven back to the zombie apocalypse that is fentanyl. Will we ever know how many mothers, fathers, sisters, brothers, daughters, sons, aunties, and uncles overdosed and died because they were kicked out of a program? The dead must be counted.

To that end, congressional hearings should be held to hold OTPs, the DEA, SAMHSA, and state opioid treatment authorities accountable for all the misery and harms their inhumane system has caused. Also essential is the creation of a truth and reconciliation commission so patients can testify about their clinic experiences to foster healing and restorative justice.

Methadone patients—for so long invisible and voiceless—need to be seen and heard. This reckoning is long overdue, *and it is coming.*

THE METHADONE CLINIC
ABOLITION COLLECTIVE

Through education, art, film, and protest, the goal of MCAC is to free methadone by abolishing the racist carceral clinic system.

If you would like to get involved, go to www.porticofilms.com.

LIST OF ABBREVIATIONS

21 CFR: Title 21 of the Code of Federal Regulations

42 CFR: Title 42 of the Code of Federal Regulations

AA: Alcoholics Anonymous

AATOD: American Association for the Treatment of Opioid Dependence

ACT UP: AIDS Coalition to Unleash Power

AMA: American Medical Association

ARC: Addiction Research Center

ARTC: Addiction Research and Treatment Corporation

ASAM: American Society of Addiction Medicine

BDC: Blackman's Development Center

CASAC: Credentialed Alcoholism and Substance Abuse Counselor

CFR: Code of Federal Regulations

CMS: Community Medical Services

COMPA: Coalition of Medication-Assisted Treatment Providers and Advocates

CSA: Controlled Substances Act

DATA 2000: Drug Addiction Treatment Act of 2000

DAWN: Drug Abuse Warning Network

D-C train: drug-crime train

DEA: Drug Enforcement Administration

FBN: Federal Bureau of Narcotics

FDA: Food and Drug Administration

GED: general equivalency diploma

GHC: Greater Harlem Coalition

HRTC: Harm Reduction Therapy Center

IoM: Institute of Medicine

MARS: Medication Assisted Recovery Services

MCAC: Methadone Clinic Abolition Collective

MDC: Manhattan Drug Court

MOTAA: Modernizing Opioid Treatment Access Act

NAMA: National Alliance for Methadone Advocates

NAMA-R: National Alliance for Medication Assisted Recovery

NASEM: National Academies of Sciences, Engineering, and Medicine

NATA: Narcotic Addict Treatment Act, 1974

NIDA: National Institute on Drug Abuse

NSW: New South Wales, Australia

NTA: Narcotics Treatment Administration

OBOT: office-based opioid treatment

OPC: overdose prevention center

OPT: opioid pharmacotherapy treatment

OTP: opioid treatment program

PBS: Pharmaceutical Benefits Scheme

PDMP: prescription drug monitoring program

SAMHSA: Substance Abuse and Mental Health Services Administration

SAODAP: Special Action Office for Drug Abuse Prevention

SSN: Stop Stigma Now

TC: therapeutic community

VANDU: Vancouver Area Network of Drug Users

YLP: Young Lords Party

NOTES

INTRODUCTION

1 Ruth Potee, "WTF Methadone—What Is the Future?" presentation at the American Society of Addiction Medicine (ASAM) 54th Annual Conference, Washington, DC, April 2, 2022, www.youtube.com/watch?v=4byAJbZiZM4.

CHAPTER 1: THE AMERICAN METHADONE CLINIC SYSTEM: "WHO DO I HAVE TO BLOW?"

1 Ethan A. Nadelmann and Jennifer McNeely, "Doing Methadone Right," *National Affairs*, no. 64 (Spring 1996): 85, www.nationalaffairs.com/public_interest/detail/doing-methadone-right.
2 Nadelmann and McNeeley, "Doing Methadone Right," 85.
3 Christopher M. Jones, Beth Han, Grant T. Baldwin, Emily B. Einstein, and Wilson M. Compton, "Use of Medication for Opioid Use Disorder Among Adults with Past-Year Opioid Use Disorder in the US, 2021," *JAMA Network Open* 6, no. 8 (August 7, 2023), https://doi.org/10.1001/jamanetworkopen.2023.27488.
4 Heather Schacht Reisinger, Robert P. Schwartz, Shannon Gwin Mitchell, James A. Peterson, Sharon M. Kelly, Kevin E. O'Grady, Erica A. Marrari, et al., "Premature Discharge from Methadone Treatment: Patient Perspectives," *Journal of Psychoactive Drugs* 41, no. 3 (September 2009): 285–96, https://doi.org/10.1080/02791072.2009.10400539. The study was conducted at six OTPs in Baltimore.
5 Noa Krawczyk, Arthur Robin Williams, Brendan Saloner, and Magdalena Cerdá, "Who Stays in Medication Treatment for Opioid Use Disorder? A National Study of Outpatient Specialty Treatment Settings," *Journal of Substance Abuse Treatment* 126 (July 2021), https://doi.org/10.1016/j.jsat.2021.108329. The study examined retention rates for methadone, buprenorphine, and naltrexone.
6 Brian Mann, "More Than a Million Americans Have Died from Overdoses During the Opioid Epidemic," NPR, December 30, 2021, www.npr.org/2021/12/30/1069062738/more-than-a-million-americans-have-died-from-overdoses-during-the-opioid-epidemi; National Institutes of Health, "Medications Reduce Risk of Death after Opioid Overdose," July 10, 2018, www.nih.gov/news-events/nih-research-matters/medications-reduce-risk-death-after-opioid-overdose.

7   Montefiore Einstein, "Security Officer," accessed May 25, 2024, https://careers
.montefiore.org.

8   Giacomo Bologna, "A West Baltimore Neighborhood Wants to Block a Methadone Clinic,"
The Baltimore Banner, April 30, 2024, www.thebaltimorebanner.com/community/public
-health/baltimore-methadone-opioid-clinic-Z66SYGNI7FAWTPFNBINTBAB53E.

9   Greater Harlem Coalition, "GHC vs Mount Sinai," blog post, January 18, 2021,
https://greaterharlem.nyc/asks/mtsinai.

10 Alison Hamburg, Alexa Kasdan, and Phil Marotta, "Beyond Methadone: Improving
Health and Empowering Patients in Opioid Treatment Programs," VOCAL-NY and
Community Development Project of the Urban Justice Center, October 2011, p. 22,
https://nyf.issuelab.org/resource/beyond-methadone-improving-health-and-empowering
-patients-in-opioid-treatment-programs-otps-hepatitis-c-overdose-prevention-syringe
-exchange-buprenorphine-other-opportunities-to-make-programs-work-for-patients.html.

11 Hamburg et al., "Beyond Methadone," 23.

12 Zoe Adams, "Unjust Treatment," *Urban Omnibus*, December 2, 2021, https://
urbanomnibus.net/2021/12/unjust-treatment.

13 "Retired City Ferryboat Used as a Methadone Clinic," *New York Times*, June 16, 1971,
www.nytimes.com/1971/06/16/archives/retired-city-ferryboat-used-as-a-methadone
-clinic.html.

14 Helen Redmond, "Boston's 'Methadone Mile' and the Wars on Drug Users, Unhoused
People," *Filter*, February 9, 2021, https://filtermag.org/bostons-methadone-mile-and
-the-wars-on-drug-users-unhoused-people.

15 Camilo J. Vergara, "Photos of Methadone Clinics," Library of Congress, Washington,
DC, accessed April 18, 2025, www.loc.gov/search/?in=&q=photos+of+methadone
+clinics&new=true&st=.

16 Urban Survivors Union, "The Methadone Manifesto," April 2021, https://sway.cloud
.microsoft/UjvQx4ZNnXAYxhe7.

17 Johnathan H. Duff and Jameson A. Carter, "Location of Medication-Assisted Treatment for Opioid Addiction: In Brief," Congressional Research Service, June 24, 2019,
www.congress.gov/crs-product/R45782.

18 Mischa Wanek-Libman, "New York State Comptroller: MTA Is Facing 'the Greatest
Crisis in Its Long History,'" Mass Transit, October 14, 2020, www.masstransitmag
.com/management/article/21158376/new-york-state-comptroller-mta-is-facing-the
-greatest-crisis-in-its-long-history.

19 Pew, "Overview of Opioid Treatment Program Regulations by State," September 19,
2022, https://pew.org/3Qw8g8c.

20 Elizabeth Brico, "They Were Opioid Addicts on Their Way to Recovery. Then the Hurricane Hit," *Vox*, September 11, 2017, www.vox.com/first-person/2017/9/8/16273590
/hurricane-harvey-irma-methadone-heroin-addiction.

21 Julia A. Dunn, Paul Grekin, James B. Darnton, Sean Soth, Elizabeth J. Austin,
Stephen Woolworth, Elenore P. Bhatraju, et al., "Disruption of Opioid Treatment
Program Services Due to an Extreme Weather Event: An Example of Climate Change

Effects on the Health of Persons Who Use Drugs," *Journal of Addiction Medicine* 19, no. 3 (2025): 245–47, https://doi.org/10.1097/ADM.0000000000001403.

22 Zach Rhoads, "What Can We Learn From the Nation's First 24/7 Methadone Clinic?," *Filter*, June 20, 2019, https://filtermag.org/what-can-we-learn-from-the-nations-first-24-7-methadone-clinic.

23 Pew, "Overview of Opioid Treatment Program Regulations by State."

24 Pew, "Overview of Opioid Treatment Program Regulations by State"; *Methadonia*, written by Nick Pappas, directed by Michel Negroponte (HBO Documentary, 2005), www.imdb.com/title/tt0485777.

25 SOAR Corp Recovery Center, "Patient Handbook," 2022, https://irp.cdn-website.com/2e728799/files/uploaded/2021-PATIENT-HANDBOOK.pdf.

26 Ashley Smith, "What Can You Get Away With at an Opioid Treatment Program?," MedMark, blog post, February 22, 2023, https://medmark.com/resources/blog/what-can-you-get-away-with-at-an-opioid-treatment-program. The original blog post, which I've quoted, has been rewritten to sound less punitive.

27 Helen Redmond, "The Tech Companies Policing Methadone Patients for Profit," *Filter*, February 14, 2023, https://filtermag.org/tech-methadone-surveillance.

28 David Segal, "In Pursuit of Liquid Gold," *New York Times*, December 27, 2017, www.nytimes.com/interactive/2017/12/27/business/urine-test-cost.html.

29 SAMHSA, *Federal Guidelines for Opioid Treatment Programs*, HHS Publication No. (SMA) PEP15-FEDGUIDEOTP, Rockville, MD: Substance Abuse and Mental Health Services Administration, January 2015, p. 53, https://www.govinfo.gov/content/pkg/GOVPUB-HE20_400-PURL-gpo139641/pdf/GOVPUB-HE20_400-PURL-gpo139641.pdf. SAMHSA updated the take-home guidelines in 2024; take-home medication is more generous and can be given on the day a person enters treatment.

30 Pew, "Overview of Opioid Treatment Program Regulations by State."

31 The number of take-home bottles that states allow fluctuates, and since the time of publication these numbers could be outdated.

32 SAMHSA, *Federal Guidelines*, 2015, pp. 53–54.

33 Athena Chapekis and Sono Shah, "Most Americans Now Live in a Legal Marijuana State—and Most Have at Least One Dispensary in Their County," Pew Research Center, February 29, 2024, www.pewresearch.org/short-reads/2024/02/29/most-americans-now-live-in-a-legal-marijuana-state-and-most-have-at-least-one-dispensary-in-their-county.

34 Lev Facher, "Rigid Rules at Methadone Clinics Are Jeopardizing Patients' Path to Recovery from Opioid Addiction," *Stat*, March 12, 2024, www.statnews.com/2024/03/12/methadone-clinics-rigid-rules-opioid-addiction-recovery.

35 Facher, "Rigid Rules."

36 SAMHSA, *Federal Guidelines*, 2015, p. 44.

37 National Alliance of Methadone Advocates, "Policy Statement: Bottle Recall," March 2002, www.methadone.org/downloads/namadocuments/ps10bottle_recall.pdf.

38 Nick Voyles, "'This Lid Is Not Right!'—Arbitrarily Losing My Methadone Take-Homes," *Filter*, June 1, 2021, https://filtermag.org/arbitrary-methadone-take-homes.

39 National Alliance of Methadone Advocates, "Policy Statement: Bottle Recall."

40 Helen Redmond, "'Horrible'—Harm Reduction Legend Discusses the Methadone System," *Filter*, June 4, 2024, https://filtermag.org/harm-reduction-methadone-system.

41 Montefiore Einstein, "Methadone Counselor," accessed March 30, 2024, https://careers.montefiore.org.

42 Robert P. Schwartz, Sharon M. Kelly, Kevin E. O'Grady, Devang Gandhi, and Jerome H. Jaffe, "Randomized Trial of Standard Methadone Treatment Compared to Initiating Methadone without Counseling: 12-Month Findings," *Addiction* 107, no. 5 (2012): 943–52, https://doi.org/10.1111/j.1360-0443.2011.03700.x.

43 Jennifer Friedman and Marixsa Alicea, *Surviving Heroin: Interviews with Women in Methadone Clinics* (University Press of Florida, 2001), 172.

44 Peter Vanderkloot, "Methadone: Medicine, Harm Reduction or Social Control," *Harm Reduction Communication* 11 (Spring 2000), www.yumpu.com/en/document/read/34312211/the-pdf-here-harm-reduction-coalition.

45 *Methadonia*. In an interview with director Michel Negroponte in 2024, he told me that he wished he had never made the documentary because it reinforced so many of the stigmatizing ideas around methadone and the patients who take it.

CHAPTER 2: SUBSTITUTING ONE DRUG FOR ANOTHER: DISCOVERING METHADONE TO TREAT OPIOID ADDICTION

1 World Health Organization, "World Health Organization Model List of Essential Medicines: 23rd List (2023)," https://iris.who.int/bitstream/handle/10665/371090/WHO-MHP-HPS-EML-2023.02-eng.pdf.

2 Melody Glenn, *Mother of Methadone: A Doctor's Quest, a Forgotten History, and a Modern-Day Crisis* (Beacon Press, 2025), 69.

3 Clary Estes, "The Narcotic Farm and the Little Known History America's First Prison for Drug Addicts," *Forbes*, November 18, 2019, www.forbes.com/sites/claryestes/2019/11/18/the-narcotic-farm-and-the-little-known-history-americas-first-prison-for-drug-addicts; Drug Enforcement Administration, "Early Years," p. 22.

4 Estes, "Narcotic Farm."

5 Nancy D. Campbell, J. P. Olsen, and Luke Walden, *The Narcotic Farm: The Rise and Fall of America's First Prison for Drug Addicts* (Abrams, 2008).

6 DEA Museum, "Narcotics Enforcement in the 1930s," https://museum.dea.gov/exhibits/online-exhibits/anslinger/narcotics-enforcement-1930s; *Grass Is Greener*, directed by Fab 5 Freddy (Netflix documentary, 2019), www.netflix.com/title/80213712.

7 *Grass Is Greener*; Natalie Papillion, "Drug War History: Anslinger, Armstrong and America's Early Anti-Cannabis Crusade," *Medium*, blog post, July 3, 2020, https://medium.com/equityorg/drug-war-history-anslinger-armstrong-and-americas-early-anti-cannabis-crusade-949022207856.

8   Rachel Chang, "How the Government Targeted 'Strange Fruit' Singer Billie Holiday with Drug Arrests," *Biography*, February 26, 2021, www.biography.com/musicians /billie-holiday-narcotics-us-government.

9   Johann Hari, *Chasing the Scream: The First and Last Days of the War on Drugs* (Bloomsbury Books, 2015), 31.

10   Campbell et al., *Narcotic Farm*, 165.

11   Campbell et al., *Narcotic Farm*, 152.

12   *The Narcotic Farm*, written by J. P. Olsen, directed by J. P. Olsen and Luke Walden (PBS documentary, 2008), https://vimeo.com/97168417.

13   David T. Courtwright, "Preventing and Treating Narcotic Addiction—A Century of Federal Drug Control," *New England Journal of Medicine* 373, no. 22 (2015): 2095–97, https://doi.org/10.1056/NEJMp1508818.

14   HBO, "The Synanon Fix: Did the Cure Become a Cult?," www.hbo.com/series /urn:hbo:series:GZgPZyA5ipcPCwwEAAAAD.

15   Lawrence Van Gelder, "Charles Dederich, 83, Synanon Founder, Dies," *New York Times*, March 4, 1997, www.nytimes.com/1997/03/04/us/charles-dederich-83-synanon -founder-dies.html.

16   HBO, "Synanon Fix."

17   Brianna Nofil, "The CIA's Appalling Human Experiments with Mind Control," History Channel, n.d., accessed April 20, 2024, www.history.com/mkultra-operation -midnight-climax-cia-lsd-experiments.

18   National Institute on Drug Abuse, "Drug Misuse and Addiction," July 2020, https:// nida.nih.gov/publications/drugs-brains-behavior-science-addiction/drug-misuse -addiction; American Society of Addiction Medicine, "What Is the Definition of Addiction?" September 15, 2019, www.asam.org/quality-care/definition-of-addiction.

19   Olsen, *Narcotic Farm*.

20   Nat Hentoff, *A Doctor Among the Addicts* (Rand McNally, 1968), 57–58.

21   Hentoff, *Doctor Among the Addicts*, 64–65. Nyswander was depressed as a result of the racial discrimination she witnessed at Narco and wanted to quit. She was convinced to finish the year by her supervisor.

22   Katie Hafner and Carol Sutton Lewis, "Marie Nyswander: The Doctor & the Fix," *Lost Women of Science*, podcast, 2023, www.lostwomenofscience.org/marie -nyswander.

23   Hentoff, *Doctor Among the Addicts*, 70.

24   Rebecca J. Anderson, "Marie Nyswander and Methadone Maintenance," *The Pharmacologist*, June 2024, https://thepharmacologist.org/methadone-maintenance.

25   Vincent P. Dole, "Addiction as a Public Health Problem," *Alcoholism: Clinical and Experimental Research* 15, no. 5 (October 1, 1991): 749–52, https://doi.org/10.1111 /j.1530-0277.1991.tb00592.x.

26   David Courtwright, Herman Joseph, and Don Des Jarlais, *Addicts Who Survived: An Oral History of Narcotic Use in America, 1923–1965* (University of Tennessee Press, 1989), 332.

27   Vincent P. Dole, Marie E. Nyswander, and Alan Warner, "Successful Treatment of 750 Criminal Addicts," *JAMA* 206, no. 12 (December 16, 1968): 2709–10, https://doi.org/10.1001/jama.1968.03150120042009.

28   Dole et al., "Successful Treatment." To their credit, Dole and Nyswander recognized the role of racism and stated in their paper that minority groups "were further handicapped by racial discrimination and by their police records" (p. 2710).

29   Hentoff, *Doctor Among the Addicts*, 71.

30   Hentoff, *Doctor Among the Addicts*, 73.

31   Courtwright et al., *Addicts Who Survived*, 336–38.

32   Aneri Pattani, "DEA Takes Aggressive Stance toward Pharmacies Trying to Dispense Addiction Medicine," NPR, November 8, 2021, www.npr.org/sections/health-shots/2021/11/08/1053579556/dea-suboxone-subutex-pharmacies-addiction.

33   Helen Redmond, "Methadone Clinics' Conference Felt Like Being Behind Enemy Lines," *Filter*, November 23, 2022, https://filtermag.org/methadone-clinics-reform-aatod. In April 2025, Heather E. Achbach, acting section chief for regulatory drafting at the DEA, spoke at the ASAM conference (https://annualconference.asam.org).

34   Jeffrey A. Singer and Trevor Burrus, "Cops Practicing Medicine," Cato Institute, November 29, 2022, www.cato.org/white-paper/cops-practicing-medicine.

35   Marie Nyswander, *The Drug Addict as a Patient* (Grune & Stratton, 1956), 148.

36   Herman Joseph and Joycelyn Sue Woods, "In the Service of Patients: The Legacy of Dr. Dole," *Heroin Addiction and Related Clinical Problems* 8, no. 4 (December 1, 2006): 9–28, www.researchgate.net/publication/255662523.

37   Ernest Drucker, Sam Rice, Gerry Ganse, Jeffrey J. Kegley, Karen Bonuck, and Ellen Tuchman, "The Lancaster Office Based Opiate Treatment Program: A Case Study and Prototype for Community Physicians and Pharmacists Providing Methadone Maintenance Treatment in the United States," *Addictive Disorders & Their Treatment* 6, no. 3 (September 2007): 121–35, https://doi.org/10.1097/ADT.0b013e31802b4ea1; Helen Redmond, "A Methadone Pioneer Who Freed People from the Cruel Clinic System," *Filter*, April 23, 2025, https://filtermag.org/methadone-pioneer-office-based-prescribing.

38   "Vincent P. Dole Treatment and Research Institute for Opiate Dependency," Weill Cornell Medicine, n.d., accessed May 6, 2024, https://medicine.weill.cornell.edu/divisions-programs/public-health-programs/vincent-p-dole-treatment-and-research-institute-opiate.

39   Vincent P. Dole and Marie E. Nyswander, "Methadone Maintenance: A Theoretical Perspective," in *Theories on Drug Abuse: Selected Contemporary Perspectives, NIDA Research Monograph 30,* eds. Dan J. Lettieri, Mollie Sayers, and Helen Wallenstein Pearson (Rockville, MD: NIDA, 1980), 256–61.

40   Joseph and Woods, "In the Service of Patients"; Hentoff, *Doctor Among the Addicts*, 120. Nyswander said, "They perceive the anxieties of new patients and can speak to them with the authority of personal experience."

41 Hentoff, *Doctor Among the Addicts*, 92.

42 Addiction Treatment Forum, "Interview with Dr. Vincent Dole, MD. Methadone: The Next 30 Years?" *AT Forum Quarterly Newsletter*, 1996, https://atforum.com /interview-dr-vincent-dole-methadone-next-30-years.

43 American Association for the Treatment of Opioid Dependence, "AATOD Award Recipients," n.d., accessed March 30, 2024, https://aatod.eventscribe.net/aaStatic.asp ?SFP=VFFZUUhVRERAMTU4MDdAQUFUT0QgQXdhcmQgUmVjaXBZW50cw.

44 National Institutes of Health, "Medications Reduce Risk of Death after Opioid Overdose," *NIH Research Matters*, July 10, 2018, www.nih.gov/news-events/nih -research-matters/medications-reduce-risk-death-after-opioid-overdose.

45 "Retro Fitness," Yelp, 2017, www.yelp.com/biz/retro-fitness-brooklyn-7?start= 40#location-and-hours. The majority of comments about Retro Fitness are not about the Dole Clinic.

46 Google Search, under "Vincent P. Dole Clinic Brooklyn," accessed April 13, 2024, www.google.com/search?q=vincent+p.+dole+clinic+brooklyn.

CHAPTER 3: RICHARD NIXON, THE WAR ON DRUGS, AND METHADONE

1 "President Nixon Declares Drug Abuse 'Public Enemy Number One,'" press conference, June 17, 1971, YouTube video, posted April 29, 2016, www.youtube.com /watch?v=y8TGLLQlD9M.

2 Mical Raz, "Treating Addiction or Reducing Crime? Methadone Maintenance and Drug Policy Under the Nixon Administration," *Journal of Policy History* 29, no. 1 (January 2017): 58–86, https://doi.org/10.1017/S089803061600035X.

3 Dan Baum, "Legalize It All: How to Win the War on Drugs," *Harper's Magazine*, April 2016, https://harpers.org/archive/2016/04/legalize-it-all.

4 David T. Courtwright, *Dark Paradise : Opiate Addiction in America before 1940* (Harvard University Press, 1982), 172.

5 Emily Dufton, "The War on Drugs: How President Nixon Tied Addiction to Crime," *The Atlantic*, March 26, 2012, www.theatlantic.com/health/archive/2012/03/the-war -on-drugs-how-president-nixon-tied-addiction-to-crime/254319.

6 Michelle Alexander, *The New Jim Crow: Mass Incarceration in the Age of Colorblindness*, rev. ed. (New Press, 2012), 43–44.

7 Nicholas J. Kozel, Robert L. DuPont, and Barry S. Brown, "Narcotics and Crime: A Study of Narcotic Involvement in an Offender Population," *International Journal of the Addictions* 7, no. 3 (1972): 443–50, https://doi.org/10.3109/10826087209028098. DuPont's research consistently tied drug treatment to crime reduction. Among the articles he published at the time: "Development of a Heroin-Addiction Treatment Program: Effect on Urban Crime" and "Heroin Addiction Treatment and Crime Reduction."

8 Raz, "Treating Addiction." The NTA offered detoxification and abstinence-based treatment.

9   Nancy D. Campbell, "Technologies of Suspicion: Coercion and Compassion in Post-Disciplinary Surveillance Regimes," *Surveillance & Society* 2, no. 1 (2004), https://doi.org/10.24908/ss.v2i1.3328.

10 Kozel et al., "Narcotics and Crime."

11 Robert L. DuPont, "Harm Reduction and Decriminalization in the United States: A Personal Perspective," *Substance Use & Misuse* 31, no. 14 (January 1996): 1929–45, https://doi.org/10.3109/10826089609066439.

12 "President Nixon Declares Drug Abuse 'Public Enemy Number One.'"

13 Michael Massing, *The Fix* (Simon & Schuster, 1998), 87.

14 Massing, *Fix*, 88.

15 Massing, *Fix*, 91.

16 Jerome H. Jaffe, "One Bite of the Apple: Establishing the Special Action Office for Drug Abuse Prevention," in *One Hundred Years of Heroin*, ed. David F. Musto (Auburn House, 2002), 44.

17 Raz, "Treating Addiction."

18 Wayne Hall and Megan Weier, "Lee Robins' Studies of Heroin Use among US Vietnam Veterans," *Addiction* 112, no. 1 (January 2017): 176–80, https://doi.org/10.1111/add.13584.

19 Jerome H. Jaffe, "A Follow-up of Vietnam Drug Users: Origins and Context of Lee Robins' Classic Study," *American Journal on Addictions* 19, no. 3 (May 1, 2010): 212–14, https://doi.org/10.1111/j.1521-0391.2010.00043.x.

20 Massing, *Fix*, 115. Dr. Beny Primm, an African American pioneer in methadone treatment in New York, accompanied Jaffe to Vietnam.

21 "Interview: Dr. Jerome Jaffe," PBS *Frontline*, 2000, www.pbs.org/wgbh/pages/frontline/shows/drugs/interviews/jaffe.html.

22 Jerome H. Jaffe, in Special Action Office for Drug Abuse Prevention, *First Annual Report*, 1973, https://babel.hathitrust.org/cgi/pt?id=uiug.30112106555144.

23 David Courtwright, Herman Joseph, and Don Des Jarlais, *Addicts Who Survived: An Oral History of Narcotic Use in America, 1923–1965* (University of Tennessee Press, 1989), 325. He also saw the clinic as controlling: "I'm on a leash. I can't travel. I would first have to get an OK from my clinic doctor. That would be readily given, but he is restricted to giving me medication for a certain number of days. . . . If there is no clinic in Venice or Naples or Paris, I can't go there. . . . That's what I mean by the leash. It's always there."

24 "Interview: Dr. Jerome Jaffe."

25 Massing, *Fix*, 126–28. Jaffe met with Governor Rockefeller to express his disagreement with imprisoning drug dealers for life. Rockefeller listened but didn't change his position.

26 Zoe Adams, "Doctors, Not Dealers," *Guernica*, February 27, 2023, www.guernicamag.com/doctors-not-dealers.

27 Richard A. Rettig and Adam Yarmolinsky, *Federal Regulation of Methadone Treatment* (National Academy Press, 1995), 132, https://nap.nationalacademies.org/read/4899.

28 Drug Policy Alliance, "The DEA: Four Decades of Impeding and Rejecting Science," June 8, 2014, https://maps.org/wp-content/uploads/2014/06/DPA-MAPS_DEA_Science_Final.pdf.

29 John Strang, Teodora Groshkova, and Nicola Metrebian, "EMCDDA Insights: New Heroin-Assisted Treatment," European Monitoring Centre for Drugs and Drug Addiction, 2012, www.drugsandalcohol.ie/17385/1/Heroin_Insight.pdf.

30 Drug Policy Alliance, "DEA."

31 Buprenorphine is in Schedule III.

32 Rettig and Yarmolinsky, *Federal Regulation*, 98.

33 The street value of illicit drugs constantly fluctuates, and availability and innovation can change pricing. Powdered cocaine is usually expensive; crack cocaine is cheap. When heroin was available in the United States, it was relatively costly; fentanyl is cheap.

34 Jeffrey Nadler, Fred Fumia, Charles Cherubin, and Francis Gearing, "Deaths of Narcotic Addicts in New York City in 1971: Those Reported to Be Using Methadone," *International Journal of the Addictions* 10, no. 1 (January 1975): 143–44, https://doi .org/10.3109/10826087509026710.

35 Rettig and Yarmolinsky, *Federal Regulation*, 101, 102.

36 Rettig and Yarmolinsky, *Federal Regulation*, 93.

37 Barry Spunt, Dana E. Hunt, Douglas S. Lipton, and Douglas S. Goldsmith, "Methadone Diversion: A New Look," *Journal of Drug Issues* 16, no. 4 (October 1986): 578, https://doi.org/10.1177/002204268601600406.

38 James A. Inciardi, *Methadone Diversion: Experiences and Issues*, Services Research Monograph Series (Rockville, MD: NIDA, 1977), 13, www.google.com/books /edition/Methadone_Diversion/ZoGbAaMxzfsC.

39 Rettig and Yarmolinsky, *Federal Regulation*, 112–13.

40 Rettig and Yarmolinsky, *Federal Regulation*, 98.

41 Rettig and Yarmolinsky, *Federal Regulation*, 93.

42 Massing, *Fix*, 121.

43 Rettig and Yarmolinsky, *Federal Regulation*, 134.

44 Spunt et al., "Methadone Diversion," 570.

45 Rettig and Yarmolinsky, *Federal Regulation*, 115.

46 Rettig and Yarmolinsky, *Federal Regulation*, 141.

47 Rettig and Yarmolinsky, *Federal Regulation*, 2.

48 American Medical Association, "Narcotics and Medical Practice: Medical Use of Morphine and Morphine-like Drugs and Management of Persons Dependent on Them," *JAMA* 218, no. 4 (October 25, 1971): 582, https://doi.org/10.1001 /jama.1971.03190170056013.

49 American Medical Association, "Narcotics and Medical Practice," 583.

50 Rettig and Yarmolinsky, *Federal Regulation*, 4.

CHAPTER 4: METHADONE IN BLACK AND BROWN COMMUNITIES: SLAVERY AND SOCIAL CONTROL

1 James Forman Jr., *Locking Up Our Own: Crime and Punishment in Black America* (Farrar, Straus and Giroux, 2017), 30.

2 Forman, *Locking Up Our Own*, 28; Gary Lindsay, "Black Man's Army in War Against Drug Abuse," *Washington Afro-American*, October 11, 1969.

3 "The Myth of Methadone," *Black News*, December 27, 1970, in Freedom Archives, https://search.freedomarchives.org/search.php?s=the+black+panther+party+community+news+service&no_digital=1&keyword[]=methadone; Zoe Adams, "Unjust Treatment," *Urban Omnibus*, December 2, 2021, https://urbanomnibus.net/2021/12/unjust-treatment.

4 Samuel Kelton Roberts, "The Politics of Stigma and Racialization in the Early Years of Methadone Maintenance Regulation," in *Methadone Treatment for Opioid Use Disorder: Improving Access Through Regulatory and Legal Change: Proceedings of a Workshop*, eds. Lisa J. Bain, Sheena M. Posey Norris, and Clare Stroud (National Academies Press, 2022), www.nationalacademies.org/documents/embed/link/LF2255DA3DD1C41C0A42D3BEF0989ACAECE3053A6A9B/file/D4F35602BCE0AD3C6FCAD4515932EF817FD6D4CB9791?noSaveAs=1.

5 Vice News, "Dope Is Death: The Short List," YouTube video, posted February 21, 2021, www.youtube.com/watch?v=Ua-m7AANkQ4.

6 Harriet A. Washington, *Medical Apartheid: The Dark History of Medical Experimentation on Black Americans from Colonial Times to the Present* (Knopf Doubleday, 2008).

7 Michel Marriott, "Needle Exchange Angers Many Minorities," *New York Times*, November 7, 1988, www.nytimes.com/1988/11/07/nyregion/needle-exchange-angers-many-minorities.html.

8 Kayla Martha Morgan, Dale Dagar Maglalang, Mollie A. Monnig, Jasjit S. Ahluwalia, Jaqueline C. Avila, and Alexander W. Sokolovsky, "Medical Mistrust, Perceived Discrimination, and Race: A Longitudinal Analysis of Predictors of COVID-19 Vaccine Hesitancy in US Adults," *Journal of Racial and Ethnic Health Disparities* 10, no. 4 (August 2023): 1846–55, https://doi.org/10.1007/s40615-022-01368-6.

9 Ruqaiijah Yearby, Brietta Clark, and José F. Figueroa, "Structural Racism in Historical and Modern US Health Care Policy," *Health Affairs* 41, no. 2 (February 2022): 187–94, https://doi.org/10.1377/hlthaff.2021.01466.

10 Jennifer Tolbert, Sammy Cervantes, Clea Bell, and Anthony Damico, "Key Facts about the Uninsured Population," KFF, December 18, 2024, www.kff.org/uninsured/issue-brief/key-facts-about-the-uninsured-population.

11 Stephanie Colombini, "For People with Opioid Addiction, Medicaid Overhaul Comes with Risks," NPR, September 16, 2024, www.npr.org/sections/shots-health-news/2024/09/14/nx-s1-5078745/for-people-with-opioid-addiction-medicaid-overhaul-comes-with-risks.

12 Christina M. Andrews and Keith Humphreys, "Investing in Medicaid to End the Opioid Epidemic," *Psychiatric Services* 70, no. 7 (July 2019): 537, https://doi.org/10.1176/appi.ps.70705.

13 Julia Dickson-Gomez, Margaret Weeks, Danielle Green, Sophie Boutouis, Carol Galletly, and Erika Christenson, "Insurance Barriers to Substance Use Disorder Treatment after Passage of Mental Health and Addiction Parity Laws and the Affordable

Care Act: A Qualitative Analysis," *Drug and Alcohol Dependence Reports* 3 (March 31, 2022): 100051, https://doi.org/10.1016/j.dadr.2022.100051.

14 Christopher M. Jones, Beth Han, Grant T. Baldwin, Emily B. Einstein, and Wilson M. Compton, "Use of Medication for Opioid Use Disorder Among Adults with Past-Year Opioid Use Disorder in the US, 2021," *JAMA Network Open* 6, no. 8 (August 7, 2023), https://doi.org/10.1001/jamanetworkopen.2023.27488.

15 German Lopez, "Methadone Can Help People Beat Opioid Addiction—If They Can Afford It," *Vox*, January 16, 2020, www.vox.com/policy-and-politics /2020/1/16/21065528/methadone-treatment-opioid-epidemic-addiction-treatment -drug-rehab.

16 Johanna Fernández, *The Young Lords: A Radical History* (University of North Carolina Press, 2020), 273.

17 Martin Tolchin, "Rage Permeates All Facets of Life in the South Bronx," *New York Times*, January 17, 1973, www.nytimes.com/1973/01/17/archives/rage-permeates -all-facets-of-life-in-the-south-bronx.html. In this article, Tolchin sneers at the politics and activism of the Young Lords.

18 Fitzhugh Mullan, *White Coat, Clenched Fist: The Political Education of an American Physician* (Macmillan, 1976), 112–13.

19 "How We Occupied a Hospital and Changed Public Health Care," *New York Times* Op-Docs, YouTube video, posted October 12, 2021, www.youtube.com/watch?v =aK_ALMA1NMk.

20 Mullan, *White Coat*. See chapter 7, "Seize the Hospital to Serve the People."

21 Mullan, *White Coat*, 147–49.

22 Fernández, *Young Lords*, 298–99.

23 Martin Tolchin, "South Bronx: A Jungle Stalked by Fear, Seized by Rage," *New York Times*, January 15, 1973, www.nytimes.com/1973/01/15/archives/south-bronx-a -jungle-stalked-by-fear-seized-by-rage-the-south-bronx.html. Tolchin wrote a fear-mongering four-part series about the South Bronx that was full of racist stereo-types and poverty porn.

24 See the outstanding documentary *Decade of Fire*, written and directed by Gretchen Hildebran and Vivian Vazquez, 2019, https://decadeoffire.com.

25 Fernández, *Young Lords*, 220.

26 Darrel Enck-Wanzer, ed., "Health and Hospitals," chap. 9 in *The Young Lords: A Reader* (New York University Press, 2010), https://caringlabor.wordpress.com/2010/12/04 /the-young-lords-reader-health-and-hospitals.

27 Eana Meng, "Use of Acupuncture by 1970s Revolutionaries of Color: The South Bronx 'Toolkit Care' Concept," *American Journal of Public Health* 111, no. 5 (May 2021): 896–906, https://doi.org/10.2105/AJPH.2020.306080.

28 Sessi Kuwabara Blanchard, "How the Young Lords Took Lincoln Hospital, Left a Health Activism Legacy," *Filter*, October 30, 2018, https://filtermag.org/how-the -young-lords-took-lincoln-hospital-and-left-a-health-activism-legacy.

29 Tolchin, "Rage Permeates."

30 Roberts, "Politics of Stigma."

31 Vice News, "Dope Is Death"; Roberts, "Politics of Stigma."

32 Claudia Voyles, Kenneth Carter, and Laura Cooley, "Back to the Future: The National Acupuncture Detoxification Association (NADA) Protocol Persists as an Agent of Social Justice and Community Healing by the People and for the People," *Open Access Journal of Complementary & Alternative Medicine* 2, no. 4 (June 23, 2020): 191–93, https://lupinepublishers.com/complementary-alternative-medicine -journal/fulltext/back-to-the-future-the-national-acupuncture-detoxification-association .ID.000143.php.

33 Mia Donovan, "Dope Is Death: The Podcast," 2020, https://dopeisdeath.com. Dr. Michael O. Smith was the medical director of Lincoln Detox. He practiced acupuncture and was founder and chairperson of the National Acupuncture Detox-ification Association (NADA).

34 Meng, "Use of Acupuncture."

35 Kenneth Carter, Michelle Olshan-Perlmutter, Jonathan Marx, Janet F. Martini, and Simon B. Cairns, "NADA Ear Acupuncture: An Adjunctive Therapy to Improve and Maintain Positive Outcomes in Substance Abuse Treatment," *Behavioral Sciences* 7, no. 2 (June 16, 2017): 37, https://doi.org/10.3390/bs7020037; Jann Bellamy, "Nada for NADA: 'Acudetox' Not Effective in Addiction Treatment," *Science-Based Medicine*, September 1, 2016, https://sciencebasedmedicine.org/nada-for-nada -auricular-acupuncture-not-effective-in-addiction-treatment.

36 Blanchard, "How the Young Lords Took Lincoln Hospital."

37 David Courtwright, Herman Joseph, and Don Des Jarlais, *Addicts Who Survived: An Oral History of Narcotic Use in America, 1923–1965* (University of Tennessee Press, 1989), 320–25.

38 Jennifer Friedman and Marixsa Alicea, *Surviving Heroin: Interviews with Women in Methadone Clinics* (University Press of Florida, 2001), 136–37.

39 Forman, *Locking Up Our Own*, 25.

40 Blackman's Development Center, "Drug Cure: The Humane Alternative to Blanket Methadone Maintenance," James Forman Papers, Box 81, Manuscript Division, Library of Congress.

41 Ryan Reft, "Heroin and Chocolate City: Black Community Responses to Drug Addiction in the Nation's Capital, 1967–1973," *The Metropole: The Official Blog of the Urban History Association*, blog post, January 24, 2024, https://themetropole .blog/2024/01/24/heroin-and-chocolate-city-black-community-responses-to-drug -addiction-in-the-nations-capital-1967-1973.

42 Reft, "Heroin and Chocolate City."

43 "Interview: Dr. Robert DuPont," PBS *Frontline*, 2000, www.pbs.org/wgbh/pages /frontline/shows/drugs/interviews/dupont.html. In this interview, DuPont reports being personally attacked and threatened with violence for promoting the use of methadone. At a gathering when it was revealed he was the head of the NTA, a

woman spit on him. DuPont asked her why and she replied that he was the person who was bringing methadone to the city. Another incident happened on a Howard University radio show: "I was talking with a young black man who was the deputy head of the local competing drug treatment program. He and I were talking, and he announced that the community had to get rid of people like me, and that he was recommending murder—that I be killed because of what I was doing to the community."

44 William White, "A Life of Clinical Activism: An Interview with Robert G. Newman," 2011, www.stopstigmanow.org/wp-content/uploads/2021/02/SSN-NEWMAN.book -pgs-2020-FINALqxp.pdf.

45 Forman, *Locking Up Our Own*, 29. The BDC engaged in vigilantism and produced a flyer that read, "Anywhere that you see them, let us know and we will deal with them ourselves. . . . If they do not stop immediately . . . WE WILL STOP THEM!!!" Jeru-Ahmed also had an anonymous hotline to report drug dealing.

46 Reft, "Heroin and Chocolate City." "The world doesn't know all the specific cases on which [Hassan] has helped," US Attorney Harold J. Sullivan said in a court deposition crediting Hassan with the imprisonment of at least one prominent local drug dealer.

47 Beny J. Primm and John S. Friedman, *The Healer: A Doctor's Crusade against Addiction and AIDS* (CreateSpace, 2014), 9–10.

48 Beny J. Primm, "Methadone No Answer for Addiction Problem," *New York Amsterdam News*, June 24, 1972. In this article Primm sends mixed messages. He argues that methadone isn't enough to solve all the problems of poor drug users, the root causes of addiction must be addressed and stigma against methadone ended. He writes: "Communities must begin to accept treatment programs in their midst, community residents must accept ex-addicts as fellow citizens and workers."

49 Dorothy Nelkin, *Methadone Maintenance: A Technological Fix* (George Braziller, 1973), 65.

50 Richard Severo, "Rumor, Intrigue and Criticism Beset City's Brooklyn Methadone Center," *New York Times*, June 11, 1970, p. 47, www.nytimes.com/1970/06/11/archives /rumor-intrigue-and-criticism-beset-citys-brooklyn-methadone-center.html.

51 "The Myth of Methadone," *Black News* 27, no. 26 (1970): 2.

52 Primm and Friedman, *The Healer*, 29.

53 Severo, "Rumor, Intrigue and Criticism."

54 Lonny Shavelson, *Hooked: Five Addicts Challenge Our Misguided Drug Rehab System* (New Press, 2001), 69.

55 William White and William Miller, "The Use of Confrontation in Addiction Treatment History, Science, and Time for Change A History of Confrontational Therapies," *Counselor* 8, no. 4 (January 1, 2007): 12–30, www.researchgate.net/publication /265148872.

56 "White Lightening," Freedom Archives, https://search.freedomarchives.org/search .php?view_collection=1025; White Lightening newsletter, "Methadone," n.d.,

accessed August 12, 2024, https://freedomarchives.org/Documents/Finder/DOC58
_scans/58.White.Lightening.Methadone.pdf.

57 Marsha Rosenbaum and Sheigla Murphy, "Always a Junkie?: The Arduous Task of
Getting Off Methadone Maintenance," *Journal of Drug Issues* 14, no. 3 (July 1, 1984):
527–52, https://doi.org/10.1177/002204268401400307; Stephen Magura and
Andrew Rosenblum, "Methadone Treatment: Lessons Learned, Lessons Forgotten,
Lessons Ignored," *Mount Sinai Journal of Medicine* 68, no. 1 (January 2001): 62–74,
https://pubmed.ncbi.nlm.nih.gov/11135508; J. B. Milby, "Methadone Maintenance
to Abstinence: How Many Make It?" *Journal of Nervous and Mental Disease* 176,
no. 7 (July 1988): 409–22, https://doi.org/10.1097/00005053-198807000-00003;
Karen L. Sees, Kevin L. Delucchi, Carmen Masson, Amy Rosen, H. Westley Clark,
Helen Robillard, Peter Banys, and Sharon M. Hall, "Methadone Maintenance vs
180-Day Psychosocially Enriched Detoxification for Treatment of Opioid Dependence: A Randomized Controlled Trial," *JAMA* 283, no. 10 (March 8, 2000):
1303–10, https://doi.org/10.1001/jama.283.10.1303.

58 Kelly R. Knight, Marsha Rosenbaum, Margaret S. Kelley, Jeanette Irwin, Allyson
Washburn, and Lynn Wenger, "Defunding the Poor: The Impact of Lost Access to
Subsidized Methadone Maintenance Treatment on Women Injection Drug Users,"
Journal of Drug Issues 26, no. 4 (October 1996): 923–42, https://doi.org/10.1177
/002204269602600411.

59 Knight et al., "Defunding the Poor."

60 Patrick Radden Keefe, "The Family That Built an Empire of Pain," *New Yorker*,
October 23, 2017, www.newyorker.com/magazine/2017/10/30/the-family
-that-built-an-empire-of-pain.

61 Daniel Ciccarone, "The Triple Wave Epidemic: Supply and Demand Drivers of the
US Opioid Overdose Crisis," *International Journal of Drug Policy* 71 (September
2019): 183–88, https://doi.org/10.1016/j.drugpo.2019.01.010.

62 Ciccarone, "Triple Wave Epidemic." There is a fourth wave of overdose deaths currently unfolding with cocaine, methamphetamine, and xylazine with or without
fentanyl.

63 Elizabeth Chiarello, *Policing Patients: Treatment and Surveillance on the Frontlines of
the Opioid Crisis* (Princeton University Press, 2024), 28–29.

64 Katharine Q. Seelye, "In Heroin Crisis, White Families Seek Gentler War on Drugs,"
New York Times, October 30, 2015, www.nytimes.com/2015/10/31/us/heroin-war-on
-drugs-parents.html.

65 Michael Shaw, "Photos Reveal Media's Softer Tone on Opioid Crisis," *Columbia Jour-
nalism Review*, July 26, 2017, www.cjr.org/criticism/opioid-crisis-photos.php.

66 Seelye, "In Heroin Crisis."

67 Helena Hansen, Jules Netherland, and David Herzberg, *Whiteout: How Racial Capitalism Changed the Color of Opioids in America* (University of California Press, 2023),
157–58. *Whiteout* is indispensable in explaining how racial disparities are baked into
opioid prescribing.

68 Hansen et al., *Whiteout*, 42.

69 Hansen et al., *Whiteout*, 42.

70 Matthew Perry, *Friends, Lovers, and the Big Terrible Thing: A Memoir* (Flatiron Books, 2024): "I had already heard about methadone, a drug that promised to remove a fifty-five-a-day Vicodin habit in one day with one little sip. The only catch was, you had to drink that little sip every day, or you would go into serious withdrawal. . . . I got on the drug immediately and was able to return to *Friends* the next day, sharp as a tack" (p. 130). Perry also took Suboxone and tapered off the medication numerous times, often feeling suicidal. Would the beloved actor be alive today if he'd understood that both medications are used for maintenance?

71 Friedman and Alicea, *Surviving Heroin*, 178. Another white patient described how taking methadone was embarrassing for her family: "We were middle class. Frank Lloyd Wright home. . . . So for them to have a daughter that does heroin and then be on a methadone program. . . . This is absurd."

72 Deborah Sontag, "Addiction Treatment With a Dark Side," *New York Times*, November 16, 2013, www.nytimes.com/2013/11/17/health/in-demand-in-clinics-and-on-the-street-bupe-can-be-savior-or-menace.html.

73 Addiction Treatment Forum, "Buprenorphine vs. Methadone," February 12, 2013, https://atforum.com/2013/02/buprenorphine-vs-methadone.

74 The drug rating system introduced by the 1970 Controlled Substances Act is medically inaccurate. For example: Schedule I drugs include heroin, cannabis, and LSD and are deemed to have no therapeutic use, but all three have evidence-based medical uses. The system of scheduling drugs needs to be abolished.

75 Jerome H. Jaffe and Charles O'Keeffe, "From Morphine Clinics to Buprenorphine: Regulating Opioid Agonist Treatment of Addiction in the United States," *Drug and Alcohol Dependence* 70, no. 2, Supplement (May 21, 2003): S3–S11, https://doi.org/10.1016/S0376-8716(03)00055-3.

76 Sontag, "Addiction Treatment."

77 Hansen et al., *Whiteout*, 44. Those super profits were enabled by US taxpayers: Reckitt Benckiser received over $23 million from NIDA to conduct clinical trials with buprenorphine, the drug received "orphan status," and patent protection was extended for seven years.

78 The second year the cap was raised to 100, then a doctor could apply to treat up to 275 patients. Physicians rarely met those caps. In 2016, prescribing authority was given to nurse practitioners and physician assistants who had to complete a twenty-four-hour training to prescribe. They should have been included in DATA 2000 to expand the pool of prescribers from the start.

79 Dima M. Qato, Jonathan H. Watanabe, and Kelly J. Clark, "Federal and State Pharmacy Regulations and Dispensing Barriers to Buprenorphine Access at Retail Pharmacies in the US," *JAMA Health Forum* 3, no. 8 (August 26, 2022): e222839, https://doi.org/10.1001/jamahealthforum.2022.2839.

80 Hansen et al., *Whiteout*, 187.

81 Wendy Kissin, Caroline McLeod, Joseph Sonnefeld, and Arlene Stanton, "Experiences of a National Sample of Qualified Addiction Specialists Who Have and Have Not Prescribed Buprenorphine for Opioid Dependence," *Journal of Addictive Diseases* 25, no. 4 (2006): 91–103, https://doi.org/10.1300/J069v25n04_09. The researchers noted: "Many waivered physicians had not provided buprenorphine treatment. Prescribers identified challenges such as induction logistics, recordkeeping requirements, the 30-patient limit, DEA involvement, and limited patient compliance."

82 Pooja A. Lagisetty, Ryan Ross, Amy Bohnert, Michael Clay, and Donovan T. Maust, "Buprenorphine Treatment Divide by Race/Ethnicity and Payment," *JAMA Psychiatry* 76, no. 9 (September 1, 2019): 979–81, https://doi.org/10.1001/jamapsychiatry.2019.0876.

83 Michael L. Barnett, Ellen Meara, Terri Lewinson, Brianna Hardy, Deanna Chyn, Moraa Onsando, Haiden A. Huskamp, et al., "Racial Inequality in Receipt of Medications for Opioid Use Disorder," *New England Journal of Medicine* 388, no. 19 (May 10, 2023): 1779–89, https://doi.org/10.1056/NEJMsa2212412; Utsha G. Khatri, Max Jordan Nguemeni Tiako, Abeselom Gebreyesus, Andre Reid, Sara F. Jacoby, and Eugenia C. South, "'A Lack of Empathy:' A Qualitative Study of Black People Seeking Treatment for Opioid Use Disorder," *SSM—Qualitative Research in Health* 4 (December 1, 2023): 100298, https://doi.org/10.1016/j.ssmqr.2023.100298.

84 "Fact Sheet: The Impact of the Overdose Crisis on Black Communities in the United States," Drug Policy Alliance, June 28, 2024, https://drugpolicy.org/resource/fact-sheet-the-impact-of-the-overdose-crisis-on-black-communities-in-the-united-states. Between 2021 and 2022, the Black overdose death rate increased by 7 percent as white rates went down. Since 2020, Black communities have had the second-highest overdose death rate after Native Americans nationally.

85 Chiarello, *Policing Patients*, 131.

86 Chiarello, *Policing Patients*, 60. See chapter 2, "Trojan Horse Technologies," for a critical analysis of PDMPs.

87 Ethan Brooks, "The Drug That Could Help End the Opioid Epidemic," *The Atlantic*, August 8, 2024, www.theatlantic.com/podcasts/archive/2024/08/drug-could-help-end-opioid-epidemic/679397; Chiarello, *Policing Patients*.

88 Patrice Wendling, "The Quest to Fill Suboxone Prescriptions," MedCentral, March 25, 2024, www.medcentral.com/addiction-med/oud/the-quest-to-fill-suboxone-prescriptions. Prior authorization is a health insurance restriction that also delays access to taking the medication and creates time-consuming paperwork or phone calls for providers, making them wary of prescribing.

89 Roberts, "Politics of Stigma."

CHAPTER 5: "WOULD YOU WANT TO LIVE NEXT TO A METHADONE CLINIC?": NIMBY MOVEMENTS

1 The Sugar Hill Gang was a US hip-hop group, famous for the 1979 blockbuster hit song "Rapper's Delight."

2   Beny J. Primm and John S. Friedman, *The Healer: A Doctor's Crusade against Addiction and AIDS* (CreateSpace, 2014), 49.

3   Mario Lotmore, "DOH and Acadia Respond to Proposed Lynnwood Methadone Clinic Concerns," *Lynnwood Times*, January 13, 2023, https://lynnwoodtimes.com /2023/01/13/lynnwood-opioid.

4   "Proposed Opioid Treatment Program (OTP) Lynnwood Comprehensive Treatment Center: Acadia Public Comment Responses," Washington State Department of Health, January 2023, https://doh.wa.gov/sites/default/files/2023-01/Lynnwood Response2023.pdf.

5   Helen Redmond, "Boston's 'Methadone Mile' and the Wars on Drug Users, Unhoused People," *Filter*, February 9, 2021, https://filtermag.org/bostons-methadone-mile-and -the-wars-on-drug-users-unhoused-people.

6   Giacomo Bologna, "A West Baltimore Neighborhood Wants to Block a Methadone Clinic," *Baltimore Banner*, April 30, 2024, www.thebaltimorebanner.com/community /public-health/baltimore-methadone-opioid-clinic-Z66SYGNI7FAWTPFNBINTBAB53E.

7   Bologna, "West Baltimore Neighborhood."

8   William White, "A Life of Clinical Activism: An Interview with Robert G. Newman," 2011, www.stopstigmanow.org/wp-content/uploads/2021/02/SSN-NEWMAN.book -pgs-2020-FINALqxp.pdf.

9   White, "Life of Clinical Activism." Before methadone could be secured from a hospital pharmacy for ferry patients, Dr. Newman stored the medication in his apartment. He delivered the methadone each morning and brought the leftovers home at night, usually in his son's stroller.

10 Jennifer Lu, "First Methadone Clinic to Open in North Dakota," *Dickinson Press*, July 30, 2016, www.thedickinsonpress.com/news/first-methadone-clinic-to-open-in-north-dakota.

11 C. Debra M. Furr-Holden, Adam J. Milam, Elizabeth D. Nesoff, Renee M. Johnson, David O. Fakunle, Jacky M. Jennings, and Roland J. Thorpe Jr., "Not in My Back Yard: A Comparative Analysis of Crime Around Publicly Funded Drug Treatment Centers, Liquor Stores, Convenience Stores, and Corner Stores in One Mid-Atlantic City," *Journal of Studies on Alcohol and Drugs* 77, no. 1 (January 2016): 17–24, https://doi.org/10.15288/jsad.2016.77.17.

12 Christine Vestal, "In Opioid Epidemic, Prejudice Persists Against Methadone," *Stateline*, November 11, 2016, https://stateline.org/2016/11/11/in-opioid-epidemic -prejudice-persists-against-methadone.

13 Alison Knopf, "Email from Staats-Combs to Clanton Mayor, Chilton County Law Enforcement," Addiction Treatment Forum, January 20, 2023, https:// atforum.com/2023/01/email-staats-combs-clanton-mayor-chilton-county-law -enforcement.

14 Johnathan H. Duff and Jameson A. Carter, "Location of Medication-Assisted Treatment for Opioid Addiction: In Brief," Congressional Research Service, June 24, 2019, www.congress.gov/crs-product/R45782.

15 Pew, "State Opioid Treatment Program Regulations Put Evidence-Based Care Out of Reach for Many," October 31, 2022, https://pew.org/3s5uPXJ; Pew, "Overview of

Opioid Treatment Program Regulations by State," September 19, 2022, https://pew.org/3Qw8g8c.

16 Pew, "State Opioid Treatment."

17 Helen Redmond, "A State-by-State Guide to the Cruelty of the Methadone Clinic System," *Filter*, September 27, 2022, https://filtermag.org/states-methadone-clinics-cruelty.

18 Lev Facher, "The Methadone Clinic Monopoly: Opioid Treatment Chains Backed by Private Equity Are Fighting Calls for Reform," *Stat*, March 19, 2024, www.statnews.com/2024/03/19/methadone-clinics-opioid-addiction-private-equity.

19 Peter Vanderkloot, "Methadone: Medicine, Harm Reduction or Social Control," *Harm Reduction Communication* 11 (Spring 2000), www.yumpu.com/en/document/read/34312211/the-pdf-here-harm-reduction-coalition.

20 Jenna is featured in my documentary *Liquid Handcuffs: A Documentary to Free Methadone*, directed by Marilena Marchetti and Helen Redmond, Portico Films, 2019, www.porticofilms.com/pastwork/liquidhandcuffs.

21 Greater Harlem Coalition, "Who We Are and Our Mission," May 31, 2023, https://greaterharlem.nyc.

22 Greater Harlem Coalition, "18% Of NYC's OTP Patients Are Treated in Harlem," November 3, 2022, https://greaterharlem.nyc/data/18-percent-of-nyc-patients-are-treated-in-harlem; Shawn Hill and Syderia Asberry-Chresfield, "Harlem Is Saturated with Methadone," *New York Daily News*, July 16, 2021, www.nydailynews.com/2021/07/16/harlem-is-saturated-with-methadone.

23 William C. Goedel, Aaron Shapiro, Magdalena Cerdá, Jennifer W. Tsai, Scott E. Hadland, and Brandon D. L. Marshall, "Association of Racial/Ethnic Segregation with Treatment Capacity for Opioid Use Disorder in Counties in the United States," *JAMA Network Open* 3, no. 4 (April 22, 2020): e203711, https://doi.org/10.1001/jamanetworkopen.2020.3711.

24 Zoe Adams, "Unjust Treatment," *Urban Omnibus*, December 2, 2021, https://urbanomnibus.net/2021/12/unjust-treatment.

25 Greater Harlem Coalition, "Nation's First Safe Injection Site Worsen Quality of Life Issues in Harlem," blog post, October 10, 2022, https://greaterharlem.nyc/asks/drug-consumption-site.

26 OnPoint NYC, n.d., accessed May 11, 2025, https://onpointnyc.org.

CHAPTER 6: THE RISE OF FOR-PROFIT METHADONE CLINIC CHAINS

1 Ethan Hawes, "I Chose Fentanyl Over the Humiliation of Methadone Treatment," *Filter*, June 15, 2023, https://filtermag.org/methadone-clinic-fentanyl.

2 National Academies of Sciences, Engineering, and Medicine, "Methadone Treatment for Opioid Use Disorder: Examining Federal Regulations and Laws: A Workshop," March 3–4, 2022, www.nationalacademies.org/event/03-03-2022/methadone-treatment-for-opioid-use-disorder-examining-federal-regulations-and-laws-a-workshop.

3   National Academies, "Methadone Treatment Workshop." Parrino's presentation was titled "OTPs as Hub Sites in Systemic Expansion."

4   Adam Gaffney, "Eight Needed Steps in the Fight Against COVID-19," *Boston Review*, April 3, 2020, www.bostonreview.net/articles/adam-gaffney-gaffney -medicine-statement.

5   Nora Volkow, "To Address the Fentanyl Crisis, Greater Access to Methadone Is Needed," National Institute on Drug Abuse, blog post, July 29, 2024, https://nida .nih.gov/about-nida/noras-blog/2024/07/to-address-the-fentanyl-crisis-greater-access -to-methadone-is-needed.

6   Lev Facher, "Rigid Rules at Methadone Clinics Are Jeopardizing Patients' Path to Recovery from Opioid Addiction," *Stat*, March 12, 2024, www.statnews.com /2024/03/12/methadone-clinics-rigid-rules-opioid-addiction-recovery; Emily Alpert Reyes, "Skid Row Is an Overdose 'Epicenter.' But Methadone Can Be Miles Away," *Los Angeles Times*, May 11, 2022, www.latimes.com/california/story/2022-05-11 /la-skid-row-overdose-epicenter-methadone-access.

7   Lev Facher, "The Methadone Clinic Monopoly: Opioid Treatment Chains Backed by Private Equity Are Fighting Calls for Reform," *Stat*, March 19, 2024, www.statnews .com/2024/03/19/methadone-clinics-opioid-addiction-private-equity.

8   Facher, "Methadone Clinic Monopoly."

9   Brian Mann, "As Addiction Deaths Surge, Profit-Driven Rehab Industry Faces 'Severe Ethical Crisis,'" NPR, February 15, 2021, www.npr.org/2021/02/15/963700736/as -addiction-deaths-surge-profit-driven-rehab-industry-faces-severe-ethical-cris.

10   German Lopez, "She Wanted Addiction Treatment. She Ended up in the Relapse Capital of America," *Vox*, March 2, 2020, www.vox.com/policy-and-politics /2020/3/2/21156327/florida-shuffle-drug-rehab-addiction-treatment-bri-jaynes; Ryan Grim, "Addiction Treatment Industry Worried Lax Ethics Could Spell Its Doom," *HuffPost*, June 17, 2016, www.huffpost.com/entry/addiction-treatment -industry-ethics_n_575f3fa5e4b0e4fe5143865c.

11   Shoshana Walter, "At Hundreds of Rehabs, Recovery Means Work without Pay," *Reveal*, July 7, 2020, https://revealnews.org/article/at-hundreds-of-rehabs-recovery -means-work-without-pay.

12   Jason Cherkis, "Dying to Be Free: There's a Treatment for Heroin Addiction That Actually Works. Why Aren't We Using It?," *HuffPost*, January 28, 2015, https://projects .huffingtonpost.com/projects/dying-to-be-free-heroin-treatment.

13   American Association for the Treatment of Opioid Dependence, "Our Board of Directors," n.d., accessed December 12, 2024, www.aatod.org/about-us/our-board -of-directors.

14   Katie Thomas and Jessica Silver-Greenberg, "Fraud and Fakery at the Country's Largest Chain of Methadone Clinics," *New York Times*, December 7, 2024, www.nytimes .com/2024/12/07/health/acadia-methadone-clinics-fraud.html.

15   BayMark Health Services, "Treatment Locations," n.d., accessed July 7, 2025, https:// baymark.com/treatment-locations.

16 Facher, "Methadone Clinic Monopoly."

17 Chicago Recovery Alliance, "A Tribute to Dan Bigg," September 27, 2018, https://anypositivechange.org/a-tribute-to-dan-bigg.

18 Zach Rhoads, "What Can We Learn From the Nation's First 24/7 Methadone Clinic?," *Filter*, June 20, 2019, https://filtermag.org/what-can-we-learn-from-the-nations-first-24-7-methadone-clinic.

19 Montefiore Einstein, "Methadone Counselor," accessed March 30, 2024, https://careers.montefiore.org.

20 BayMark Health Services, "BayMark Innovates with BAART Programs 24/7 Access to Opioid Treatment Services in Los Angeles," May 18, 2021, https://baymark.com/blog/baart-programs-24-7-access-to-opioid-treatment-services-in-los-angeles; San Francisco Department of Public Health, "Annual Report 2022–2023," 2024, p. 16, www.sf.gov/sites/default/files/2024-02/FY22-23%20DPH%20Annual%20Report_0.pdf.

21 Helen Redmond, "Watch: Former Methadone Clinic Director Slams Culture of Cruelty," *Filter*, August 7, 2023, https://filtermag.org/methadone-clinic-director. Urdahl also terminated the employment of counselors who had no education or experience providing counseling.

22 Yuhua Bao, Megan A. O'Grady, Kayla Hutchings, Ju-Chen Hu, Kristen Campbell, Elizabeth Knopf, Shazia Hussaine, et al., "Payment and Billing Strategies to Support Methadone Take-Home Medication: Perspectives of Financial Leaders of Opioid Treatment Program Organizations in New York State," *Journal of Substance Use and Addiction Treatment* 168 (January 2025): 209547, https://doi.org/10.1016/j.josat.2024.209547.

23 BayMark headquarters are located in Lewisville, Texas.

24 Thomas and Silver-Greenberg, "Fraud and Fakery."

25 Michael Fenne, "Private Equity-Owned SUD Clinics Settle False Claims Allegations," Private Equity Stakeholder Project, August 7, 2024, https://pestakeholder.org/news/private-equity-owned-sud-clinics-settle-false-claims-allegations; US Department of Justice, "Substance Use Disorder Treatment Clinics to Pay More than $850,000 to Resolve Allegations They Knowingly Overbilled Medicaid for Office Visits," news release, July 25, 2024, www.justice.gov/opa/pr/substance-use-disorder-treatment-clinics-pay-more-850000-resolve-allegations-they-knowingly.

26 Connecticut Attorney General, "Settlement Reached with Opioid Treatment Provider to Resolve Medicaid Overpayment Claim Allegations," news release, 2017, https://portal.ct.gov/ag/press-releases-archived/2017-press-releases/settlement-reached-with-opioid-treatment-provider-to-resolve-medicaid-overpayment-claim-allegations.

27 KFF Health News, "Payback: Tracking the Opioid Settlement Cash," n.d., accessed May 11, 2025, https://kffhealthnews.org/opioid-settlements.

28 Thomas and Silver-Greenberg, "Fraud and Fakery."

29 Liz Weber, "As a Methadone Patient, I Demand No Return to the Pre-COVID Status Quo," *Filter*, April 20, 2022, https://filtermag.org/methadone-patient-covid-rules.

30 Helen Redmond, "The Tech Companies Policing Methadone Patients for Profit," *Filter*, February 14, 2023, https://filtermag.org/tech-methadone-surveillance.

31 Alison Knopf, "Sonara: A Digitized Label for Methadone Take-Homes," Addiction Treatment Forum, November 4, 2022, https://atforum.com/2022/11/sonara -digitized-label-methadone-take-homes.

32 Michael Hegarty worked at a BayMark OTP, where the app was piloted, and shared this information with me. He personally witnessed how the app works from both the patient and provider side. Curiously, the Sonara website doesn't mention that patients have to recite "The quick brown fox jumps over the lazy dog" post dose. The sentence is an English-language pangram—it contains all the letters of the alphabet.

33 Sam Blum, "Addiction-Treatment Startups Are Raking in VC Money—and Amassing Millions in Fines," *Inc.*, June 7, 2024, www.inc.com/sam-blum/addiction-treatment -startups-are-raking-in-vc-money-and-amassing-millions-in-fines.html. Cuban is the former owner of the Dallas Mavericks basketball team, co-owner of 2929 Entertainment, and was one of the main "sharks" on the ABC reality television series *Shark Tank*.

34 David Sjostedt, "Mark Cuban-Backed Methadone Startup Helps People Kick Opioids," *San Francisco Standard*, September 14, 2022, https://sfstandard.com/2022/09/14/mark -cuban-backed-methadone-startup-helps-people-kick-opioids-in-sf.

35 Erin Schumaker, Carmen Paun, Daniel Payne, and Ruth Reader, "Hearts Travel Better in a Box," *Politico*, December 24, 2024, www.politico.com/newsletters/future -pulse/2024/08/22/hearts-travel-better-in-a-box-00175700.

36 Olivia Solon, "'Digital Shackles': The Unexpected Cruelty of Ankle Monitors," *Guardian*, August 28, 2018, www.theguardian.com/technology/2018/aug/28 /digital-shackles-the-unexpected-cruelty-of-ankle-monitors.

37 Zachary Kletter works for Sonara as a customer success manager. His father is Jason Kletter, the CEO of BayMark. See www.sonarahealth.com/about-us.

38 Michael Giles, Lucy Reynales, Avinash Jayaraman, Omer Kaplan, Kshitij Verma, Katharina Wiest, Samuel Denney, et al., "Usability and Feasibility of a Take-Home Methadone Web-Application for Opioid Treatment Program Patients: A Small Business Innovation Research Mixed Methods Study," *Journal of Substance Use and Addiction Treatment* 157 (February 2024): 209181, https://doi.org/10.1016/j .josat.2023.209181.

39 Sonara Health, "Translating Research into Practice," n.d., accessed December 27, 2024, www.sonarahealth.com/research. The "Responsibly Expanding Access to Life-Saving Methadone" study was a conducted in spring 2022 to help facilitate increased access to take-home methadone in response to SAMHSA's relaxed take-home guidelines. The study was administered in partnership with BayMark, researchers at Oregon Health and Science University and Stanford University, and with support from NIDA.

40 Jamie Grill-Goodman, "New Pilot Program Aims to Curb Opioid Abuse Through Innovative Treatment," *Commerce*, October 17, 2024, https://www.tapinto.net/towns/madison /articles/new-pilot-program-aims-to-curb-opioid-abuse-through-innovative-treatment-5.

41 Lilo H. Stainton, "Taking the Handcuffs Off Methadone Treatment, 'Game-Changer' for Patients," *NJ Spotlight News*, June 9, 2025, www.njspotlightnews.org/2025/06 /methadone-online-treatment-innovation-game-changer-for-patients.

42 Sonara Health, "Using Opioid Settlement Funds to Support OTP Innovation," You-Tube video, posted February 28, 2024, www.youtube.com/watch?v=ipjLAHsdZw0.

43 Sonara Health, "Sonara Health Partners with MedMark Treatment Centers to Expand Take-Home Methadone Access to Pennsylvania," 2024, www.sonarahealth.com /articles-1/sonara-health-partners-with-medmark-treatment-centers-to-expand-take -home-methadone-access-to-pennsylvania.

44 Redmond, "Tech Companies."

45 Verinetics, "The Solution," 2024, www.verinetics.com/the-solution.

46 WRAL TechWire, "RTP's Verinetics Awarded $1.5M Contract to Expand Access to Medications to Treat Opioid Use Disorder," November 30, 2021, https://wraltechwire .com/2021/11/30/rtps-verinetics-awarded-1-5m-contract-to-expand-access-to -medications-to-treat-opioid-use-disorder. Verinetics also seeks funding from private investors: "We continue to seek impact-minded investors and strategic collaboration partners interested in facilitating a paradigm shift in the packaging, distribution, and control of high-risk prescription medications" (Verinetics, n.d., accessed June 12, 2025, www.verinetics.com/investors).

47 MedMinder, "Automatic Pill Dispenser," n.d., accessed January 3, 2025, https:// medminder.com.

48 Kelly E. Dunn, Robert K. Brooner, and Kenneth B. Stoller, "Technology-Assisted Methadone Take-Home Dosing for Dispensing Methadone to Persons with Opioid Use Disorder during the Covid-19 Pandemic," *Journal of Substance Abuse Treatment* 121 (February 2021): 108197, https://doi.org/10.1016/j.jsat.2020.108197. Dr. Stoller serves on the Board of Directors of AATOD.

49 Redmond, "Tech Companies." Ferguson is the harm reduction coordinator for CMS, a methadone clinic chain.

CHAPTER 7: JUST SAY NO TO METHADONE IN DRUG TREATMENT COURT, JAIL, OR PRISON

1 Manhattan Treatment Court, "Handbook: Guidelines and Program Information for Drug Court Participants," April 23, 2023, p. 17, https://nycourts.gov/courts/nyc /drug_treatment/publications_pdf/MDC%20Handbook%20-%20ENGLISH.pdf.

2 Drug Policy Alliance, "Drug Courts Are Not the Answer: Toward a Health-Centered Approach to Drug Use," March 21, 2011, p. 2, https://drugpolicy.org/resource/drug -courts-are-not-the-answer-toward-a-health-centered-approach-to-drug-use.

3 Rebecca Tiger, *Judging Addicts: Drug Courts and Coercion in the Justice System*, Alternative Criminology Series (New York University Press, 2013), 4.

4 Tiger, *Judging Addicts*, 19–20.

5 Newt Gingrich and Van Jones, "Drug Courts Can Help Solve the Opioid Crisis," *Time*, August 1, 2017, https://time.com/4882507/newt-gingrich-van-opioid-epidemic -drug-courts.

6   Prison Policy Initiative, "New Report Mass Incarceration: The Whole Pie 2023 Shows That as the Pandemic Subsides, Criminal Legal System Returning to 'Business as Usual,'" blog post, March 14, 2023, www.prisonpolicy.org/blog/2023/03/14 /whole_pie_2023.

7   All Rise, "About Treatment Courts," n.d., accessed May 13, 2025, https://allrise.org /about/treatment-courts.

8   Aaron Arnold, "Navigating Harm Reduction in Treatment Courts," webinar, All Rise, 2024.

9   National Harm Reduction Coalition, "Principles of Harm Reduction," 2024, https:// harmreduction.org/about-us/principles-of-harm-reduction.

10   Sheila P. Vakharia, *The Harm Reduction Gap: Helping Individuals Left Behind by Conventional Drug Prevention and Abstinence-Only Addiction Treatment* (Routledge, 2024), 157. While Vakharia worked in a community-based drug treatment program, she became a drug court representative, which required her to appear in court several times a month to report client updates to the judge.

11   Alec Karakatsanis, "The Punishment Bureaucracy: How to Think About 'Criminal Justice Reform,'" *Yale Law Journal* 128 (March 2019), www.yalelawjournal.org/forum /the-punishment-bureaucracy. Karakatsanis is the founder and executive director of Civil Rights Corps.

12   Drug Policy Alliance, "Drug Courts," 8.

13   Kerwin Kaye, *Enforcing Freedom: Drug Courts, Therapeutic Communities, and the Intimacies of the State* (Columbia University Press, 2020), 10; Timothy Ho, Shannon M. Carey, and Anna M. Malsch, "Racial and Gender Disparities in Treatment Courts: Do They Exist and Is There Anything We Can Do to Change Them?" *Journal for Advancing Justice* 1 (2018): 5–34, https://advancejustice.org/wp-content /uploads/2018/06/AJ-Journal.pdf.

14   Manhattan Treatment Court, "Handbook," p. 9; Allison Jordan, "Methadone, the Early Pandemic and the Terror of a Poppyseed Positive," *Filter*, August 18, 2022, https://filtermag.org/methadone-covid-pandemic-positive.

15   Manhattan Treatment Court, "Handbook," p. 9.

16   National Association of Drug Court Professionals, "Adult Drug Court Best Practice Standards, Volume II," 2018, p. 28, https://allrise.org/wp-content/uploads/2024/05 /Adult-Drug-Court-Best-Practice-Standards-Volume-2_Standard-VII_Text-Revision -December-2018-1.pdf.

17   Joanne Csete and Holly Catania, "Methadone Treatment Providers' Views of Drug Court Policy and Practice: A Case Study of New York State," *Harm Reduction Journal* 10, no. 1 (December 5, 2013): 35, https://doi.org/10.1186/1477-7517 -10-35.

18   Lacey Fosburgh, "Methadone Clinic Head Sentenced for Contempt," *New York Times*, July 26, 1972, www.nytimes.com/1972/07/26/archives/methadone-clinic -head-sentenced-for-contempt.html.

19 Nina Feldman, "Many 'Recovery Houses' Won't Let Residents Use Medicine to Quit Opioids," NPR, September 12, 2018, www.npr.org/sections/health-shots /2018/09/12/644685850/many-recovery-houses-wont-let-residents-use-medicine -to-quit-opioids; German Lopez, "We Have a Solution for the Opioid Epidemic. It's Dramatically Underused," *Vox*, December 17, 2019, www.vox.com/policy-and -politics/2019/12/17/18292021/opioid-epidemic-methadone-buprenorphine -naltrexone-drug-rehab.

20 Jillian Bauer-Reese, "There's a New 12-Step Group: Medication-Assisted Recovery Anonymous," *Slate*, April 17, 2018, https://slate.com/technology/2018/04/theres -a-new-12-step-group-for-people-in-recovery-who-are-prescribed-medications-like -methadone.html.

21 Manhattan Treatment Court, "Handbook," p. 15.

22 Maia Szalavitz, "Every Drug Court Should Allow Methadone Treatment," *New York Times*, July 20, 2015, www.nytimes.com/2015/07/20/opinion/every-drug-court-should -allow-methadone-treatment.html.

23 Drug Policy Alliance, "Report: The Drug Treatment Debate: Why Accessible and Vol-untary Treatment Wins," September 30, 2024, p. 12, https://drugpolicy.org/resource /report-the-drug-treatment-debate-why-accessible-and-voluntary-treatment-wins -out-over-forced.

24 Manhattan Treatment Court, "Handbook," p. 18.

25 Benjamin R. Nordstrom and Douglas B. Marlowe, "Medication-Assisted Treatment for Opioid Use Disorders in Drug Courts," National Drug Court Institute, *Drug Court Practitioner Fact Sheet* 11, no. 2 (August 2016): 6, https://allrise.org/wp-content /uploads/2022/07/mat_fact_sheet-1.pdf.

26 Harlan Matusow, Samuel L. Dickman, Josiah D. Rich, Chunki Fong, Dora M. Dumont, Carolyn Hardin, Douglas Marlowe, et al., "Medication Assisted Treatment in US Drug Courts: Results from a Nationwide Survey of Availability, Barriers and Attitudes," *Journal of Substance Abuse Treatment* 44, no. 5 (May 2013): 473–80, https://doi.org/10.1016/j.jsat.2012.10.004.

27 National Association of Drug Court Professionals, "Adult Drug Court Best Practice Standards," p. 25.

28 Phalguni Deswal, "Alkermes Fends off Generic Versions of Vivitrol until 2027," *Phar-maceutical Technology*, August 31, 2023, www.pharmaceutical-technology.com/news /alkermes-fends-off-generic-versions-of-vivitrol-until-2027. Methadone costs about $350 per month, and Suboxone $400.

29 Jake Harper, "To Grow Market Share, a Drugmaker Pitches Its Product to Judges," NPR, August 3, 2017, www.npr.org/sections/health-shots/2017/08/03/540029500 /to-grow-market-share-a-drugmaker-pitches-its-product-to-judges.

30 Jonathan Kirkpatrick, "Naltrexone as Opioid Treatment: Who Does It Work For, Besides Cops?," *Filter*, December 22, 2023, https://filtermag.org/naltrexone-opioid -use-disorder.

31 Drug Policy Alliance, "Drug Courts."

32 The Harm Reduction Therapy Center, n.d., accessed May 14, 2025, https://harm reductiontherapy.org. Denning and Little started offering harm reduction-based therapy in 2000 at locations in San Francisco and Oakland. In 2021 they opened the drop-in center in the SoMa neighborhood in San Franciso. Since 2018, HRTC has set up weekly pop-up "clinics without walls" on the street in four different neighborhoods in San Francisco. This is truly meeting people where they are at.

33 Mardet Homans, Denise M. Allen, and Yesenia Mazariegos, "A Review of Medication Assisted Treatment (MAT) in United States Jails and Prisons," University of California, Irvine, Center for Evidence-Based Corrections, July 2023, p. 3, https://ucicorrections .seweb.uci.edu/files/2023/07/MAT-in-United-States-Jails-and-Prisons.pdf.

34 Jail & Prison Opioid Project (https://prisonopioidproject.org), cited in Josh Rising, Sara Whaley, and Brendan Saloner, "How the Drug Enforcement Administration Can Improve Access to Methadone in Correctional Facilities and Save Lives," Johns Hopkins Bloomberg School of Public Health, 2022, p. 8, https://americanhealth.jhu.edu /sites/default/files/JHU-026%20Methadone%20White%20Paper-r1.pdf.

35 Legal Action Center, "Care for Opioid Use Disorder in the Criminal Justice System," chap. 4 in *Evidence Based Strategies for Abatement of Harms from the Opioid Epidemic*, October 2020, www.lac.org/resource/evidence-based-strategies-for-abatement-of-harms -from-the-o, www.lac.org/assets/files/OpioidAbatementFactSheet-Chapter4-v1.pdf.

36 Ingrid A Binswanger, Carolyn Nowels, Karen F. Corsi, Jason Glanz, Jeremy Long, Robert E. Booth, and John F. Steiner, "Return to Drug Use and Overdose after Release from Prison: A Qualitative Study of Risk and Protective Factors," *Addiction Science & Clinical Practice* 7, no. 1 (December 2012): 3, https://doi.org/10 .1186/1940-0640-7-3.

37 Beth Schwartzapfel and Keri Blakinger, "Federal Prisons Are Supposed to Provide Suboxone. They Dole Out Punishment Instead," Marshall Project, December 12, 2022, www.themarshallproject.org/2022/12/12/suboxone-federal-prison-opioid-addiction -treatment-overdose.

38 Schwartzapfel and Blakinger, "Federal Prisons."

39 Felice J. Freyer, "Drug May Give Those Leaving Jail a Better Shot at Recovery," *Boston Globe*, December 5, 2015, www.bostonglobe.com/metro/2015/12/08/long-lasting -addiction-treatment-raises-hopes-for-inmates-return-community/l8I3jvI3DmY7N J2n7AtaCP/story.html. Alkermes gives away the first dose for free with the hope the person will continuing taking the medication post incarceration and insurance will pick up the exorbitant cost.

40 Legal Action Center, "Cases Involving Discrimination Based on Treatment with Medication for Opioid Use Disorder (MOUD)," February 6, 2024, www.lac.org/search ?query=Cases%20Involving%20Discrimination%20Based%20on%20Treatment%20 with%20Medication%20for%20Opioid%20Use%20Disorder%20(MOUD).

41 Abby Goodnough, "Methadone Helped Her Quit Heroin. Now She's Suing U.S. Prisons to Allow the Treatment," *New York Times*, March 15, 2019, www.nytimes.com /2019/03/15/health/methadone-prisons-opioids.html.

42 Rising et al., "How the Drug Enforcement Administration Can Improve Access."

43 Ruth Potee, "WTF Methadone—What Is the Future?," presentation at the American Society of Addiction Medicine (ASAM) 54th Annual Conference, Washington, DC, April 2, 2022, YouTube video, posted May 26, 2022, www.youtube.com/watch?v =4byAJbZiZM4.

44 Sara Whaley, Brendan Saloner, and Josh Rising, "Providing Methadone in Jails and Prisons: An Explanation of a New Approach to Increase Access to Methadone in Carceral Settings," Johns Hopkins Bloomberg School of Public Health, 2022, https://opioidprinciples.jhsph.edu/wp-content/uploads/2023/05/Methadone-Fact -Sheet.pdf.

45 Helen Redmond, "Can Methadone Vans Deliver the Goods?," *Filter*, April 2024, https://filtermag.org/methadone-vans-new-york.

46 Alison Knopf, "The Importance of Paying More for Mobile Than Brick and Mortar Methadone," Addiction Treatment Forum, February 4, 2025, https://atforum.com /2025/02/codac-mobile-unit. CODAC operates numerous OTPs throughout Rhode Island.

47 Gail Groves Scott, "Handcuffing Participants (!) in a PA Jail MOUD Program," Comment, Opioid Safety and Naloxone Network, April 15, 2024. Groves Scott is a public health and addiction policy researcher. When she found out that inmates at the local jail in Lancaster, Pennsylvania, were being handcuffed while receiving medication, she contacted the warden to complain. He told her that they would continue the restraint protocol.

CHAPTER 8: "IF THE CHEMIST LIKES YOU": METHADONE DISPENSING IN AUSTRALIA, CANADA, AND BRITAIN

1 Harm Reduction International, "The Global State of Harm Reduction 2024," 2024, https://hri.global/wp-content/uploads/2024/10/GSR24_full-document_12.12.24 _B.pdf.

2 Keith Bradsher, "Shake-Up on Opium Island," *New York Times*, July 19, 2014, www .nytimes.com/2014/07/20/business/international/tasmania-big-supplier-to-drug -companies-faces-changes.html.

3 National Drug Research Institute, "The Cost of Opioid Use to Australia: $15.7 Billion and 2,203 Deaths," media release, May 14, 2020, https://ndri.curtin.edu.au /news-events/ndri-news/media-release-the-cost-of-opioid-use-to-australia; Penington Institute, "Opioid Pharmacotherapy at the Crossroads: Enduring Barriers and New Opportunities," 2023, www.penington.org.au/wp-content/uploads/2023/08/PEN _Pharmacotherapy-at-Crossroads_FINAL.pdf.

4 Penington Institute, "Opioid Pharmacotherapy."

5 Linda Gowing, Robert Ali, Adrian Dunlop, Mike Farrell, and Nick Lintzeris, "National Guidelines for Medication-Assisted Treatment of Opioid Dependence," Australian Commonwealth Department of Health, 2014, www.health.gov.au/sites

/default/files/national-guidelines-for-medication-assisted-treatment-of-opioid
-dependence_0.pdf.

6 Harm Reduction Victoria, "Pharmacotherapy Advocacy Mediation Support (PAMS)," n.d., accessed February 7, 2025, www.hrvic.org.au/pams. Harm Reduction Victoria is a peer-based organization.

7 Pew, "In Australia, Primary Care and Pharmacies Deliver Methadone," May 17, 2023, https://pew.org/3BwTVU4. Leah McLeod disagrees that dosing privacy is possible for most methadone patients at community pharmacies and told me, "Everybody knows that if you go to *that* counter, that's what you're getting."

8 Penington Institute, "Opioid Pharmacotherapy."

9 Sarah Lord told me that prior to 2004, doctors couldn't make decisions about take-home doses. They had to submit an application to the government for the patient to get them. A government representative had to approve the application and then decide how many bottles of medication could be given, never having seen the patient.

10 Danielle Russell, "After Years of US Clinics, I Get Methadone with Dignity in Australia," *Filter*, December 11, 2023, https://filtermag.org/methadone-clinic-pharmacy -australia; Danielle Russell, "To a US Methadone Recipient, Visiting Australia Was Shocking," *Filter*, December 20, 2022, https://filtermag.org/methadone-clinic -australia-pharmacy.

11 B. B. Chaar, J. R. Hanrahan, and C. Day, "Provision of Opioid Substitution Therapy Services in Australian Pharmacies," *Australasian Medical Journal* 4, no. 4 (May 1, 2011): 210–16, https://pubmed.ncbi.nlm.nih.gov/23393513.

12 Natassia Chrysanthos, "This Medication Has Cost Leah's Family $180,000, and Counting," *Sydney Morning Herald*, April 27, 2023, www.smh.com.au/politics /federal/this-medication-has-cost-leah-s-family-180-000-and-counting-20230425 -p5d334.html.

13 Chaar et al., "Provision of Opioid Substitution Therapy Services."

14 Penington Institute, "Australia's Annual Overdose Report 2024," August 2024, www .penington.org.au/wp-content/uploads/2024/08/PEN_Annual-Overdose-Report -2024.pdf.

15 Harm Reduction Australia, "Treatment Equity," n.d., accessed February 8, 2025, www.harmreductionaustralia.org.au/treatment-equity.

16 Penington Institute, "Opioid Pharmacotherapy."

17 Health Canada, "Canada's Overdose Crisis and the Toxic Illegal Drug Supply," March 25, 2024, www.canada.ca/en/health-canada/services/opioids/overdose-crisis-toxic -illegal-drug-supply.html.

18 Government of Canada, "Final Report of the Commission of Inquiry into the Non-Medical Use of Drugs," 1973, https://publications.gc.ca/site/eng/9.699765 /publication.html. The commission saw heroin maintenance "as a last resort in selected difficult cases when every reasonable effort has been made to withdraw the addict from the illicit market by other means."

19 Canadian Medical Association, "Methadone and the Care of the Narcotic Addict: Report of a Special Joint Committee of C.M.A. and the D.N.H.W. Food and Drug Directorate," *CMAJ* 105, no. 11 (December 4, 1971): 1193–96, https://pmc.ncbi .nlm.nih.gov/articles/PMC1931366.

20 Benedikt Fischer, "Prescriptions, Power and Politics: The Turbulent History of Methadone Maintenance in Canada," *Journal of Public Health Policy* 21, no. 2 (2000): 187–210, https://doi.org/10.2307/3343343.

21 Fischer, "Prescriptions."

22 PHS Community Services Society, n.d., accessed April 11, 2025, www.phs.ca.

23 Robert A. Kleinman, Thomas D. Brothers, Marlon Danilewitz, and Anees Bahji, "Office-Based Methadone Prescribing for Opioid Use Disorder: The Canadian Model," *Journal of Addiction Medicine* 16, no. 5 (September 2022): 499–504, https:// doi.org/10.1097/ADM.0000000000000950.

24 Garth Mullins, *Crackdown: Surviving and Resisting the War on Drugs* (Doubleday Canada, 2025), 129.

25 Mullins, *Crackdown*, 129.

26 Mullins, *Crackdown*, 130.

27 Mullins, *Crackdown*, 137.

28 SAMHSA, *Federal Guidelines for Opioid Treatment Programs*, HHS Publication No. (SMA) PEP15-FEDGUIDEOTP, Rockville, MD: Substance Abuse and Mental Health Services Administration, January 2015, pp. 53–54, https://www.govinfo .gov/content/pkg/GOVPUB-HE20_400-PURL-gpo139641/pdf/GOVPUB-HE20 _400-PURL-gpo139641.pdf.

29 Health Canada, "Provincial and Territorial Public Drug Benefit Programs," May 8, 2025, www.canada.ca/en/health-canada/services/health-care-system/pharmaceuticals /access-insurance-coverage-prescription-medicines/provincial-territorial-public-drug -benefit-programs.html.

30 Kleinman et al., "Office-Based Methadone Prescribing."

31 Lien Yeung, "Pharmacies Still Paying Patients Kickbacks, DTES Sources Say," CBC News, March 27, 2024, www.cbc.ca/news/canada/british-columbia/pharmacies-downtown -eastside-kickbacks-1.7076276.

32 Andrea Woo, "Special Investigation Finds Some 60 Pharmacies Accused in Kickback Scheme, Say B.C. Health Ministry Documents," *Globe and Mail*, February 5, 2025, www .theglobeandmail.com/canada/article-special-investigation-finds-some-60-pharmacies -accused-in-kickback. Patients on other medications were also offered financial incentives.

33 Yeung, "Pharmacies Still Paying."

34 Health Canada, "Safer Supply: Prescribed Medications as a Safer Alternative to Toxic Illegal Drugs," April 25, 2023, www.canada.ca/en/health-canada/services/opioids /responding-canada-opioid-crisis/safer-supply.html.

35 Vice News, "Inside a Free Fentanyl and Heroin Clinic," YouTube video, posted December 16, 2022, www.youtube.com/watch?v=Je3YADbep9w.

36 Doug Johnson, "Vancouver Safe Supply Program Begins Prescribing Take-Home Fentanyl," *Filter*, April 13, 2022, https://filtermag.org/safe-supply-phs-vancouver-prescription-fentanyl.

37 William Turvill, "Opioid Vending Machine Opens in Vancouver," *Guardian*, February 17, 2020, www.theguardian.com/science/2020/feb/17/opioid-vending-machine -opens-vancouver-mysafe-canada.

38 MySafe Society, "MySafe," YouTube video, posted January 23, 2020, www.youtube .com/watch?v=wxFg8R5Tq8A.

39 CATIE, "MySafe Safer Opioid Supply Program Using Biometric Dispensing Machines," August 15, 2023, www.catie.ca/programming-connection/mysafe-safer -opioid-supply-program-using-biometric-dispensing-machines.

40 Mark Tyndall, "A Safer Drug Supply: A Pragmatic and Ethical Response to the Overdose Crisis," *CMAJ* 192, no. 34 (August 24, 2020): E986–87, https://doi.org /10.1503/cmaj.201618.

41 Matthew Bonn, "Fentanyl Patches Are Saving My Life. We Need to Make Them Accessible," *Filter*, June 1, 2023, https://filtermag.org/fentanyl-patch-safe-supply.

42 CBC News, "9 Ontario Supervised Drug Consumption Sites Set to Close under New Law Will Become Treatment Hubs," January 2, 2025, www.cbc.ca/news/canada/toronto /supervised-consumption-sites-hart-hubs-ontario-1.7421744. The treatment hubs won't provide safe supply medications, supervised consumption, or syringe services.

43 British Columbia Centre on Substance Use, "Prescribed Alternatives," n.d., accessed February 20, 2025, www.bccsu.ca/clinical-care-guidance/prescribed-alternatives.

44 Wolf Depner, "B.C. Tightens 'Safe Supply', Only Giving Drugs under Health Worker Supervision," *Chilliwack Progress*, February 19, 2025, www.theprogress.com/news/bc -government-announces-steps-to-tighten-safe-supply-program-7830786.

45 Garth Mullins (@garthmullins), "A witness-only safe supply program in BC is a mistake," X, February 19, 2025, https://x.com/garthmullins/status/1892324902595674267.

46 Marie Nyswander, *The Drug Addict as a Patient* (Grune & Stratton, 1956), 148.

47 J. S. Rafaeli, "When Boots Prescribed Heroin, the UK Did Drug Policy Right," *Vice*, October 4, 2018, www.vice.com/en/article/when-boots-prescribed-heroin-the-uk -did-drug-policy-right.

48 Virginia Berridge, "Drugs and Social Policy: The Establishment of Drug Control in Britain 1900–30," *British Journal of Addiction* 79 (April 1, 1984): 18, https://doi.org /10.1111/j.1360-0443.1984.tb00244.x.

49 The Home Office is the lead government department for crime, the police, drugs policy, immigration and passports, and counterterrorism.

50 Berridge, "Drugs and Social Policy," 25.

51 Virginia Berridge, "The Making of the Rolleston Report, 1908–1926," *Journal of Drug Issues* 10, no. 1 (January 1980): 20–21, https://doi.org/10.1177 /002204268001000102.

52 Mike Ashton, "The Rolleston Legacy," *Drug And Alcohol Findings* 15 (2006), https:// findings.org.uk/docs/Ashton_M_28.pdf?s=eb&r=&c=&sf=sfnos.

53 Berridge, "Drugs and Social Policy," 18.

54 Ashton, "Rolleston Legacy."

55 Keith Richards and James Fox, *Life* (Little, Brown and Company, 2010). The Rolling Stones's song "Brown Sugar" is said to be about heroin.

56 Berridge, "Drugs and Social Policy," 28.

57 Mark Monaghan, "The Recent Evolution of UK Drug Strategies: From Maintenance to Behaviour Change?," *People, Place and Policy Online* 6, no. 1 (March 30, 2012): 29–40, https://doi.org/10.3351/ppp.0006.0001.0004.

58 Audit Commission, "Changing Habits: The Commissioning and Management of Community Drug Treatment Services for Adults," 2002, p. 5, www.drugsandalcohol.ie/5220/1/Audit_committee_changing_habits.pdf. Doctors reporting drug dependent patients to the police resulted in many not seeking treatment for fear of punishment or arrest.

59 Nicola J. Kalk, J. Roy Robertson, Brian Kidd, Edward Day, Michael J. Kelleher, Eilish Gilvarry, and John Strang, "Treatment and Intervention for Opiate Dependence in the United Kingdom: Lessons from Triumph and Failure," *European Journal on Criminal Policy and Research* 24, no. 2 (June 1, 2018): 183–200, https://doi.org/10.1007/s10610-017-9364-z.

60 John Strang, Janie Sheridan, and Nick Barber, "Prescribing Injectable and Oral Methadone to Opiate Addicts: Results from the 1995 National Postal Survey of Community Pharmacies in England and Wales," *BMJ* 313, no. 7052 (August 3, 1996): 270–72, https://doi.org/10.1136/bmj.313.7052.270.

61 Gerry V. Stimson, "AIDS and Injecting Drug Use in the United Kingdom, 1987–1993: The Policy Response and the Prevention of the Epidemic," *Social Science & Medicine* 41, no. 5 (September 1995): 711–12, https://doi.org/10.1016/0277-9536(94)00435-V. The United Kingdom pioneered another vital harm reduction practice: making sterile syringes available to drug users at no cost.

62 John Strang and Matt Hickman, "Impact of Supervision of Methadone Consumption on Deaths Related to Methadone Overdose (1993–2008): Analyses Using OD4 Index in England and Scotland," *BMJ* 341, no. c4851 (September 16, 2010), https://doi.org/10.1136/bmj.c4851.

63 Working with Everyone, n.d., accessed June 28, 2024, https://workingwitheveryone.org.uk.

64 According to Mark Gilman, "Some of the more progressive clinics don't bother to urine test at all."

65 *Liquid Handcuffs: A Documentary to Free Methadone*, directed by Marilena Marchetti and Helen Redmond (Portico Films, 2019), www.porticofilms.com/pastwork/liquidhandcuffs.

66 Diane Taylor, "Let Junkies Fix Themselves," *Guardian*, October 19, 1999, www.theguardian.com/lifeandstyle/1999/oct/19/healthandwellbeing.health1.

67 Neil McKeganey, "Clear Rhetoric and Blurred Reality: The Development of a Recovery Focus in UK Drug Treatment Policy and Practice," *International Journal of Drug Policy* 25, no. 5 (September 2014): 957, 960, https://doi.org/10.1016/j.drugpo.2014.01.014.

CHAPTER 9: "IT TOOK A PANDEMIC TO GET MORE TAKE-HOMES": METHADONE AND COVID-19

1 National Academies of Sciences, Engineering, and Medicine, "Methadone Treatment for Opioid Use Disorder: Examining Federal Regulations and Laws: A Workshop,"

March 3, 2022, www.nationalacademies.org/event/03-03-2022/methadone-treatment
-for-opioid-use-disorder-examining-federal-regulations-and-laws-a-workshop.

2 Helena Hansen, Jules Netherland, and David Herzberg, *Whiteout: How Racial Capitalism Changed the Color of Opioids in America* (University of California Press, 2023), 42. Leschner stressed that buprenorphine was uniquely appropriate for a new kind of opioid user, as opposed to methadone "which tends to concentrate in urban areas, [and] is a poor fit for the suburban spread of narcotic addiction."

3 Lisa Bain, Sheena M. Posey Norris, and Clare Stroud, eds., *Methadone Treatment for Opioid Use Disorder: Improving Access Through Regulatory and Legal Change: Proceedings of a Workshop* (National Academies Press, 2022), https://doi.org/10.17226/26635. One of the reviewers of the report was Jason Kletter, the president of the methadone clinic chain BayMark. Despite presentations on methadone dispensing in Australia and New Zealand, there was no recommendation that the United States transition to that model.

4 American Association for the Treatment of Opioid Dependence (AATOD), n.d., accessed March 27, 2025, www.aatod.org.

5 AATOD, "Our Board of Directors," n.d., accessed March 22, 2025, www.aatod.org/about-us/our-board-of-directors.

6 Richard A. Rettig and Adam Yarmolinsky, *Federal Regulation of Methadone Treatment* (National Academy Press, 1995), https://nap.nationalacademies.org/read/4899; Ethan A. Nadelmann and Jennifer McNeely, "Doing Methadone Right," *National Affairs*, Spring 1996, www.nationalaffairs.com/public_interest/detail/doing-methadone-right.

7 Emily Alpert Reyes, "Skid Row Is an Overdose 'Epicenter.' But Methadone Can Be Miles Away," *Los Angeles Times*, May 11, 2022, www.latimes.com/california/story/2022-05-11/la-skid-row-overdose-epicenter-methadone-access.

8 Lev Facher, "Q&A: Mark Parrino Says It's Time to 'Completely Re-Examine' Methadone Treatment for Opioid Addiction," *Stat*, March 19, 2024, www.statnews.com/2024/03/19/methadone-clinics-aatod-mark-parrino.

9 Helen Redmond, "Methadone Clinics' Conference Felt Like Being Behind Enemy Lines," *Filter*, November 23, 2022, https://filtermag.org/methadone-clinics-reform-aatod.

10 Jason Kletter, "Allowing Pharmacies to Dispense Methadone Is Dangerous for Patients and Communities," *Stat*, December 23, 2022, www.statnews.com/2022/12/23/pharmacies-shouldnt-be-allowed-to-dispense-methadone; Lev Facher, "At Las Vegas Conference, Methadone Clinics Blast Idea of Doctors Prescribing Directly," *Stat*, May 28, 2024, www.statnews.com/2024/05/28/addiction-methadone-clinics-doctor-prescription-markey.

11 Ofer Amram, Solmaz Amiria, Elson S. Floyd, Victoria Panwala, Robert Lutz, Paul J. Joudrey, and Eugenia Socias, "The Impact of Relaxation of Methadone Take-Home Protocols on Treatment Outcomes in the COVID-19 Era," *American Journal of Drug and Alcohol Abuse* 47, no. 6 (November 2, 2021): 722–29, https://doi.org/10.1080/00952990.2021.1979991; Sarah Brothers, Adam Viera, and Robert Heimer, "Changes in Methadone Program Practices and Fatal Methadone Overdose Rates in

Connecticut during COVID-19," *Journal of Substance Abuse Treatment* 131 (December 1, 2021): 108449, https://doi.org/10.1016/j.jsat.2021.108449.

12 National Archives and Records Administration, Code of Federal Regulations, Title 42, Chapter I, Subchapter A, Part 8, "Medications for the Treatment of Opioid Use Disorder," accessed March 2, 2025, www.ecfr.gov/current/title-42/chapter-I /subchapter-A/part-8?toc=1.

13 Ruth Potee, "The Four Walls That Built Methadone Clinics," video, https://ruthpotee .com/videos. Dr. Potee made this remark on the panel "Methadone in the Modern Era" at the American Society of Addiction Medicine Annual Conference, April 6, 2024, in Dallas.

14 National Institutes of Health, "Methadone and Buprenorphine Reduce Risk of Death after Opioid Overdose," news release, June 19, 2018, www.nih.gov/news-events/news -releases/methadone-buprenorphine-reduce-risk-death-after-opioid-overdose.

15 Beth E. Meyerson, Keith G. Bentele, Danielle M. Russell, Benjamin R. Brady, Missy Downer, Roberto C. Garcia, Irene Garnett, et al., "Nothing Really Changed: Arizona Patient Experience of Methadone and Buprenorphine Access during COVID," *PLOS One* 17, no. 10 (2022): e0274094, https://doi.org/10.1371/journal.pone.0274094.

16 SAMHSA, *Federal Guidelines for Opioid Treatment Programs*, HHS Publication No. PEP24-02-011, Rockville, MD: Substance Abuse and Mental Health Services Administration, 2024, pp. vii, 38, https://www.med.unc.edu/fammed/nctac/wp-content /uploads/sites/1256/2025/01/federal-guidelines-opioid-treatment-pep24-02-011-1.pdf.

17 SAMHSA, *Federal Guidelines*, 2024, p. 89. States can choose not to follow federal guidelines for take-home medication and determine their own schedule.

18 SAMHSA, *Federal Guidelines for Opioid Treatment Programs*, HHS Publication No. (SMA) PEP15-FEDGUIDEOTP, Rockville, MD: Substance Abuse and Mental Health Services Administration, January 2015, p. 54, https://www.govinfo.gov/content/pkg /GOVPUB-HE20_400-PURL-gpo139641/pdf/GOVPUB-HE20_400-PURL-gpo139641 .pdf. State regulations can disregard SAMHSA take-home guidelines and create their own, often allowing less.

19 SAMHSA, *Federal Guidelines*, 2024, p. 7.

20 SAMHSA, *Federal Guidelines*, 2024, pp. 28–29.

21 SAMHSA, *Federal Guidelines*, 2024, p. 89.

22 SAMHSA, *Federal Guidelines*, 2015, pp. 53–54.

23 Alison Knopf, "AATOD Releases Guidance for OTPs on Coronavirus/COVID-19," Addiction Treatment Forum, March 25, 2020, https://atforum.com/2020/03/aatod -releases-guidance-for-otps-on-coronavirus-covid-19.

24 Helen Redmond, "With New Final Methadone Rule, SAMHSA Isn't Coming to Save Us," *Filter*, February 13, 2024, https://filtermag.org/samhsa-methadone-final-rule.

25 SAMHSA, *Federal Guidelines*, 2015, p. 70.

26 SAMHSA, *Federal Guidelines*, 2024, p. 89.

27 SAMHSA, *Federal Guidelines*, 2024, p. vii.

28 SAMHSA, *Federal Guidelines*, 2024, pp. x, 106.

29 Helen Redmond, "Methadone Clinics Angry at Bad PR, but Not Afraid of SAMHSA," *Filter*, April 4, 2023, https://filtermag.org/methadone-clinics-samhsa-aatod.

30 Bridget C. E. Dooling and Laura E. Stanley, "A Vast and Discretionary Regime: Federal Regulation of Methadone as a Treatment for Opioid Use Disorder," George Washington University, Regulatory Studies Center, August 11, 2022, https://regulatorystudies.columbian.gwu.edu/federal-regulation-of-methadone.

31 SAMHSA, *Federal Guidelines*, 2024, p. 37.

32 AATOD, "HHS/SAMHSA Releases New Opioid Treatment Program (OTP) Regulations," news release, February 5, 2024, www.prweb.com/releases/hhssamhsa-releases-new-opioid-treatment-program-otp-regulations-302052890.html.

33 Donald Norcross (D-NJ), "HR 1359: Modernizing Opioid Treatment Access Act," legislation, March 10, 2023, www.congress.gov/bill/118th-congress/house-bill/1359. The first iteration of the bill was named the Opioid Treatment Access Act of 2022.

34 US Rep. Donald Norcross, "Reps. Norcross, Bacon Lead Introduction of the Modernizing Opioid Treatment Access Act," media release, March 6, 2023, https://norcross.house.gov/2023/3/reps-norcross-bacon-lead-introduction-of-the-modernizing-opioid-treatment-access-act.

35 US Senator Ed Markey, "Senator Markey on New Methadone Rules: We Need Even More Expansion to Access," media release, February 1, 2024, www.markey.senate.gov/news/press-releases/senator-markey-on-new-methadone-rules-we-need-even-more-expansion-to-access.

36 Jeffrey A. Singer and Sofia Hamilton, "Expand Access to Methadone Treatment: Remove Barriers to Primary Care Practitioners Prescribing Methadone," Cato Institute, September 7, 2023, p. 13, www.cato.org/sites/cato.org/files/2023-08/policy-analysis-960.pdf.

37 Helen Redmond, "Did ASAM Push to Limit Federal Methadone Reform Bill?," *Filter*, July 25, 2023, https://filtermag.org/asam-methadone-reform-bill.

38 Kayla Holgash and Martha Heberlein, "Physician Acceptance of New Medicaid Patients: What Matters and What Doesn't," *Health Affairs Forefront*, April 10, 2019, https://doi.org/10.1377/forefront.20190401.678690.

39 Norcross, "HR 1359."

40 American Society of Addiction Medicine, "Statement of Stephen M. Taylor to the US Senate Committee on Health, Education, Labor, and Pensions (HELP) Subcommittee on Primary Health and Retirement Security," May 17, 2023, www.help.senate.gov/imo/media/doc/23.05.17%20Dr.%20Stephen%20Taylor%20(ASAM)%20-%20Written%20Testimony%20-%20Senate%20HELP%20Subcommittee%20on%20Primary%20Health.pdf.

41 Terance M. Hughes, Joan Chen, and Utsha G. Khatri, "Liberate Methadone: An Introduction for the Emergency Medicine Physician," *ACEP Now*, April 14, 2025, www.acepnow.com/article/liberate-methadone-an-introduction-for-the-emergency-medicine-physician.

42 William White, A Life of Clinical Activism: An Interview with Robert G. Newman," 2011, p. 11, www.stopstigmanow.org/wp-content/uploads/2021/02/SSN-NEWMAN .book-pgs-2020-FINALqxp.pdf.

43 Cato Institute, "Expanding Access to Methadone Treatment," policy forum, September 13, 2023, www.cato.org/events/expanding-access-methadone-treatment; Helen Redmond, "Rep. Norcross Admits His Methadone Bill Isn't Enough. We Should, Too," *Filter*, November 20, 2023, https://filtermag.org/norcross-methadone-bill -not-enough.

44 Redmond, "Did ASAM Push."

CHAPTER 10: METHADONE PATIENT ADVOCACY GROUPS, UNHOLY ALLIANCES, AND THE FUTURE OF METHADONE

1 NAMA Recovery, "About Us," n.d., accessed March 27, 2025, https://namarecovery .org/about.

2 Joycelyn Sue Woods, "A Voice for Methadone Patients," *Journal of Maintenance in the Addictions* 1, no. 1 (March 15, 1997): 135–36, https://doi.org/10.1300 /J126v01n01_18.

3 NAMA Recovery, "About Us."

4 Woods, "Voice for Methadone Patients." My co-filmmaker and I met with Joycelyn Woods and Zachary Talbott to discuss our documentary, *Liquid Handcuffs: A Documentary to Free Methadone* (directed by Marilena Marchetti and Helen Redmond, Portico Films, 2019, www.porticofilms.com/pastwork/liquidhandcuffs). Woods thought it was a terrible film that stigmatized patients. She said that we only interviewed patients who were unstable, nonworking, and were "hang-out-in-the-park problem patients."

5 Methadone.org, "MARS Medicated Assisted Recovery Services Project," n.d., accessed June 11, 2025, www.methadone.org/mars/mars-index.html.

6 Anita Kennedy, "Registration for the 2022 CMA Training Course Is Now Open!" NAMA Recovery, September 9, 2022, https://namarecovery.org/2022-cma -registration.

7 Methadone.org, "National Alliance for Medication Assisted Recovery: Grievance /Compliment Report," n.d., accessed June 11, 2025, www.methadone.org/library /grievance_report_print.html.

8 Robert Newman, "Response to 'Methadone Maintenance vs. Methadone Taper during Pregnancy' Paper," *American Journal on Addictions* 18, no. 3 (May 6, 2009): 250, https://doi.org/10.1080/10550490902786892.

9 Leadership of NAMA-R in conversations with the author.

10 NAMA-R letter to Mark Parrino, president of AATOD, April 8, 2020, www .methadone.org/downloads/documents/2020%200408NAMAR%20AATOD%20 re%20COVID19%20signed.pdf. Complaints came from nurses who considered resigning because there was not enough personal protective equipment.

11 Alison Knopf, "From Starter OTP to Acquisition by BayMark: A 3-Year Journey," *Alcoholism & Drug Abuse Weekly* 30, no. 34 (2018): 5–6, https://doi.org/10.1002 /adaw.32095.

12 Alison Knopf, "OTPs, Profit, and Not-for-Profit: What's the Fuss About?," *Addiction Treatment Forum*, June 4, 2019, https://atforum.com/2019/06/otps-profit-not -profit-fuss.

13 Talbott Legacy Centers, "Leadership," n.d., accessed March 12, 2025, www.talbottlegacy .org/about-us/leadership.

14 *Swallow THIS: A Documentary About Methadone & COVID-19*, directed by Marilena Marchetti and Helen Redmond (Portico Films, 2022), www.porticofilms.com /swallowthis.

15 Anita Kennedy, "ASAM and NAMA Recovery Applaud Introduction of the Modernizing Opioid Treatment Access Act," NAMA Recovery, March 8, 2023, https:// namarecovery.org/asam-and-nama-recovery-applaud-introduction-of-m-otaa.

16 Schorr is the president of the New York state Coalition of Medication-Assisted Treatment Providers and Advocates. COMPA, "Board Biographies," n.d., accessed April 4, 2025, https://compa-ny.org/board-profiles.

17 Alison Knopf, "Next Steps for OTPs: Three Executives on Their Vision for the Future," Addiction Treatment Forum, January 12, 2023, https://atforum.com/2023/01 /next-steps-otps-vision.

18 Kennedy, Anita, "Call for Nominations for the Richard Lane/Robert Holden Patient Advocacy Award 2025," NAMA Recovery, January 31, 2025, https://namarecovery .org/call-for-nominations-for-the-richard-lane-robert-holden-patient-advocacy-award -2025. The AATOD Conference Awards Committee has final approval of who wins the Lane/Holden award.

19 National Academies of Sciences, Engineering, and Medicine, "Methadone Treatment for Opioid Use Disorder: A Workshop," March 3, 2022, www.nationalacademies.org /event/03-03-2022/methadone-treatment-for-opioid-use-disorder-examining-federal -regulations-and-laws-a-workshop.

20 Stop Stigma Now, "About Us," n.d., accessed April 1, 2025, www.stopstigmanow.org /about-us-2.

21 Stop Stigma Now, "About Us."

22 Stop Stigma Now, "About Us."

23 Sarah Schulman, *Let the Record Show: A Political History of ACT UP New York, 1987– 1993* (Farrar, Straus and Giroux, 2021), 5.

24 Schulman, *Let the Record Show*, 99.

25 Schulman, *Let the Record Show*, 208. The federal government, via taxpayer money, conducted most of the research for AZT that Burroughs Wellcome then profited from.

26 Schulman, *Let the Record Show*, 211–12.

27 Maia Szalavitz, *Undoing Drugs: How Harm Reduction Is Changing the Future of Drugs and Addiction* (Hachette, 2021), 91.

28 Helen Redmond, "A Methadone Pioneer Who Freed People from the Cruel Clinic System," *Filter*, April 23, 2025, https://filtermag.org/methadone-pioneer-office -based-prescribing.
29 Peter Vanderkloot, "Methadone: Medicine, Harm Reduction or Social Control," *Harm Reduction Communication* 11 (Spring 2000), www.yumpu.com/en/document /read/34312211/the-pdf-here-harm-reduction-coalition.

INDEX

ACKNOWLEDGMENTS

Thanks to the following people, places, music, and restaurants:

Peter Vanderkloot. His article "Methadone: Medicine, Harm Reduction or Social Control" profoundly changed how I thought about methadone. He made the case for clinic abolition and prescription parity in 2001! We stand on his shoulders.

All the people who take or used to take methadone that I've interviewed and have learned from over the years: Jenna Abazia, Melissa Burkholder, Sarah Clingan, Abby Coulter, Brenda Davis, Magda Ferreira, David Frank, Walter Ginter, Peter Gumprecht, David Herzberg, Louie Jones, Anita Kennedy, Bill Kinkle, Erin O'Mara, Jerry Otero, Danielle Russell, Knina Strichartz, Zachary Talbott, Jess Tilley, Louise Vincent, Nick Voyles, and Joycelyn Woods. There are many more whose names I cannot use for privacy reasons.

Dr. Robert Newman, the "Pope of Methadone." He was the most passionate and unapologetic defender of the power of methadone to transform lives. I was lucky to interview Bob on camera in his home a few years before he died. We stand on his shoulders.

Marilena Marchetti, co-filmmaker and fellow clinic abolitionist.

All the folks, harm reduction organizations, churches, conferences, and universities involved in the cross-country tour of *Swallow THIS: A Documentary about Methadone and COVID-19*.

The trio of harm reduction goddesses in the United States: Edith Springer, Patt Denning, and Jeannie Little. We stand on their shoulders. I heard Edith speak at the Harm Reduction Coalition conference in 2004, and her presentation forever altered my beliefs about drug addiction. I became a harm reductionist and started working with people who use drugs. Over two decades, I've had the good fortune to be friends with Patt and Jeannie. We've spent countless hours discussing all things harm reduction and ranting about the war on drugs while drinking cocktails in their front yard in Oakland. Their two groundbreaking books, plus the Harm Reduction Therapy Center in San Francisco, influenced my book and my life. Much love. Extra shout-out to Patt for constructive criticism and advice on several chapters, and lots of encouragement.

Deborah Small, the fiercest, most brilliant critic of the War on Drugs and racial capitalism. Deborah was featured in my first documentary about methadone, *Liquid Handcuffs: A Documentary to Free Methadone*. We stand on her shoulders.

Helena Hansen and Samuel Kelton Roberts, for scholarship on the intersection of race, class, addiction, and medication. Hansen's book, *Whiteout*, taught me how buprenorphine was intentionally marketed to distinguish it pharmacologically and symbolically from methadone.

Will Godfrey, my editor at *Filter*. He always makes my writing better. His kindness, incredible knowledge about drugs, and honest feedback and suggestions about the book were invaluable. I could not have written this book without Will's support. Full stop.

Aden McCracken, research assistant and fellow methadone clinic abolitionist. Special shout-out for help with the section on methadone diversion.

Bella Berg, research assistant—she can find any source, seriously, in no time flat.

Margeaux Weston, for acquiring my book and taking a chance on a first-time author. And to all the publishers who didn't think my book could "attract wider commercial interest," fuck off!

Shayna Keyles, my editor at North Atlantic Books, for rearranging paragraphs, toning down my "opinionated language," finding wiggle room for delivering the manuscript, and for keeping me organized and motivated so I could finish the book.

Christopher Church for copyedits.

The team at North Atlantic Books, for doing the heavy lifting to get my book ready to publish, and for the dope book cover.

Dao Tran, for all-around book publishing wisdom, advice, and for being in my corner.

Bruce Trigg, my teacher, for the informative and fun conversations about the politics and pharmacology of methadone.

Janet Urdahl, a fellow social worker, for trying to change the culture of cruelty in an OTP, despite all odds.

Elizabeth Chiarello, for her book *Policing Patients*, which helped me think through the issues of pharmacy dispensing of methadone in the United States.

Emily Dufton, for clarifying the origins of the methadone clinic system.

Corey Davis, for explaining unfathomable SAMHSA and DEA regulations and how to get rid of them.

Michael Hegarty, for breaking down how surveillance technology is disrupting and transforming the for-profit methadone clinic system in the United States of Addiction.

Michel Negroponte, for having the courage to admit to me that he wishes he never made the documentary *Methadonia*.

Paul D'Amato and Alan Maass, for giving me the opportunity to write about drugs for *Socialist Review* and *Socialist Worker* back in the day.

Lindsey Alexander, Syderia Asberry-Chresfield, Mary Buser, Brandon Carr, Pedro Catita, Kathleen Cochran, Hiawatha Collins, Elisa Correa, Harry Cullens, Adriana Curado, Sy Demsky, Sheri Doyle, Ernie Drucker, Robert DuPont, Hugo Faria, Johann Hari, John Hamilton, Paul Harkin, Shawn Hill, Jerome Jaffe, Manisha Krishnan, Stephen Maher, Ethan Nadelmann, Dinah Ortiz, José Queiroz, Kelly Ramsey, Marsha Rosenbaum, Edwin Salsitz, Roxanne Saucier, Jeffrey Singer, Maia Szalavitz, Daphna Thier, Uri Thier, Sheila Vakharia, Daniel Wolfe, and Lisa Zitzmann.

Australia: Companions of the Order of Good People: Sarah Lord, Leah McLeod, John Ryan.

Canada: Neighbors to the north: Liz Evans, Joshua Fletcher, Garth Mullins, Brett Wolfson-Stofko. Special shout-out to Garth for sharing a galley copy of his badass memoir with me, *Crackdown: Surviving and Resisting the War on Drugs*.

Britain: Keep calm and carry on: Julia Buxton, Judy Chang, Mark Gilman, David MacKintosh.

Agência Piaget para o Desenvolvimento, British Columbia Association of People on Opiate Maintenance, Cato Institute, Drug Policy Alliance, *Filter*, Greater Harlem Coalition, Grupo de Ativistas em Tratamiento, Harm Reduction Australia, Harm Reduction International, Harm Reduction Victoria, International Network of People Who Use Drugs, Mount Sinai, National Alliance for Medication Assisted Recovery, National Harm Reduction Coalition, National Survivors Union, New England Users Union, Open Society Foundations, Pew Charitable Trusts, Silver School of Social Work, Stop Stigma Now, Vancouver Area Network of Drug Users, VOCAL-NY, Working With Everyone.

Quiet places and cities: Bobst Library, Countee Cullen Library, New York University Madrid and Washington Square campuses, Schomburg Center for Research in Black Culture, The Harlem Collective. Catania, Lisbon, Oakland, San Francisco.

Takeout: Falafel Tarboosh, Manhattanville Coffee, Mumbai Masala Indian Grill, River Thai, The Handpulled Noodle.

Music: Jon Batiste, Kari Faux, Childish Gambino, Patty Griffin, Talib Kweli, Madison McFerrin, Mos Def, Nas, Caroline Polachek, James Taylor, The Cinematic Orchestra, Tour-Maubourg, Susumu Yokota, Kali Uchis.

ABOUT THE AUTHOR

Photo by Uri Thier

Helen Redmond is a Harlem-based documentary filmmaker, journalist, and licensed clinical social worker. She has worked with people who use drugs for over two decades in medical, harm reduction-based housing, and community mental health settings. She is an expert on drug addiction and treatment.

Redmond is a senior editor and a multimedia journalist at *Filter* and writes about drugs, with a focus on methadone, nicotine, and tobacco harm reduction. Her short videos appear on the website (https://filtermag.org /author/helen-redmond).

She is the co-director of the feature-length film *Liquid Handcuffs: A Documentary to Free Methadone* and the short documentary *Swallow THIS: A*

Documentary About Methadone and COVID-19 (www.porticofilms.com). Both have screened across the United States and internationally.

Redmond is an adjunct assistant professor at New York University's Silver School of Social Work.

ABOUT NORTH ATLANTIC BOOKS

North Atlantic Books (NAB) is an independent, nonprofit publisher committed to a bold exploration of the relationships between mind, body, spirit, and nature. Founded in 1974, NAB aims to nurture a holistic view of the arts, sciences, humanities, and healing. To make a donation or to learn more about our books, authors, events, and newsletter, please visit www.northatlanticbooks.com.